ASPECTS OF

PACIFIC ETHNOHISTORY

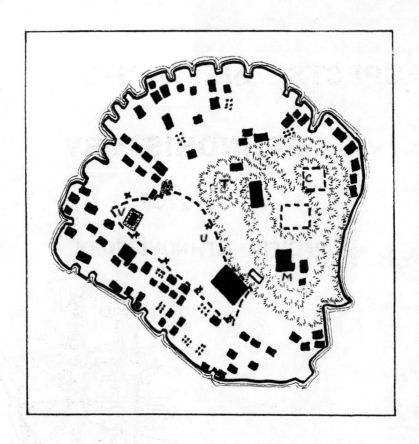

The writer's rough plan of Bau Island at the time of the
Pig's Head Ceremony, showing the distribution of occupied
houses and unoccupied house-foundations. The large encircled
area (U) is Na Ulunivuaka, the crosses indicating the position of the warrior-guards. V is Vatanitawake. The two
circular hill-tops are burial grounds, showing the graves
of Tanoa (T) and Cakobau (C). The large building (M) is the
mission house, but this was the original land of the people
who were expelled, as recorded in the narrative. The other
large building on Na Ulunivuaka is the Cakobau Memorial
Church.

[See Pages 91-103]

THE ISLAND OF BAU

ASPECTS of PACIFIC

ETHNOHISTORY

A.R. Tippett

William Carey Library

In accord with some of the most recent thinking in the academic press, the William Carey Library is pleased to present this scholarly book which has been prepared from an author-edited and author-prepared camera-ready manuscript.

Library of Congress Cataloging in Publication Data

Tippett, Alan Richard
    Aspects of Pacific ethnohistory

    Includes bibliographies
    1. Ethnology--Oceanica 2. Ethnology--Methodology
    3. Oceanica--History I. Title
GN 663.T56   301.2'07'22   73-8820
ISBN 0-87808-132-1

Published by the William Carey Library
305 Pasadena Ave.
South Pasadena, Calif. 91030
Telephone: 213-799-4559

PRINTED IN THE UNITED STATES OF AMERICA

CONTENTS

History may partake of the nature of the social sciences, and it is to be hoped that as such it may improve... If the historian who considers himself a guardian of the cultural heritage and an interpreter of human development also seeks to reach generalizations that appear to be valid and to provide credible explanations of the development of contemporary events, thoughts, manners and institutions, he is, by the extra effort, no less, and he may be the more, a historian. ... The historian as social scientist and the historian as a humanist, need not be two separate persons; they may easily be the same one. And the usefulness of that one to both the humanities and the social sciences would be greatly increased if he were not to act schizophrenically.

Louis Gottschalk:
Understanding History, *p. 31*

PLATES

1

ETHNOHISTORY AS
RESEARCH METHODOLOGY

"Ethnohistory," said William N. Fenton, "is a way
of getting at certain problems in culture history" (1962: 2).
Ethnohistory is neither a discipline in itself nor an inter-
disciplinary field. It is neither an anthropological view
of history, nor an historical view of anthropology. It is a
synthesis of methodologies but not merely the sum of the two
(Cf. Dovring, 1960: 75), for there is a precise quality in
their symbiotic interrelationship and this can only come into existence in the research experience itself.

In this book we shall attempt to focus on a number
of problems in Pacific culture history. These have been selected to permit discussion of the research procedures util-
ized, as much as to arrive at solution to the problems.   I
have selected a wide range of problems deliberately to employ
a wide range of critical methods of approach.

Perhaps we should begin with a brief presentation
of the anthropological theory which lies behind ethnohistorical method.

Theory of Ethnohistorical Method

Ethnohistory is a technique for considering cultural
data *spatially* and *sequentially*. The data itself is organized into *traits* or *elements,* and these in turn into spatial
patterns which we term *complexes,* and maybe into even larger
configurations sometimes called *activities* (Linton, 1964:403;
Fenton, 1962: 6). This frame of reference permits the study
of *function* and *meaning* at various levels.

Any of these configurations may be studied as sequences through time. This sequence we call a *cultural continuum* (Linton, 1964:294-296; Barnett, 1942: 30), which Linton points out is "not only a continuum but a continuum in a

1

constant state of change." This process of cultural complexes each in dynamic equilibrium within itself yet moving like
a gyroscope through time is the subject of ethnohistorical
investigation.

The study of a cohesive but dynamic complex may be
made over a wide area spatially *at a point of time,* which
for ethnohistorical purposes may be a day, or a decade, or a
generation, so that it is within the focus and memory of an
informant - this we speak of as a *synchronic* analysis. Or it
may be researched as the movement of dynamic change within
any cohesive process of the cultural continuum, *through time.*
This is called *diachronic* research. These notions came to me
through S.F. Nadel's study of social processes, in which
methodologically he spoke of "synchronic and diachronic en-
quiry" (1951:100).

We are struggling with a number of anthropological
problems in the study of society, like *continuity* and *change,*
and *function* and *meaning.* This is anthropology - the dynamics of cultural change. But in that change can only be
studied through time it is also history. Ethnohistory is a
research methodology for exploring the regions where history
phases out into anthropology.

The distinction of diachronic from synchronic research is intended to remind us, as Linton pointed out that
the cultural continuum is never static. Change of some kind
is going on all the time. Societies are equipped with mech-
anisims for stimulating, and regulating the speed of change.
These changes reflect not only the character and values of
a people but also the material culture. To study material
culture diachronically is to see the reflection of human development through the generations, just as much as changes
in language and customs. Every artifact has meaning only in
its context - it relates both to individuals and to society
at any given point of time, and if such synchronic analyses
are investigated diachronically we may observe the momentum
of culture change throughout a cultural continuum.

There are at least three kinds of cultural reconstruction used in ethnohistorical research. These were defined by Dark (1957:231-278), as (1) *Cross-sectional* (2)
Institutional and (3) *Culture Continuum.* In the first type
the synthesis is synchronic; in the second it is diachronic
and in the third it is both spatial and temporal (synchronic-
diachronic).

Each of the patterns of synthesis has been used
for effective ethnohistorical reconstructions. Dark takes
a number of such research projects or "constellations" and
analyses them into sub-types.

In the writer's Fijian research he has used all
three methods of reconstruction. Most of the articles in
this volume are synchronic in that they are constellations
at some historic point of time - the study of Fijian war is
cross-sectional, 1839-1846; the Fijian letters from Papua
depict the initial Fiji/Papua value encounter, 1894-1905;
and Geddie's New Hebrides, 1848-1857. These are synchronic
in that they were the observations in a period of time which
could be seen whole in the lifetime of one man. Recently
the writer produced a paper for an anthropological society
which traced the institution of sorcery from pre-Christian
times to the present day with a different body of primary
sources for each generation. The book *Fijian Material Culture: A Study in Culture Context, Function and Change* covers
a spatial anthropological study at three or four levels of
temporal analysis across Fiji, coving four different institutions - war clubs, canoes and boats, turtle-fishing and
house-building. This method of synthesis (cultural-contin-
uum), brought to light during the research a definite strat-
um of Tongan influence before the arrival of the white man,
and quite independent of the Christian Tongan impact.   The
existence of this Tongan level in Fiji explains the process
of diffusion of Christianity into the Fiji Group. This is a
good example of how the study of artifacts may throw light
on dynamic and personality factors (Tippett, 1968).

Somehow or other we have to get beyond the merely
material artifact. Often when we go to a museum or to some
antiquarian's collection we look at meaningless things. They
have to have a *context* both in an institution and in a period
of history. If we can bring these factors together in a synthesis the *meaning* immediately becomes apparent. Furthermore,
even to members of one society and at one point of time the
context will be different, as for example, a beautifully made
war club will mean one thing to the craftsman, but something
quite different to the warrior. Likewise we have to identify
the *generation*. To one warrior the same war club (say, a
bowai) is a well-balanced weapon, his strength and protection
for a particular offensive stroke; but after his death, and
when because of his war exploits he has been deified, the
club may be the religious shrine for his spirit *(waqawaqa)* to
his son, who no longer calls it a *bowai*, but oils it reverent-
ly and presents an offering before it before he himself goes

to war with another war club, which is a *bowai*, or a *cali*, or
a *waka*, or whatever kind of club it happens to be. Here the
meaning and *function* have changed because the generational
context has changed.

So we have one *relativity of contemporaries* and a
relativity of generations, the former in the synchronic sequences and the latter in the diachronic. The last one especially raises a real problem for museum typologies. Barnett calls the latter the *relativity of needs* (1942: 30), a
phrase which came to him as he reconstructed ethnohistoric-
ally the experiences of certain American Indians under culture contact. His work could be classed as history as he
reconstructed from documents; but he drew also from anthropological data, and sought valid generalizations about human
behaviour.

Another example of the relativity of generations
on an international (rather than personal) level comes from
Barnett's research on Palau (Micronesia). Palauan religion,
for example, may be studied diachronically as changing under
the forces of acculturation through periods of Spanish, German, Japanese and American domination (1949:227-240; 1960:
82-84). Diachronic studies of this type are a natural method
for Western Pacific research.

Another quite imaginitive use of the diachronic
approach, is the fictionalized reconstruction around an artifact. I remember as a schoolboy reading a British public
school story *The Adventures of a Ten-guinea Watch*. Was this
perhaps the prototype for Wallace Deane's *The Strange Adventures of a Whale's Tooth?* This is a story for young people,
the tale of a whale's tooth *(tabua)*, the artifact used in Fijian ceremonial life for making requests for assistance in
war, for burning a village, for obtaining a favour, for ar-
ranging a marriage, for atonement, for mourning the dead and
so on, *ad infinitum*. Deane weaves all these different functions of a real tabua into an imaginary story running from
pagan whaling days into Christian times. It is a diachronic
study of the functional role of a whale's tooth in Fijian
ceremonial and an accurate synthesis. This is true ethnohistorical fiction (Deane, 1919).

Upstreaming

Another form of ethnohistorical reconstruction is
known as *upstreaming*. This term was innovated by Fenton,

who describes it as restructuring by direct sequence "against the tide of history going from the known present to the unknown past" (1962:12). He used it first in a study of suicide, but has made other uses of it since. I used it myself for a reconstruction of Fijian cannibalism. The pattern has two advantages. First, it is easier to go back step by step reconstructing slowly because of the continuity of many cultural features and interpretations. It is easier for me to interpret my father's experiences than those of my great-great-grandfather. So I proceed from father, to grandfather, to great-grandfather, and so on, and thereby eliminate the long time jump. This gives us a better *historic sense*. Second, one makes most interesting discoveries as he works back through his source material in the reverse chronology, to suddenly find that some significant culture trait disappears. It is like an archaeologist discovering an older form of pottery, or a cruder design, which can only be explained by the invention of the wheel or brush.

Thus one moves from the point of law and order to the war to suppress the cannibalism in the mountain regions (1870s). As one goes back you can trace the spread of cannibalism, the distribution of Christian and cannibal villages (back to 1854, the conversion of Cakobau the most famous cannibal of all). Before 1854 you find Christianity a really small thing except in Lau. One by one the little Christian groups disappear until 1835 when the Christian mission is no longer there at all. It is like the flood line in Middle East archaeology. But what this 'upstreaming' really brings to light is the period from 1835 back to about 1809, when the Fijian wars were under the control of escaped convicts and deserters from sandalwood and whaling ships. Beyond that you are in the period of pre-contact ceremonial cannibalism. It was the introduction of western arms and ammunition and renegade whites to service them as gunsmiths and marksmen that cannibalism underwent its dramatic *secularization*. The religious taboos and controls broke down and there was a surplus of bodies for the oven, and women and children indulged as they had not done before, and sometimes bodies were eaten without even presentation at the temple. It was a period of secularization before the missionary arrived. Cannibalism there was as far back as the myths go for the Fijian gods were cannibal gods, and they required human sacrifices for scores of purposes.

I very much doubt if this stratification could ever have been observed without 'upstreaming', through the source

Major Sources for the Study of Fijian Cannibalism

20th Century	No Cannibalism
4th Period of Acculturation Post Cession Period	Government and Mission Records Memoirs of Government Servants – Brewster, Im Thurn, Thomson Missionary Researcher Deane
3rd Period of Acculturation 1854-74. After Cakobau's Conversion	Missionary Writers, Fison, Langham, Carey, Baker Recorders of Fijian Traditions, Tatawaqa, Toganivalu, Sokiveta, Bulu Official Travellers, Smyth, Seemann Australian Missionary Notices, Letters Circuit Reports British Consular Records. Transactions Fijian Society
2nd Period of Acculturation 1835-54. Mission Contact Period	Missionary Records, Annual Reports of Circuits (especially Bau 1854) *Wesleyan Magazine* Missionary writings of Joseph Water- house and Carey Missionary Journals: Hunt, Jaggar, Lyth, Cross, Cargill, Williams, Lawry Sea Captains, Erskine, Endicott Seamen who resided with Fijians, Jackson, Diapea Beche de mer Trader's wife Mrs Wallis
Period of Culture Contact c1800-1835	Sea Captains, Wrecked Sailors and Sandalwooders: Siddons, Lockerby. Patterson, Dillon Missionary Journals & Letters: Cross, Cargill, Hunt, Lyth, Waterhouse, Wil- liams, Jaggar, Watsford, Hazelwood
Pre-contact Period Before 1800	First analyses of pre-Christian Relig- ious World View. Cargill, Cross, Hunt, Lyth, Williams Myths and Chants: Hunt, Hazelwood, Quain, Carey, *Transactions of Fijian Society*

Major Sources for Vocabulary of Cannibalism - Hazelwood,
Cargill, Hunt, Fison

material. This helps the researcher to "get into the act" himself, and he is truly exploring as he upstreams from the 'estuary' to the 'source'.

An Ethnohistorical Lexicon

A good ethnohistorian must have a wide knowledge of the language of the documents he is studying. This means that he should be able to recognize and date semantic change, and identify dialect words, especially in oral traditions and chants. In doing my studies of Fijian cannibalism, honourable and dishonourable killing, and sorcery, I found I had to work out my own lexicon of obsolete and modified words, phrases and symbolic terms and circumlocutions. It stands at about 400 entries at present, and had to be discovered by internal evidence, but once extracted from the documents and put into use as a tool, one knows these subjects could never be properly researched without the lexical key.

Every speaker of Fijian knows, for instance, that *beru* means rubbish. Not everyone knows that it meant food or body refuse sought by a sorcerer for applying his arts against a victim, or that in another context it meant a widow who escaped from the strangling cord. Or *ai cula*, commonly meaning a fork or needle in acculturated times, might under certain circumstances have represented small wooden pins set in the footprints of the intended victim to make him feel the prick of pain at night, and even to kill him if pushed deeply into the footprints. Or what do we mean by *luvedra ni mate* (children of the dead)? One's guess might be "an orphan". Set in its location of time and context it indicates men who have not yet avenged the death of their father. Or when does *qa ni vivili* mean a sea-shell, and when does it indicate the dead body from which the 'soul' has fled? Or when is a dead body for the cannibal called long pig *(vuaka balavu)*, and when a trussed frog *(botoualai)*. One could go on and on with these terms. Certainly one has to master first a symbolic system. Marc Block said that the "vocabulary of documents" is "form of evidence" (1964:168). So to, is the vocabulary of oral traditions, chants, dirges and proverbs.

Artifact or 'Document'

Lucey (1958: 28) distinguishes between *remains* and

records, and defines the former in this way -
    Remains are tangible evidences of the life of man
    in society. They are products (artifacts) of man's
    daily needs and hence are infinite in variety; they
    were not made with the intent of informing posterity,
    of man and his activities. The transmission of his-
    tory was not their primary purpose....
Yet every artifact tells a story of man in society. Just as
it is an index to society, so society has to interpret it.
Gottschalk says "a piece of pottery or a coin, an ancient
seal or a recent stamp may well be a personal document
(1969: 87). Sometimes an artifact does count in lieu of a
document, to signify an agreement.

    The Greeks had a custom of two men with a close
attachment parting company breaking a small white stone as
they separated. If in the fortunes of their descendants
two should ever meet again with the evidence of the fitting
stones the personal friendship of their forebears could be
taken up as if these descendants were themselves the con-
tracting parties. The stone was an agreement.

    The first offer of the cession of Fiji to Britain
was declined on the advice of a military man who feared the
cost in men and money of what the missionaries were accom-
plishing anyway by slow and peaceful means (Smyth, 1864:193,
208). Fiji then turned to the United States. The offer of
Cession was made by the presentation of a great whale's
tooth - the biggest I have seen. It is currently preserved
in National Archives in Washington, D.C., as part of an interesting collection of unusual artifacts which are counted
as documents, because they tell of important historical
events and have the symbolic meaning of agreements and con-
tracts.

    On page 44 of *Fijian Material Culture* the Fijian
mace is illustrated. Originally it was a war club of Ratu
Cakobau who surrendered it to Queen Victoria upon the Cession of the islands to Britain. This club, symbol of the
authority of the cannibal king, subsequently became the symbol of law and order under the colonial system. For the
people of the Kingdom of Bau the surrender of the artifact
signified the transfer of the government, and was far more
meaningful to them than the formal signing of the Deed of
Cession which the westerners alone fully understood.

    But only very few such artifacts have become housed

in archives, and many have now lost their meaning, like those
in the museums which have no identification of context.   We
are now in the anthropological area of history.   I recall
some of the talking points for data collecting of my Fiji
days - a turtle skull over the door of a house, a few remains
of tapa cloth spread over a grave, a row of notches on the
handle of a war club (scoring kills), a row of stones each
marking a body which ended in a cannibal oven, a weather-
eaten whale's tooth at Nakauvadra, petroglyphs on the rock
face at Dedevolevu. These are all ethnohistorical evidence;
but only if we can locate them in their cultural context.
Once they interpret *function* and *meaning* they become evidence.
Until then they are raw material for investigation.   The
stick charts of Micronesia have no evidential value until we
identify the waters of the northwest Pacific, the position
of the Marshall Islands represented by the shells (i.e. we
identify the context) and understand that they are used for
navigation, and how the Micronesian sailors used them to
achieve this purpose. Once their function and meaning are
clear the stick chart is as much a genuine map as any other
prepared with the most scientific instruments, and it tells
as historically significant a story.

Oral Tradition

Oral tradition has many forms, one of which is *myth*.
This requires a book for itself. I mention it merely to distinguish it from that form of oral tradition which is sometimes called proto-history and to which I shall devote a
chapter in this book. By this I am eliminating myth at two
levels. First there are the origin myths which frequently
assimilate historical characters and events and adapt themselves to political and social changes. If they have any
historical value it is as reflections of the process of change
itself. They produce numerous local variations and are often
reinterpretations rather than truly origin myths. Second
there are the myths associated with natural formations like
peculiarly shaped rocks along the coast. A whole volume
could be written on these for the Fijian island of Kadavu
alone.

Hocart makes the claim that "Custom and myth are
inseparable." Myth relates to the serious business of life,
is a precedent, is necessary because it gives ritual its intention (1952: 17,21).

These forms I shall have to bypass in this book.

I do so with the hope of coming back to them as an anthropological study at some future date. In this book, Oral
Tradition shall be taken to mean sub-recent traditions iden-
tifiable with historical events - floods, eclipses, pesti-
lences, and the first white men's ships. And this we shall
examine with the hope of identifying some of the local criteria for testing their reliability inherent within the society itself (Sturtevant, 1966: 26).

Pacific Research Today

Washburn pointed out that we do ethnohistory a dis-
service "when we expect it to contain within itself a whole
new philosophy." It is a method of approaching problems.
"What we can do, however, is to refine and exploit the method...." (1961: 33). And for the Pacific this most certainly
needs to be done. Ethnologists have appropriated descriptive
material from both primary and secondary sources uncritically.
Much of the literature on which they depend, posing as history or historical fiction, is itself unreliable.   Modern
myths emerge even in our own days and are communicated in
interviews, to be 'swallowed hook, line and sinker' by gullible researchers - Captain James Cook, Napoleon Bonepart and
Thomas Baker are passing into Pacific mythology and can be
historically studied as part of the mythmaking process itself.
And fictitious characters like those of Michener's novel *Hawaii,* are emerging as historical people. There never was a
time like this when Pacific history so needed to protect itself and so needed anthropological methods to do so (See Dening, 1966:32).

A number of these problems of historical reliability are dealt with in the article, "Skeletons in the Literary Closet."

Other articles explore different types of data base.
The reconstruction of Fijian war (1839-1846) and the New Hebridean study (1848-1857) are based on missionary journals. I
wish to press the point of the great historical and anthropological value of these manuscripts. Anthropology, in particular, has bypassed these resources, very much to its loss,
The exception has been Katherine Luomala who has written on
the subject (1947: 5-31), but much more remains to be said.

Davidson in an article on "Problems of Pacific History" (1966: 20) raises the question of the island mission-

aries (I mean island people, not westerners) who went to
other islands - "How did they evaluate the cultures of the
islands other than their own, when they travelled abroad as
mission teachers.....?" It is a good question, and has led
me to include one such study in this book. It is based on
a corpus of over 40 letters in the Fijian language, written
by Fijians in Papua to their folk at home (1894-1905) and
related to Davidson's question of the encounter of island
cultures.

    One of the most exciting things in Pacific studies
in the last decade is the new accessibility of historical
documents. One could write a whole article on it were there
space. There is the termination of colonial restrictions
on the time a document should be regarded as of restricted
use. There is the discovery of many journals of traders,
missionaries and other westerners who lived in the islands
and spoke the language. There is the publication of many of
these with annotations. There is the availability of many
extremely valuable manuscripts on microfilm through such
bodies as the Pacific Manuscripts Bureau (including their
most valuable listings in *Pambu*). There is the new interest
of islanders in their own culture history. There is just so
much material available for research that one can hardly expect to cover the material of his own immediate interest.

    One is reminded of Butterfield's comment that Lord
Acton's development as a historian coincided with the period
when European archives were successively opened more to
scholars. Ranke also "enjoyed the happiness of these harvest
days" and large areas of history were suddenly transfromed
(Butterfield, 1948: 15). With the emergence of young uni-
versities in the Pacific we have hopes of meeting more and
more island scholars. Without doubt there are scores of island biographies and cultural histories waiting to be written by ethnohistorians who are themselves islanders.

References Cited:

Barnett, H.G.
    1942   "Culture Growth by Substitution" *Research Stud-
                ies in the State College of Washington,* 10:26-30
    1949   *Palauan Society: A Study of Contemporary Native
                Life in the Palauan Islands,* Eugene, University
                of Oregon Publications
    1960   *Being a Palauan,* New York, Holt, Rinehart &
                Winston Inc.

12   ASPECTS OF PACIFIC ETHNOHISTORY

Bloch, Marc
1964   *The Historian's Craft,* New York, Vintage
            Books (Translated by Joseph R. Strayer).
Butterfield, Herbert
1948   *Lord Action,* London, G. Philip, for the His-
            torical Association
Dark, Philip
1957   "Methods of Synthesis in Ethnohistory"
            Ethnohistory 4. 231-278
Davidson, J.W.
1966   "Problems of Pacific History" *The Journal of
            Pacific History,* Vol. 1 5-21
Deane, Wallace
1919   *The Strange Adventures of a Whale's Tooth,*
            Sydney, Epworth Printing and Publishing House
Dening, Gregory
1966   "Ethnohistory in Polynesia: The Value of
            Ethnohistorical Evidence" *The Journal of
            Pacific History,* 1:23-42
Dovring, Folke
1960   *History as a Social Science: An Essay on the
            Nature and Purpose of Historical Studies.*
            The Hague, Martinus Nijhoff
Fenton, William N.
1962   "Ethnohistory and its Problems" *Ethnohistory*
            9: 1-23
Gottschalk, Louis
1969   *Understanding History,* New York, Knoff
Hocart, A.M.
1952   *The Life-giving Myth and Other Essays,* London,
            Methuen & Co.
Linton, Ralph
1953   *The Study of Man,* New York, Appleton-Century-
            Crofts
Lucey, Williams Leo. S.J.
1958   *History:Methods and Interpretation,* Chicago,
            Loyola University Press
Luomala, Katharine
1947   "Missionary Contributions to Polynesian An-
            thropology" in *Specialized Studies in Poly-
            nesian Anthropology,* Honolulu, Bishop Museum
            Press   5-31
Pambu
1968-73   Monthly Newsletter of the Pacific Manuscripts
            Bureau, Research School of Pacific Studies,
            Australian National University, Canberra

Smyth, Col. W.J.
   1861   Col. Smyth's "Report" and "Covering Letter"
                 App. in Mrs. Smyth's *Ten Months in the Fiji
                 Islands,* Oxford, John Henry & James Parker
                 1864,   197-210
Sturtevant, Wm. E.
   1966   "Anthropology, History and Ethnohistory"
                 Ethnohistory   13, 1:1-51
Tippett, A.R.
   1968   *Fijian Material Culture: A Study in Cultural
                 Context, Function and Change,* Honolulu,
                 Bishop Museum Press   Bull.   232
Washburn, Wilcomb E.
   1961   "Ethnohistory: History 'in the Round'"
                 Ethnohistory 8, 1:31-48

E NA [illegible] ... na Vale Vakaniu'a Vakaguvutania, ma [illegible]
A WILLIAM THOMAS PRITCHARD ESQUIRE, a noma Ko... a Mar... P...
A RATU EPENISA CAKOBAU, ko ira na Turaga ei veiwatanitu e [illegible]

Ni sa [illegible] me lewai na ka ena yaco kina na [illegible] dodonu, ka vakara ta... ...ka a...
katui ... rawa [illegible] Viti, kei na ka ena tubu kina na nodra tiko kei na [illegible] ...aka ... ka Na
sa [illegible] na nodra tiko vinaka vakaveiwekani kei na veimataca... Vakapoi a Na... ... ...
[illegible] avata, ka [illegible] yaco na veika sa volai a qo,—

I   NA caka cake a vanua kei na veivolavolai kecega ko Viti kei Pajai'a... ...na ... ...
d aga ko WILLIAM THOMAS PRITCHARD.

II   KEITOU sa solia e nai vola a qo kivei WILLIAM THOMAS PRITCHARD na k[illegible]
kecega me lewai Viti me vaka nai valavala e dodonu ka amcala, me sa rawata, me cakava ka [illegible]
vuivu, kei nai valavala e so sa nanumi e yaga ka dodonu, me sa rawata me kacivi keit[illegible] yabia, sa ka
[illegible] keitou kecega, kei ira na neitou kecega, me keitou saqonivata e na vale Vakaniu'a Vakagovi... a
ia na soqonivata kecega vakaoqo, ena sa yacana, Na Soqonivata ni Veibose, me lui kina ko WILLIAM
THOMAS PRITCHARD. Keitou sa vauci keitou kei ira talega na neitou, me talairawarawa sa[illegible]
keitou sa kacivi me soqonivata mai.

III.   KEI na ka kecega e dodonu ka tautaurata, kei na vanau ena kitaka ko WILLIAM THOMAS
PRITCHARD, sa tala na tani me kitaka e na vuku i keitou se e na yaca i keitou, keitou sa qai vauci
keitou, me vakadinata, ka talairawarawa kina, ka vakayacora; ia na veiyalayalati, kei na cakacaka ei
vanua, kei na vunau, e nanuma ko WILLIAM THOMAS PRITCHARD e yaga me caka, se me veivaka-
valatitaka, se me tukuna yani, e na vuku i keitou, se e na yaca i keitou, me tubu cake ka vinaka kina
ko Viti; keitou sa vauci keitou, me vaka keitou sa lewa yadua, se lewa vata, keitou na cakava, ka vakayacora, ka veiyalayalatitaka, ka tukuna.

IV.   ME sa tu dei na veika o qo, keitou sa qai loma vata kina, ka yacova na gauna ena sa kilai
vakamacala kina ni sa vakadonuya na neitou soli Viti yani, ko koya na Marama ni Piritania, sa ia e na
kenai ka 12 ni siga e na vula ko Okatopa, 1858, keitou sa vakadinadina tale kina e na kenai ka 14 ni
siga e na vula ko Tiseba, 1859, ni keitou sa soqonivata me bosea.

Keitou sa vola na yaca i keitou ki nai vola o qo e na aiga edaidai, na kenai ka 16 ni siga ni
vula ko Tiseba, 1859, me neitoui vakadinadina.

CAKOBAU (nonai X vola), Na Vunivalu.	Roko Tui Dreketi (nonai X vola), mai Rewa.
Roko Tui Veikau (nonai X vola), mai Namara.	Lewelloma (nonai X vola), mai Verata.
Ratu Isikeli, mai Viwa.	Ragata (nonai X vola), mai Nakelo.
Tudrau (nonai X vola), mai Dravo.	Navaqalevu (nonai X vola), mai Rakiraki.
Ko mai Mataiovea (nonai X vola), mai Namara.	Nai Kiuva (nonai X vola), mai Kiuva.
Koroi Raivolita (nonai X vola), mai Dutetu.	[illegible] (nonai X vola), mai Noco.
Maqala (nonai X vola), mai Verata.	Lora Dreketi (nonai X vola), mai Tokatoka.
Dabea (nonai X vola), mai Kuku.	Koroi Koyanamalo (nonai X vola), mai Cautata.
Koroi Ravuso (nonai X vola), mai Nakalawaca.	Koroi Rai [illegible] (nonai X vola), mai Lacokau.
Jioji Nanovo (nonai X vola), mai Nadroga.	Sesebualala (nonai X vola), mai Nakorotubu.

Keirau sa vola o qo na yaca i keirau, mei vakadinadina ni keirau sa vakatusa na vosa ni vola o
qo kivei ira na Turaga era sa vola kina na yacadra, ia ka ra sa kila vinaka na kenai balebale.

W. COLLIS,
Wesleyan Training Master.

E. P. MARTIN,
Wesleyan Mission Printer.

Maafu.	Tui Cakau (nonai X vola), mai Taviuni kei Ca-
	kaudrove.
Tui Nayau (nonai X vola), mai Lakeba.	Ritova (nonai X vola), mai Macuata.
Bete (nonai X vola), mai Macuata.	Tui Bua (nonai X vola), mai Bua.

Au sa vola o qo na yacaqu mei vakadinadina ni ka'u a vakatusa na vosa ni vola o qo kivei ira
na Turaga era sa vola kina na yacadra.

JOHN BINNER.

Koroi Duadua (nonai X vola), mai Navua.

Vakatusa vosa,

CHARLES WISE.

Ai vakadinadina ni ka vola na yacana ko Charles Wise.

BERTHOLD SEEMAN.

SA TABA NAI VOLA O QO ME NEI W. T. PRICHARD ESQUIRE, A KONISULA NI MARAMA NI PIRITANIA.
SA TABAKI MAI VIWA, E VITI. 1860.

First Offer of Cession from Fiji, 1859, showing
the names of the Chiefs who signed it. (See p.8)

2

ORAL TRADITION
and
HISTORICAL RECONSTRUCTION

Certain methodological changes in both history and anthropology are now being initiated because of pressures
brought upon them by ethnohistorical research and awareness.
Possibly the most apparent area of this pressure is that of
oral tradition. What is the evidential value of oral tradition? The argument over the status of ethnohistory has at
least awakened both historians and anthropologists to their
need for a determined effort at synthesis.

The Historicity of Oral Tradition

When A.L. Kroeber had worked through what the Mohave
Indians believed to be their historical traditions he described them as *"pseudohistory* and products of the imagination, of literary interest but not historical" (1951:71-176;
Sturtevant, 1966:27).

Robert Lowie protested against the treatment of oral
traditions as history, although he accepted them as of "psy-
chological significance" and admitted that their distribution,
like that of artifacts and ritual forms, might have some historical connection; but this was as far as he would go - oral
tradition is just not history (1960:202-3). Certain elements
might be regarded as the primitive counterpart of what we
call history, but he would not validate oral tradition as
such for the same reason that he would not validate aboriginal
pathology or biology (ibid:204). "We accept primitive observations" he said of astronomy, flora and fauna, "in so far
as they conform to what we independently ascertain by our own
methods." Then he went on to make the astonishing statement
(and this was in his retiring presidential address before the
American Folklore Society):
> However we neither derive the least increment of know-
> ledge from this primitive science, nor are we in the
> slightest measure strengthened in our convictions by

15

such coincidence. Exactly the same principle applies
in the domain of history (ibid. 205).
He wanted history to be a completely 'objective' examination
within his own ethnocentric criteria, and went so far as to
say -

I deny utterly that primitive man is endowed with historical sense or perspective" (ibid:206)[1]

Just as I would challenge Lowie, on a basis of my personal experience of what he (wrongly I think) calls primitive people, that we can derive no valuable knowledge from
their botany, for example (true, it does not fit the Linnean
system, but it has its own classifications and offers us
much genuine information of value to medicine), so too the
historical value of their oral tradition is immediately manifest once we cross the cultural barrier far enough to discover what it is about - its goals, its forms, its values
and its concept of time. It cannot be studied objectively
by a foreigner. One has to enter the spirit and language.
It is not a mere chronological record based on a foreign
calendar. One has to distinguish between the *times of the
gods*, the *times of the ancestors and heroes*, and *recent
time*.[2] One has to tune himself with the media of communication - song, dirge, proverb, riddle, story - the symbolism
of the form, the social situations, occasions and institutions within which the communication operated of its own
natural accord, its enculturative function, and many other
things. It is the researcher's obligation to "get into the
act" if he wants to understand it, and this will be more a
subjective than an objective exercise. To appreciate the
historical value of oral traditions requires an *experience*.

So, while I would agree with Lowie that "we cannot substitute primitive tradition for scientific history" I would
add the comment that we do not want to do so. But, if we
know the language and can get into the act enough to *feel*
it, we will discover a rich field of historical and scientific data. Indeed there is no other way of reconstructing
the cultural milieu, the world view, the value system, which
together form the context within which the history of these
people has been enacted. The historical judgements of the
cross-cultural historian have to be made within the values
and thought-forms of the people he studies - not his own.

Since Lowie's time the folklorists have gone their own
way and collected tales, classifying the various kinds functionally - origin tales, explanatory tales, trickster tales,
cultural themes and so forth. Some interesting collections

have been put together, which have considerable entertainment value and reveal commonalities of human nature in fables
and other literary forms, but the emphasis has been more on
the tale as a reflection of culture and as a type of literature than on history, and no adequate chronology has been
recognized.

Before Lowie died in 1957 the methodology of *ethnohistory* had emerged. Strangely enough it has been developed
mostly by students of the American Indians, of whom Lowie,
an Indian specialist, said "Indian tradition is historically
worthless." I know of no revision of this opinion in his
later life and the journal *Ethnohistory* published no notice
of his death. To attend the annual meeting of the American
Association for Ethnohistory is to find oneself almost entirely confined to papers on Indian studies. Neither historians nor anthropologists at large express much interest.
Furthermore their work tended to be obviously historical or
anthropological. There was little synthesis.

Dorson complained of the gulf between folklore and history, which continues without fraternization in spite of efforts like the Oral History Project, because professional
historians equate oral tradition with untruth and distortion,
and because U.S. folklorists are not historically minded,
using formal classifications rather than historical periods
(1961:12-13). In 1966 the first national colloquium on oral
history tried to bring anthropologists and historians together
and published a report. The reviewer in the *American Historical Review* doubted if oral history had yet crystalized sufficiently to be called a field. He found them concerned for
their entity, and worried about the validity of their ap-
proaches, although the reviewer thought they do have a role
to play and wished them well (Kahn, 1967).[3]

In America, history, anthropology and folklore go their
own sweet ways and the journal, *Ethnohistory,* seems to me
to be the only serious effort to bring about a synthesis.
The journal badly needs a special emphasis beyond the limi-
tations of the American Indians.

Now let us take a look at the matter in Britain. One
of the earliest men to take a serious look at oral traditions was E.B. Tylor. He distinguished between the mythical
and historical elements, and claimed that things could be
true either factually in the historical sense, or symbolically true in the ritual or religious sense. In either case
he regarded them as of historical value. Let me give an example of each.

Seventy years ago, after his early works had become well known he argued for a recognition of the remarkable memory element in many oral traditions:

... the South Sea Islanders, who till quite recently had no writing, were intelligent barbarians, much given to handing down recollections of bygone days, and in one or two cases, which it has been possible to test among them, it seems as though memory may really keep a historical record long and correctly (1904:292).

Among the supporting data he told of a community of Ellice Islanders who claimed to have originated from Samoa, but offered no more evidence than a worm-eaten staff, pieced together and tied. It was used by the orator in their communal assembly, and was so old that it was falling to pieces. The wood from which it was made did not grow on their island. It must have come from some other place: why not Samoa? The structure of the assembly was Samoan, and the role of the orator. But there was no other memory - just the notion that they had come from Samoa as the staff 'proved'. In time that staff was actually taken to Samoa and two things immediately came to light. First it was indeed made of a Samoan wood and recognized by the people as such; and second there was in Samoa an old tradition of a large party of Samoans who went to sea a number of generations before and had never returned. Although not proved, the oral tradition is immediately credible (ibid:293).

Another contribution of E.B. Tylor was in the reconstruction of 'primitive' religion, which he regarded also as history. I recall a passage in which he described the flowing wine and burning meat sacrifice and the gods meeting in council. Yet of this obviously mythical episode he wrote:

All this is not only history, but history of the finest kind. Looked at by the student of culture, even the wild mixture of the natural and supernatural, so bewildering to the modern mind is the record of an early stage of religious thought (ibid. 296).

There is truth and error in this statement. It is false because he was reconstructing the history of religion on an *a priori* frame of reference which was shortly to be discredited by anthropological research. He was right in assuming that the study of myths is basic evidence for religious reconstruction. He performed a great service for posterity by recording much data for the use of his successors, whatever they should think of his theoretical use of it.

Eighty years ago when George Laurence Gomme was presi-
dent of the Folklore Society in England he wrote a book for
Lubbock's *Series in Modern Science.* He bemoaned the obses-
sion of anthropologists with evolutionary landmarks at the
expense of folklore. Even the historians who occasionally
drew on craniology, archaeology and philology, rarely turned
to folklore, which Gomme believed contained many ethnological
facts which called for historical investigation, and that "a
method for discovering them" had to be developed by scholars
(1892:vi). Gomme found obstruction to the study of folklore
because of the polular notion of its location in the nursery,
and it being beneath the dignity of academic historians and
philogists. He argued that the tale had value as a repository of information on beliefs, customs and traditions, and he
bemoaned the occupation of historians with only the political
and commercial progress of nations (ibid. 1-2).

Gomme himself had been much influenced by E.B. Tylor and
was aware of the fact that folklore housed a body of significant data that needed some kind of classification. From this
his own efforts as a folklorist turned to the matter of reconstructing religious belief and ethnic genealogies. Yet in
spite of his enthusiasm and the inclusion of his work in Lubbock's series, Lubbock himself was cautious about the value
and use of folklore. Grudgingly he admitted that it might
"solve many difficult problems in ethnology" but there needs
to be very careful study "before this class of evidence can
be used with safety."

The functionalists both helped and hindered the acceptance of oral tradition. Malinowski, with his synchronic
rather than diachronic approach, discarded the historical
potential of myths and concentrated on their relationships
to social procedures and belief. The same applies to Radcliffe-Brown, who, in his study of the Andaman Islanders,
saw myth as a "way of thinking and feeling about society and
its relation to the world of nature". These men stressed
the function of myth and/or oral tradition for maintaining
social cohesion. Legends which relate the invention of weapons and customs may be related back to origin myths or hero
stories - how the social order and practices came into being
(Radcliffe-Brown, 1922:376-405), but they relate to current
life and its artifacts and have no historical significance.
Malinowski argued -
> They have no idea of a long vista of historical occur-
> ances, narrowing down and dimming as they recede...
> Whenever they speak of some event, they distinguish
> whether it happened within their own memory or that
> of their fathers', or not.

There are only two 'time' categories - (1) that of their
fathers or grandfathers (the number of generations the oldest inhabitant can remember or narrate), and (2) long ago,
which is designated by an expletive, *lili'u* (1961:301). This
would agree with my own Fijian experience (*supra*, and end
note 2) except that I found the time depth of the recent period a little greater and recalled by physical events - epidemic, comet, eclipse, flood, etc. The same conception of
time has since been reported from Africa (Jones,1965:153,160)
and in Alaska (Hudson, 1966:56-58). Always there is a time
gap between the remote past and the recent past. The great
potential for ethnohistorians lies in the oral traditions of
the recent past. It seems to me that we may have a pre-exis-
tent state (timeless before the beginnings), the beginnings
(hero stories), then a gap of which the islander does not
seem to be aware until he is confronted with the problem by
the investigator, and finally the recent (and perhaps sub-
recent) period for which he can produce epics, songs, dirges,
proverbs and narratives.

At this point in our discussion I have to differentiate
between origin stories (which may have symbolic and exagger-
ated features), wonder tales, animal tales (maybe totemic or
maybe literary imagination) and fairy tales (all of which may
have great anthropological value), its function being religious, legal, educational or for entertainment, on the one
hand, and material which purports to be historical on the
other, even though it may be used to accompany a dance for
entertainment: what the Fijians would call *ai talanoa* and
ai tukuni on the one hand and *ai tukutuku* on the other.

Formulation of a Methodology

Having eliminated the religious and symbolic or mythical
element of oral tradition, and having brought our focus upon
that which actually purports to be historical, we shall now
turn back to the question of reliability.
"Written sources are better than oral ones." This is
the maxim of a non-historian,
declares Vansina (1960:52).
For the practitioner sources are sources. These can be
good or bad, but there is nothing intrinsically less
valuable in an oral source than in a written one. The
only advantage of a written source is that it is at the
same time an archaeological document....

Most encouraging results are coming out of new Africa,

where many historians, including some highly competent Afri-
cans, are working on the oral traditions and exposing much
of truly historical value (Boston, 1969; Shelton, 1968;
Alagoa, 1966, 1968; Berger, 1966; Vansina, 1960; Jones, 1965;
Ogot, 1966; Gray, 1965 et al.), and working out an appropriate methodology for handling their material.

In 1966 Ogot took certain scholars to task for writing
on African social institutions - family, clan, religious
cults, kingship, etc. - without paying adequate attention to
their historical traditions, both written and oral. He pointed
out how the functions of these institutions change through
time, and that such changes are normally embodied in the
traditions and require historical investigation. He insisted that one has precisely the same problems with both oral
and written traditions - bias, reliability, conflicting accounts, and so forth - so there are no reasons for accepting
one and rejecting the other (1966:140-145).[4]

Vansina, who researched the history of the Chiefdoms of
Kubu, and found his sources almost entirely oral traditions,
formulated a set of theoretical rules for evaluating this
kind of source. He began by identifying oral tradition as
different from reporting eye-witnesses (which would make the
product *news* rather than records intended for *transmission*).
He felt the researcher had to acquire a knowledge of (1) the
language of the traditions (2) the society, and (3) the culture of the kingdom. Then he asked why this society had oral traditions at all, and why they were preserved in these
particular forms and not in some other. He sought to find
the organic bonds which linked the forms of transmission to
the rest of culture. Eventually he classified the sources -
formulae, poetry, genealogies, tales, commentaries and pre-
cedents in law. Some of these, but not all, had historical
intention; but they all had some historical value once the
researcher understood their form and function. Vansina laid
down an important foundation and discussed procedures and
problems of data collection. He found that village and clan
records could be checked against each other, and that sometimes traditions are preserved by specialized bodies, such
as tribal councils, and their recitation is checked (1960:
43-53, 257-270).

Berger (1966:149-158), working in Karagwe, used stories
of the kings, genealogical lists, songs and recitations,
and also found institutions for preserving traditions. She
used regular anthropological open-ended interviewing, working with the old men and with groups and starting with the

genealogy. Alagoa (1966:405-417; 1968:235-242) worked among
the Ijo of the Niger delta, following Vansina's methods and
working on proverbs which were built on historical persons
and events. He stresses the importance of knowing the language and thinks that one reason why oral traditions are ne-
glected is the difficulty of the field work in data collecting. Shelton (1968:243-257) studied an historical figure and
wrote of the problems he encountered in identifying the traditions, verifying their historicity, and the importance of
identifying the purpose of the tradition before trying to interpret it - is it religious or historical, for instance?
Boston (1969:29-43) programmed his research on the oral traditions of the Igala by dealing with three critical problems,
(1) variants in the traditions, (2) chronology (because of
gaps in the time span), and (3) separating political facts
from their historical functions.

These are some of the ways in which African research is
continuing with the use of oral tradition. It will be seen
immediately that it implies a sympathetic attitude on the
part of the researchers, a positive attempt to explore its
hidden value, rather than that of "a detective trying to find
fault with a text in order to condemn it" (Vansina, 1960:49).

One of the most fascinating pieces of ethnohistorical
research to come my way was Raymond Firth's *History and Traditions of Tikopia,* (1961), which will serve in this paper
to bring us back to the Pacific. It throws light on the nature of change in traditional tales. Firth collected a body
of traditional tales in Tikopia in 1928-29. About a generation later (1952) he returned and worked over the same material again, dwelling particularly on the revisions and modifications since his earlier visit. He found the tales represented continuity and discontinuity and revealed an impor-
ant aspect of interpretation. One had to allow for variant
traditions being the reflection of variables in the socio-
political structure - the adaptation of tales to social and
political events or changing situations. The tales can be
regarded as true and interpreted symbolically, or they can
be told for recreation, but they "belong to the group" and
serve functionally as an "identity badge and a social rally-
ing point." The material is controlled by the approved leader
of the group, and for him it held ritual power, which condi-
tioned his health and prosperity. Not only do the tales
reflect the unity of the social structure, but they also permit competitive elements and organizational pressures within
the unity of that society. Firth stresses the fact that
variations may not necessarily be "defects in the memory" or

"embriodery of imagination" but rather "remoulding" due to
the "social situation" of the narrator and his times.   He
goes on to argue that "realistic appraisal of Polynesian
traditions in sociological terms" should strengthen the approach of scholars to this kind of oral tale for purposes of
interpretation.

Two Fijian Dirges:
The Wasting Sickness and the Dysentery

One of the most valuable of the forms of oral tradition
for historical reconstructions in Fiji is the *dirge (lele)*.
This is a form currently still in use.   I mean, not merely
used as a background for the *vakamololo*[5] for 'classical' entertainment tragedy, but the creation of dirges is still an
active art.   They are frequently prepared for the memorial
service *(lotu ni vakananumi)*, or end of mourning *(burua)*. If
the sexy cannibal victory dances *(wate* and *dele)* disappeared
with the coming of Christianity, this was not so with the majority of dance forms and their accompanying songs, epics and
dirges.   I have spent some hundreds of hours watching and
listening to these performances in seven or eight different
provinces of Fiji.   Sometimes the themes are local and recent,
sometimes they are archaic and from other parts of Fiji.There
is some exchange of these.   A region may send to another district for a renowned dancing-master *(dau-ni-vucu)*, who will
be entertained and given a presentation of some kind for his
services (survival of the exchange economy).   In pre-Christian times this kind of exchange served as a bridge between
Melanesia and Polynesia.   Josua Mateinaniu, the Fijian converted in the Tonga awakening, who helped the first missionaries with the Fijian language and returned with them to Fiji
to serve as their herald *(mata-ni-vanua)*according to chiefly
custom before Tui Nayau, was in Tonga as a dancing-master to
teach the Tongans a Fijian war-dance *(wesi)*.[6]

I recall a dirge performed by the young people of a village in Kadavu to honour the memory of one of their number who
lost his life in Guadalcanal in World War II.   Of all the
dirges there is none more dramatic and powerful in its effect
than the biblical lament of David over Absalom, presented in
a church service by the old women of the congregation. If the
preacher determines beforehand that he wants to end his service with this rendition that will certainly be a powerful
act of worship.   If the researcher has the language and sympathy with the mood and function of the worship service, getting into the act and sharing the experience, dirges will

never again be just forms of expression to be objectively
analyzed. You get away from the sense of time, even with an
ancient dirge, and you are there in the timeless present.
The true Fijian dirge of the olden days was not written in
the past tense with the verbal sign *'a'*, but either with the
continuous present *'sa'* (not 'e') or with no verbal sign at
all. The past, present, future time trichotomy is a recent
innovation of the education department of somewhere around
the 1930s. The grammatical change is reflected in the newspapers, books, hymns and other printed material in the forties. I lived in the Group when change was taking place.

The study of a cultural institution or trait, which has
continuity from pre-Christian to modern times can often be
understood better by the ethnohistorical approach known as
"upstreaming" (Fenton, 1962: 12).   If one gets into the
act today and goes back in reverse chronology one can identify the discontinuities and often ascribe them an approxi-
mate date. One can do this with the Fijian dances and dirges.
As you 'peel off the layers' and get back beyond the Christian period the cultural configuration contains non-Christian
elements. There will be references to the pre-Christian eschatology - *Bulotu* or *Bulu* (the abode of the dead), or the
waiting-place of souls *(nai cibaciba)*[7] or this may be specifically named, or the vocabulary of the strangling of the widows
of the dead or of the sick, or live burial, and so on[8] - yet
the forms and much of the funerary terminology will remain
the same. This is the kind of historical information,
as of the changing continuum for example, which Tylor and
Gomme longed to preserve and catalogue. I can do no more
than mention it here, and to agree that it is of vital historical importance, not only for purpose of information but
because it depicts the context of the historical dirge, marks
its genuineness, and often may be used to date events. Thus
I would agree with Dening that the problem with many of our
finest Pacific primary sources is how to use them properly:
that anthropologists have dipped into them to suit their own
purposes and "in a most unhistorical manner" (1966:26-27);
and I might add that historians have bypassed the cultural
dynamics they reflect.

To draw together a number of the points already suggested
in this paper I purpose now to take two famous Fijian dirges,
which mourned the dead on the occasions of the wasting sickness and the dysentery epidemic that fell on Fiji in Fiji in
the first two decades of culture contact when the Fijian
people were non-literate, and to pin-point some of the problems of Pacific ethnohistory to which the dirges speak. I

shall speak only of precise problems of events and chronology, not the cultural information like the linguistics and burial customs, for example.

The dirge of the wasting sickness *(lila balavu)* was widespread in Fiji all through the last century. It crops up in many places, fortunately in its Fijian form. It was published in the government paper *Na Mata,* and also in the report of the Royal Commission which investigated the decrease of native population in the 1890s, when it was analyzed and commented on by a Fijian scribe, Ilai Motonicocoko. He was sufficiently acculturated to know what western historians looked for, and pointed out some of the historical *identifiers* in the following words:

> Two things are known about the year in which the *lila balavu* attacked our ancestors; it was the year in which the first European ship came, and it was the year in which the comet with three tails appeared.

In addition to noting these two identifiers he also commented on the origin of the dirge, information which must have been common knowledge in Fiji, which we might call the Fijian 'copyright' as it were. He declared it to be -

> composed by two women, who were captured in war from Buretu, and brought into captivity to Ratu Mara, the grandfather of Ratu Jope, native magistrate of Serua, when he was living at Soso in Bau.

This oral tradition would count with the Fijians as (1) a demonstration of the integrity of the dirge and (2) the ownership of the performance rights.[9]

He also adds the comment that ultimately a medicinal cure was found for the plague by some native herbalist, and because it cured the chiefly family at Naitasiri, the herb was called *Vueti Naitasiri* (Healing of Naitasiri). The song itself describes the physical symptoms of the disease and death (as in most dirges) and mentions a number of items of material culture and some of its institutions, like strangling the sick.

Another dirge, somewhat similar in style and subject-matter, which also interested the Commission was the "Dirge of the Dysentery Epidemic" *(Cokadra).* This also dated to the pre-literate period, but was well remembered in 1875 when the measles epidemic hit Fiji and carried off 40,000 Fijians.[10] At that time there were still a few old men alive who compared it with an epidemic of their youth which, they said, worked even greater destruction. This would put it back somewhere near the turn of the century. The oral

narrative which accompanied this second dirge, declared that
the disease came from a European vessel, which came into the
Group from the direction of Lau. Furthermore, at this time
the ancestors are said to have spoken of this as the second
white man ship:
    The captain has anchored for the second time
    The origin of our sickness is among us again.
This probably does not mean literally and exclusively the "second" ship. It means - there were two epidemics, both associated with a white man's ship.[11] This information is historically valuable for the first incident also. The tradition
also confirms the sequence - the *lila balavu* first, the *cokadra* later.

    Other traditions like the death of Banuve, War Lord
(Vunivalu) of Bau, with the dysentery epidemic, (for his
dirge was lost or forgotten, except for odd fragments of information about it), gave him the name, Baleivavalagi, a
yaca vakaibalebale - a name-with-a-meaning, indicating as it
does that he died of the foreigners' disease. These names
are highly significant as historical informants.[12]

    The contextual terminology of this second dirge is
strongly nautical and reflects the orientation of the coast-
al people, who were the navigators of Fiji. From the place
names we learn the wide distribution of the epidemic and a
few features of Fijian pre-Christian eschatology and world
view validate its antiquity.

    Ilai Motonicocoko went back in his mind to the "raising
of the flag" (1875) and said that in the following fifteen
years under the new colonial administration these old traditions were fast being forgotten.
    There remain only a few today in each province, who know
    these five things - 1. the wasting sickness, 2. the comet
    with three tails, 3. the dysentery, 4. the eclipse and
    5. the tidal wave.
Possibly this was oratorical exaggeration because in the enquiries of the Royal Commission information about the dysentery at least was widespread, but always the most persistent
fact was the association of the epidemic with a white man's
ship, and many of the older informants linked it with the
death of Banuve. The Report of the Commission records in
quotation marks as the unified testimony of "the old men and
women":
    Before the white men came no one died of acute diseases:
    all the people who died were emaciated by lingering in-
    firmities before death. Coughs came with white men, so

did dysentery. Ratu Banuve is said to have died from
a foreign disease resembling dysentery soon after it
was first brought here. That is what we have always
heard from our elders (30-31).
W.S. Carew, Resident Commissioner of Colo East always obtained
the same testimony from Fijian informants and was never able to
rebut their arguments.[13]

The first whites known to have been wrecked in Fiji came
to grief on the Bukatatanoa Reef, Oneata, and were killed
and eaten, but they passed on a disease which spread through
the whole Group and proved very destructive. William Cross
picked up this tradition when he arrived in Fiji in 1835. He
passed it on to John Hunt, his later biographer, and we have
his word in print (1846:80). From the description Cross and
Hunt thought it might have been dysentery or cholera. The islanders (in terms of their world view) interpreted it as
punishment for killing the white men, and for some time
thereafter those people did not claim their rights to eat
people with "salt-water eyes". Hazelwood also worked in
this locality and identified the vessel as *Argo*, and the reef
is often now called Argo Reef (1850:308).

David Wilkinson, a prominent early figure in Fiji wrote
a paper (which I have not seen) on Fijian epidemics before
the measles. He too used a traditional dirge which came to
him from the mother of Ra Esekaia, who was heir to the paramount chieftaincy in Bua, until he surrendered it to his
younger brother upon his conversion, the country still being
pagan. These events can be dated from the missionary journals and reports. His mother's memory must have gone back
to the early 1800s. The events of the dirge went back before her memory. Its narrative covered the visit of a ship
to the Macauta coast, and again links the event with a comet.
The song spoke of a town, Koroma - "town of a thousand foundations" - completely depopulated by the epidemic. Wilkinson
visited the locality in 1860-2 and found the foundations
overgrown with timber "of the second order of rotation and
advanced girth, estimated by him to be from sixty to seventy
years old."

In fixing precise dates for the requirements of history
as the westerner likes it, we thus have a good identifier for
each epidemic, the comet for the first and the death of Banuve for the second, as these two facts recurred in various
accounts of the events from different parts of the group.

Ratu Matanikutu, also known as Naulivou, was the ruling

chief in Bau, when the notorious Charles Savage (whose adventures are well documented)[14] arrived in the Group and began the period of devastation that followed the introduction
of western arms and ammunition. His vessel was the *Eliza*,
wrecked on the reef at Nairai in 1808, and after a brief period as a fugitive he was found in Bau where he had established
himself with Naulivou's patronage in 1809. Naulivou was the
successor of Banuve, and this would place the dysentery in or
before 1808. 1808.

In the ceremonies of the installation of Naulivou as
War Lord, an institution performed by the responsible *mataqali*, the Levuka-Oneata people, among the ceremonial gifts
they presented was a canvas tent - the first European property seen at Bau. These people from Oneata had apparently
salvaged it from a wreck. This constellation of relating
facts would suggest it was the *Argo*.

On the day that Naulivou was installed by the *mataqali*,
Levuka, from Oneata, the world of nature "did honour to the
occasion" by means of an eclipse of the sun. Some day, we
hope, the astronomers will do for the Pacific what they have
recently done for Africa - chart the courses of the solar
eclipses for a thousand years across the continent on a
series of maps, for the purpose of identifying the eclipses
mentioned in the oral traditions (Gray, 1965:251-62).[15]
Thus, for example, Vansina's study of Bakuba chronology featured a solar eclipse of 1680 A.D. as a focal point for dating a genealogy from the sixteenth century to the twentieth
(1960:258), thus putting a new tool beside the zero-varve[16]
and tree-ring pattern[17] for long range dating.

Another line of tradition comes through Joseph Waterhouse who was in Bau at the time of Cakobau's conversion in
1854. This was the hub of Fiji as he collected all kinds
of information, among it, traditions of a wreck in Lau about
1800. Broken plates, buttons and other artifacts eventually
found their way to Bau, and at the same time an epidemic,
which from the native description he took to be Asiatic cholera. The effects were disastrous and the dead were simply
buried in a common grave. Banuve, the War Lord, was named
"Victim of the Foreign Disease". Somewhere in this collection of information Waterhouse picked up a myth of falling
stars, which melted in the hands of the people, and was of
course interpreted in terms of the Fijian world view. Waterhouse believed there had been a hail storm - an extremely
rare event for Fiji - an interesting case of the problem of
separating myth from history (Waterhouse, 1866:22).

The three-tailed comet was visible for 37 nights, a tradition which is credible because 37 has no sacred significance, like the Hebrew 40 days and nights, or 40 years. Donati's comet (1811) was too late. The only other reported close to that time was the comet of 1803. This is close to the wreck of the *Argo*. The Royal Commission accepted this reasoning.

A tradition from Noco, supported by another from Nakelo suggest that a sufficient space of time lay between the two epidemics to allow some population adjustment.

If we exclude Tasman and Bligh, who sailed through Fiji, the earliest land contacts we have on record were the *Pandora* (1791) and *Arthur* (1794). An individual, Komaibole, also known as Nalila, a name-with-a-meaning that identifies him with the wasting sickness and marking it as at the time of his birth, lived at Lasakau, Bau. A native informant testified before the Commission (she was about 70 years of age) that she was taken to Bau when she was about 16. Nalila was about 45 at the time. This would give us a rough date about the time of the *Pandora's* visit.

I have mentioned that the disease was cured by means of a herb. Beside Vueti Naitasiri, the name-with-a-meaning, two other herbs are mentioned in the oral traditions, *laqaiqai*, which I cannot identify; and *wavuwavu*, a currently known medicinal herb *(Erigeron albidum)*, also known as *conivavalagi*, which can be translated as "herb for the foreigners' disease". It is used now for ophthalmia, the juice being extracted and applied to the eyes as drops. I prefer the above translation to "foreigners' grass" as I can document its use before 1850.

Nakelo traditions, which concern the narrative as it influenced the Rewa delta, depicts the Rewa villages as previously overcrowded, but being left empty by the plague, the people departing and leaving the sick behind. This tradition speaks of a great flood, the highest they ever remembered, which swept the stricken villages out to sea and buried the mangroves in silt. The lower delta of the Rewa was supposedly built up by this event. This could very well be true. I know the characteristics of this river and the delta. I lived for nine years on Davuilevu land, only a few miles from Nakelo. This was possible because that land came up early for sale to foreigners: it had belonged to the Davuilevu tribe, exterminated in the *lila balavu*, as was also another nearby tribe, the Korolevu.

Most of the information about these two epidemics was
gathered about 1890 for the Royal Commission, when the epidemics were the subject of intensive investigation, as related to the subject of population decline. The research
was well done, and I have used this freely as my basic data.
Nevertheless I have been able to discover just enough related material to realize that this kind of research is never
finished.

Some Guidelines for the Validation of Fijian Oral Tradition

The study of Fijian oral traditions needs to be done
seriously, even the mythical and magico-religious material.
It is adult composition and should not be treated as for
children.

The *form* must first be identified, and then the *function* and validation must proceed within the expectations and
values of this cultural form and function.

Can the occasion for the use of the tradition be identified by internal or external information?

The researcher should understand the language of the
tradition, and hopefully be able to identify periods of semantic change. It would be ideal for him to build his own
vocabulary of specialized semantic change. This has to be
done over the years from documents rather than dictionaries.

The research should not proceed on some theoretical *a
priori* grid or frame of reference, anthropological or historical theory. Any grid used for writing up should come
out of the data itself: e.g. Fijian concept of time.

Every case is unique, even among traditions with a similar form and function: e.g. dirges. Therefore each stands
on its own merits.

Research should be positive. Commence by assuming the
tradition is accurate. Look for validations rather than
errors. This is basic in gaining rapport with one's informants.

Look for comparisons and similarities in oral traditions. Compare one tradition with another. Identify the
kinds of evidence one finds in each functional form of tradition.

Enquire of informants what testimonies or indigenous validations accompany the one being investigated. Is there another kind of oral tradition which relates to it: e.g., tradition of origin or ownership of a dirge or song for a dance.

What natural phenomena, events, catastrophes, &c., are mentioned? Can these be identified by external evidence - ship logs, &c., or by modern technology like astronomical calculations? Were these things witnessed in nearby islands and reported in their tradition?

What events in the tradition being investigated can be related to other traditional reports? Are they the same or similar? Can they be put in sequence, like the two Fijian epidemics? Can they be related to ship movements, migrating people and such things which may be dated?

Does the tradition identify names of people on known genealogies, or places on the map, especially places no longer occupied?

Do the events link up with any features of culture contact - introduction of arms and ammunition, international rivalry, cultural borrowings and innovations, &c.

What Fijian customs are buried in oral tradition that have value for interpretation: e.g., the name-with-a-meaning?

And, of course, it should go without saying, that the oral tradition has to be seen within the Fijian world view at the time, not within a system of western logic. Unless the tradition is in rhythmic form and handed down as such, its form will change and details may be omitted, for example, after conversion to Christianity.

This is by no means an exhaustive list, but merely the result of reflection on two Fijian dirges of epidemics about a decade apart, tentative dates 1791 and 1802-3, at the very beginning of the contact period of pre-literate Fiji. As I have already indicated, every case is unique and offers the researcher some new combination of problems for investigation. For such investigation ethnohistorical methods are appropriate - neither history nor anthropology is adequate alone.

Notes:

1   One could dismiss this merely as evidence of how ethnocentric even the best anthropologists could be in 1916,
when the statement was first made, but for the fact that
DuBois in 1960, in a volume of selected writings of Lowie,
choosing 33 from 300 options, selected this to include in
the section entitled "Relation of Ethnology to Other Disciplines", and presented it on its own merits, without
editorial comment, as if it were a recent article.

2   These are my own categories, and they came out of the
data itself. The material I collected in Fiji over 20
years fell into one of three types. Some material was
more theological than historical. It was historical only
in a sense of a notion of pre-existence (non-human) before
the beginnings *(ai vakatekivu)*. There are creation stories, divine validations of customs and procedures, that
speak out of the timelessness before the beginnings. The
link between this and the historical period is that the
gods were worshipped by men, but distinguished from the
deified ancestors. Olden times *(na gauna makawa)*, former
times *(na gauna eliu)*, the times of our ancestors *(na
gauna ni noda qase eliu*, or *na nodra gauna na vu)* go back
to the origin of the present lineages, and can be numbered by generations according to the lineage genealogies.
The people speak of themselves as the descendants *(kawa)*
of the *vu*. This is the historical period of their residence in the locality. Beyond that history is a blank.
More recently, say, from the first culture contact in the
late 18th century, which I have called recent times, the
Fijians identify periods by events - "times of wars", or
"cannibal times" or "Christian times", or maybe something
is described as before or after the "coming of the Church"
"the raising of the flag" or "the measles epidemic".

3   This is as viewed by an outsider. From inside I believe
the Columbia University oral history program has operated
for 25 years, and there are now 250 programs in the U.S.-
LC Information Bulletin, Mar. 30, 1973, p. 110.

4   In passing he points out that the documentary sources
for early British history - Gildas, Bede, Nennius and the
Anglo Saxon Chronicle - were all compiled from oral sources. The same point was made by Lucey (1958:30) for the
United States. In claiming that oral records are often
written down, he cited *The American West* (Ed. Wm. Targ:
Cleveland, World Publishing Co., 1946) as an example, of
a work compiled from legends, songs and ballads.

5   A *vakamololo* is a rhythmic dance-like presentation from
a seated posture. The rhythm of the performers *(matana)*

symbolizes the words *(kena vosa)* of the song, which is
either narrative or descriptive.

6   Josua Mateinaniu was a petty chief from Fulaga. Subsequently he was the spearhead of the mission thrust into
pagan Fiji, preceding the missionaries to several new
locations.

7   Every community had its local waiting-place, sometimes
called by name. This should not be confused with Naicobocobo, a place name, a place with a similar function
but known to people all over Fiji. It is in the oral
traditions and sayings as the locality where the dead
plant *tarawau*. To go to Naicobocobo to plant *tarawau*,
means to die.

8   My own vocabulary of honourable and dishonourable means
of killing, sorcery, and funerary rites comprises nearly 400 words and phrases, gathered over the years in
reading early Fijian archival material.

9   I remember on one occasion asking my herald how to go
about obtaining a bulk lot of fans of a particular design. He told me that almost any woman could make one,
but as an honourable person I should negotiate with the
chief of Daku, as a woman of that village had originally
worked out the pattern. I followed his advice and was
rewarded with the finest workmanship for honouring the
ownership of performance rights.

10   The statistics of certain areas of Fiji were carefully
kept by the missionaries. Fison's figures for Lau are a
good extant example.

11   The linguistic expletives or functors of the dirge are
of significance. *Baki* and *baci* (same word, two dialects)
imply a continuing action - "the event has occurred before". The emphasis is not on the numeral two (two
ships), but on the fact that what happened once has happened a second time.

12   I once challenged the age given by a Fijian girl on her
marriage application. She had the name "Sukunaivalu"
(return from the war) a name given to many born in that
year. She did not argue but conceded the point immediately and we set things in order.

13   A letter from Carew, Feb. 11, 1892, tells of a collection of small pots discovered during the surveying of a
location near Nausori ten years earlier. The Fijian official with them identified them as surviving from the
lila balavu, as the sick were left to die in this locality with only a supply of water and a yam or two. He
was a man of about 50 at the time, and apparently had
heard the story from his elders.

14   The story of Charlie Savage holds together well. The
      evidence of missionaries, of secular white adventurers
      and Fijian oral traditions tell very much the same story.
15   Photographic copies and a master grid are available
      for a moderate fee. The lines of the course of an ec-
      lipse are marked with symbols to indicate sunrise, mid-
      day and sunset. Dr. Gray is calling for information of
      traditions reporting eclipses.
16   Long-range dating by glacial varves (annual sediment
      deposit of retreating ice) has been fixed from a thick
      varve taken to be the ice bi-partition marking the be-
      ginning of the postglacial. This zero-varve has been
      dated at 6839 BC, at least for Sweden and Finland. It
      becomes a kind of 'historic anchor' for the calculation
      of sequences (Heizer, 1957).
17   Long-range dating is done by the dendrochronologists,
      by having reconstructed the calendar of wet and dry
      years by tree-rings. Thus they can identify the pattern
      of a piece of timber found, say, in the remains of an
      ancient house (Douglas, 1931).

References Cited:

Alagoa, Ebiegberi Joe
    1966   "Oral Tradition among the Ijo of the Niger
              Delta" *Journ. of African Hist.* 7.3: 405-17
    1968   "The Use of Oral Literary Data for History"
              Journ. Amer. Folklore, 81 235-42
Berger, Ruth C.
    1966   "Field Work Methods in the Study of Oral Tra-
              ditions in Karagwe" in Posnansky 1966 149-158
Boston, J.S.
    1969   "Oral Tradition and the History of the Igala"
              Journ. of African Hist. x.1: 29-43
Colony of Fiji
    1896   *Report of the Commission appointed to inquire
              into the Decrease of the Native Population,*
              Suva, E.J. March, Govt. Printer.
                    The basic source, especially sections 69 to
                    104; relevant replies to circular letter,
                    App.III; Ilai Motonicocoko's material on the
                    Wasting Sickness and Dysentery, App.I
Dening, Gregory
    1966   "Ethnohistory in Polynesia: The Value of Ethno-
              historical Evidence", *The Journal of Pacific
              History,* 1: 23-42

Dorson, Richard M.
1961   "Ethnohistory & Ethnic Folklore" *Ethnohistory*,
          8.1: 12-30
Douglas, A.E.
1931   "Tree Growth and Chronology of Pueblo Pre-
          history" in Kroeber & Waterman 1931:177-187
Eggan, F.R.
1954   "Social Anthropology and its Method of Control-
          led Comparison", *American Anthropologist*, 56.5:
          743-763
Fenton, William N.
1962   "Ethnohistory and its Problems", *Ethnohistory*,
          9.1:1-23
Firth, Raymond W.
1961   *History and Traditions of Tikopia*, Wellington,
          Polynesian Society
Gomme, Laurence George
1892   *Ethnohistory in Folklore*, London, Kegan Paul,
          Trench, Trübner & Co
Gray, Richard
1965   "Eclipse Maps", *Journ. of African History*, 6.3:
          251-62
Hazlewood, David
1850   *A Feejeean and English Dictionary*, Vewa, Wes-
          leyan Mission Press
          "List of Botanical and Zoological Productions
          of the Feejee Islands (omitted from dictionary)
1852   List of Wrecks in Feejee
Heizer, Robert F
1957   "Long-range Dating in Archaeology" in Kroeber
          1957:3-42
Hudson, Charles
1966   "Folk History and Ethnohistory" *Ethnohistory*,
          13.1-2:52-70
Hunt, John
1846   *Memoir of Rev. William Cross, Wesleyan Mission-
          ary to the Friendly and Feejee Islands*, London,
          John Mason
Jones, G.I.
1965   "Time and Oral Tradition with Special Reference
          to Eastern Nigeria" *Journ. of African History*,
          vi.2:153-160
Kahn, Herman
1968   Review of *Oral History at Arrowhead*, Proc. 1st
          Nat. Colloquium on Oral History. ed. E.I. Dixon
          and J.V. Mink. Los Angeles, Oral Hist. Assn.
          1967, in *American Historical Review* 73.5:1471
          June

Kroeber, A.L.
   1951   "A Mohave Historical Epic", *Anthropological
             Records,* 11.2:71-176   University of California
Kroeber, A.L. (Ed.)
   1957   *Anthropology Today: An Encyclopedic Inventory,*
             Chicago, University of Chicago Press
Kroeber, A.L. and T.T. Waterman, (Ed.)
   1931   *Source Book in Anthropology,* New York, Harcourt,
             Brace & Co.
Lowie, Robt. H.
   1960   "Oral Tradition and History" Lecture delivered
             to American Folklore Society 1916, in *Lowie's
             Selected Papers in Anthropology,* edited by Cora
             DuBois, Berkeley, University of California Press
Lucey, Willian Leo. S.J.
   1958   *History: Methods and Interpretation,* Chicago,
             Loyola University Press
Malinowski, Bronislaw
   1961   *Argonauts of the Western Pacific,* New York,
             E.P. Dutton & Co. (First published 1922)
Motonicocoka, Ilai
   1896   "The Wasting Sickness and Dysentry" See App. I
             in Colony of Fiji, 1896
Ogot, Alan B.
   1966   "Oral Traditions and the Historian" in *Prelude
             to East African History,* Ed. Merrick Posnansky.
             Ibadan, O.U.P. 1966
Parham, H.B.R.
   1943   *Fiji Native Plants with their Medicinal and
             Other Uses,* Wellington, Polynesian Society
Posnansky, Merrick (Ed.)
   1966   *Prelude to East African History,* Ibadan, O.U.P.
Radcliffe-Brown, A.R.
   1964   *The Andaman Islanders,* New York, Free Press of
             Glencoe. (Originally published 1932 but re-
             searched 1906-8)
Shelton, Austin J.
   1968   "Onojo Ogboni" *Journ. Amer. Folklore,* v.81:
             243-57
Sturtevant, Wm. C.
   1966   "Anthropology, History and Ethnohistory"
             Ethnohistory, 13.1-2:1-51
Tylor, Edward B.
   1904   *Anthropology: An Introduction to the Study of
             Man and Civilization,* New York, J.A. Hill & Co.
             Ch. xv "History & Mythology" 292-312
Vasina, J.
   1960   "Recording the Oral History of the Bakuba"

Journal of African History, I.1:43-53;
I.2:257-270
Waterhouse, Joseph
1866   *The King and People of Fiji etc.,*..... London.
         Wesleyan Conference Office

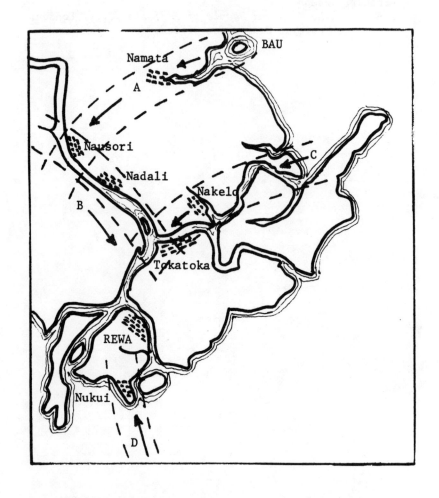

CAKOBAU'S CAMPAIGN AGAINST REWA AND HER ALLIES

3

FIJIAN WAR
in the
MISSIONARY JOURNALS[1]

This article explores the nature and social function
of Fijian warfare at the point of missionary contact. Within a few years the missionaries had distributed themselves
over four different localities and all of them kept journals
as they observed the wars. The methodology of this article
is to test one journal against another; and where possible
to call in sea captains and sailors for the same purpose.

1. Past Research on the Subject: Many references
to the nature of Fijian warfare exist in early original works,
for those who are willing to search for them, but few constructive attempts have been made to present a comprehensive
statement on the subject. The parent statement from which
most students have drawn freely is a chapter on "War" in
Thomas Williams' *Fiji and the Fijians* (1860). There are also
many scattered references to war in Wilkes' account of the
United States Exploring Expedition, of 1838-42 (1845). Basil
Thompson's work on the decay of custom in Fiji (1908) devotes
a chapter to this, and draws almost entirely from these two
primary sources, and from Fison. The most recent statement
was made by R.A. Derrick before this Society in his Presidential address in 1942.[1] In addition to these three, he used
several others of varied nature, and among other things
brought facts regarding the later wars of the seventies under
review. Much has also been written about the wars of Cakobau
in the fifties, under the head of general history and local
politics, but these references are not in systematic studies
of the nature of Fijian warfare. The most constructive account of these campaigns is that of Waterhouse (1866), who
lived in Bau during those eventful years of 1854 and 1855.
Much of Williams' description, mentioned above, was based on
his own observations in Taveuni and Vanua Levu and is therefore coloured by the peculiarities of those places. This is
especially apparent in the vocabulary of war words he mentions,
and in Fijian customs. Some of his material is Lauan. He

knew very little of Viti Levu - i.e., Bau, Rewa, Ba, Nadroga
or the interior. This should be allowed for in all cultural
studies based on his valuable work (the original of which is
in the Mitchell Library, Sydney). Together with this should
be placed his journal, published and annotated in two volumes by Henderson (1931). Scores of entries in this throw
light on the nature of Fijian warfare. Other early records
by mariners and others like Jackson (in Erskine, 1853) and
Dillon (in Wallis, 1851) are worth close examination.

2. *Scope of this Paper:* My aim is to attempt the
formulation of a statement on the nature and social function
of Fijian warfare, *per se,* and eliminate some of those factors for which the white man was responsible. The wars of
the seventies, for example, were quite acculturated. Even
in the fifties the white man had been responsible for many
modifications of the primary function of native war - both
the naval commanders and the missionaries. I purpose going
back as far as I can, but not so far that I pass beyond the
period of sound documentation. The wars of the fifties are
well documented, but the modifications caused by the rapid
acceptance of Christianity spoils the study of the real nature and function of primitive war. Furthermore I have already dealt with this in a monograph (Tippett, 1954). The
earliest missionary efforts were centred in Lakeba - not the
best place for the observation of war. When the missionaries moved into central Fiji in 1838 (Rewa), and across into Somosomo in 1839, and into Viwa in 1842, there they lived
in the midst of war. A study of this sort is perhaps best
limited to a brief period, as it allows greater concentra-
tion of research into the primary documents, and for this
reason I am confining myself to the period 1839-45. It is,
I believe the best period for study of the social function
of war: earlier there would be speculation, later too much
acculturation.

3. *Sources Used:* My basic source is the original
Journal of John Hunt, a typescript copy of which I have been
able to borrow for a limited period. It runs to over 600
pages of script. Hunt came to Fiji in 1838 and died in 1848.
He was on some occasions the interpreter used by naval officers, including Wilkes; and made copious notes on a wide
range of subjects. He was an eye-witness of two wars - that
between Somosomo and Vuna, and the 1st Bau-Rewa War - and
many petty skirmishes. His journal entries, descriptions of
ceremonial associated with war and opinions are extremely
valuable to both historian and anthropologist.   He also
throws interesting light on what the people of Somosomo

really thought of Bau in those eventful days. I understand
the original of this Journal is now in the Mitchell Library
in Sydney. Also in the Mitchell Library will be found the
Lyth Journals and papers. From these I have drawn a quantity of information to clear up doubts left in my mind by
Hunt. My limited time in Sydeny prevented a thorough examination of the Lyth material, and possibly at some later
time I will be able to add much to this paper from that
source. I have also drawn some information from missionary
correspondence as published at the time in the *Wesleyan Magazine* in Britain. Some of these letters are valuable, particularly those written by Jaggar from Rewa during the 1st
Bau-Rewa War from 1840 on. With Hunt observing from Viwa
and Jaggar from Rewa we are able to reconstruct much of the
state of that war, that has hitherto been partly conjecture.
Several original publications of the period have also been
used.

The Nature of Fijian Wars

        Much has been written of the cowardly nature of Fijian
warfare, of the insignificance of events declared to be glorious victories, of large manoeuvres which resulted in very few
very few casualties. Both naval captains and missionaries
wrote of it.

        Yet at the same time they also wrote of terrible mas-
sacres and extensive wars of a very different nature.[2]
Against the many tales of personal cowardice may be set others of great heroism. No student goes far in the study of
the documents of the period without being confronted by this
apparent contradiction in his sources.

        There is only one possible explanation of this -
clearly there were two entirely different kinds of warfare.
The discovery of this truth means a readjustment of our thinking on the matter. The small scale local skirmishes, petty
ambushes, and cowardly assaults on gardeners, fishing-women
and children, were one thing, but the war between Tanoa and
Tui Dreketi (1st Bau-Rewa War) and that between Cakobau and
Qaraniqio (2nd Bau-Rewa War) and that between Tui Bua and
Ritova, were something entirely different. Even though the
latter were regional in extent, they were waged in a different spirit, and were viewed in a different light by the Fijians,
and defined by them in different terminology.

        War of the former type was undertaken lightly, for
more or less insignificant reasons, often causes had to be

manufactured for the purpose, and they might be terminated
by an act of retaliation, or an atonement offering, and
friendly relationship continued as before. But the bitter
warfare of the more serious character was undertaken only
with extreme reluctance.

It is the thesis of this paper that the former type
of warfare was practised principally because it fulfilled a
necessary social function in Fijian society, and should be
examined in that light.

The remainder of what I have to say falls in two
parts. We shall firstly examine some of these more serious
wars, causes, events, manoeuvres, political consequences and
so on; and then by way of contrast we shall examine the precise nature of the social function of these petty skirmishes.

A War of the Chiefs

John Hunt has given us the term, by means of which
the Fijians distinguished the kind of war Tanoa asked Cakobau to wage on his account against Tui Dreketi in 1843 -
"a war of the chiefs" (Hunt *Journ. II:* 318). That is, he
goes on to explain, a war which is not terminated by any
other means than the death of the high chief of one side,
and the complete humiliation of his forces.

When this particular war began neither Hunt at Viwa,
nor Jaggar at Rewa, expected it to last long, and as the
months went by they found they were facing a different kind
of warfare. After five months Hunt wrote, "The war between
Bau and Rewa is of the most malignant kind. Nothing but a
revolution in one of the places can settle it" (Hunt *Journ.*
15/4/44). A fortnight later he had come to the conclusion
that the pace was so hot that neither side could last out
much longer (*ibid.* 29/4/44). For months on end the missionaries at Rewa and Viwa, but a few miles apart, were completely
cut off from each other (Jaggar/LC 9/7/44; Hunt/LC 26/2/45).

Causes of First Bau-Rewa War: 1843-5

About 1841 Qaraniqio, Tui Dreketi's younger brother,
was caught in forbidden relationship with the Queen of Rewa,
his brother's wife, and fled from his wrath to Bau; where he
attempted to engage the help of the Bauan chiefs against the
Tui Dreketi. Bau and Rewa had been friendly, on the whole,

the chiefly houses being related by marriage. Jackson said
the Rewan brothers were of Bauan origin (Jackson, 1853:462).
If so that explains much of their behaviour, especially that
of Cokanauto, the youngest of the three brothers, later on.
It is true that Bauan and Rewan villages would make war on
each other at the village level, but Bau as a kingdom did not
war on a Rewan village, or vice versa, without first communicating the reasons and seeking the others approval. So the
Bauan chiefs refused to touch Qaraniqio's request, and en-
deavoured to pacify the King by sending him an atonement, to
show they had no sympathies with the offending brother. Tui
Dreketi refused this atonement *(soro)* - an insult to the Bau
chiefs in a way; more especially so, since Qaraniqio, finding no support in Bau determined to risk return to Rewa, and
was received by his brother on his own account, in spite of
the rejection of the *soro*. This offended the Bauans, who
expected civil war in Rewa, and it showed their atonement
was despised. Hunt is specific on this point, that Tui Dreketi's reconciliation with Qaraniqio after rejection of the
atonement, was the cause of the growing ill-will between Bau
and Rewa. Rewa certainly had been clumsy *(sakasakā)* in its
failure to observe inter-kingdom political courtesies. It
was aggravated because he made no attempt to set the matter
right (Hunt *Journ. II:* 314).

        Waterhouse, writing from a greater time distance,
claimed there always had been enmity between Seru (Cakobau)
and Qaraniqio, from the days of their boyhood (1866:110-1).
This may have been so, but it is difficult to see how it
could have been the cause of this particular war, which was
specifically stated as "a war of the Chiefs" and terminated
in the death of Tui Dreketi, not that of Qaraniqio. No doubt
he would have shared the same fate had the Bauans laid hands
on him, but it was the second war that was waged against him.
True the second war was more or less inevitable as long as
he lived, and though he and Cakobau were prime actors in the
first war, it was a struggle between Tanoa and Tui Dreketi.

        Qaraniqio, annoyed with Bau for refusing to take
his side in the family argument determined to make an attack
on the Bau town of Dravo, but information reached Cakobau,
who advised the Dravo people to build a *bai-ni-vuaka* (pig
fence). This serves to show us something of the reasoning
powers of Cakobau. A *bai-ni-vuaka* was made of sticks and
timber, and was a peacetime occupation, but could be effectively used for defence in war. A *bai-ni-valu* (war-fence)
would have been much more carefully made, and perhaps better
protection; but the erection of a war-fence, was in Fijian
eyes, a legitimate reason for inquiry. The possibility of

war was increasing, but Cakobau had no intention of starting
it. Trouble now began at a town called Suva, with a quarrel
and some exchange of insults between the people and the Rewans. The town was attacked, but successfully defended itself, and Qaraniqio returned to Rewa for reinforcements. Cakobau sent one of his principal men to ask why, and pointing
out that it was their custom to communicate with each other
before so dealing with the other's subject towns or allies.
The messenger was received with but little ceremony and told
that the expedition was bound for Kadavu; but after its departure he was told plainly enough that it was heading for
Suva, whereupon he returned to Bau with his report. Suva was
taken and burned and the people massacred with savage barbar-
ity. Hunt's account is confirmed by Mrs. Wallis, wife of a
beche-de-mer trader here at the time (Wallis, 1851:162ff).
Bau still made no move. Hunt had a long conversation with
Tanoa at the time, and left him satisfied that Bau would not
move unless something else happened, and he writes in his
journal that Bau seemed to be "particularly anxious to make
it plain to all parties that they had nothing to do with commencing the war" (II: 314-316). At the same time it was
quite apparent that Cakobau and Tanoa had made up their minds
that if there was war it would be no petty skirmish, yet they
did not at this stage make any obvious preparations for such
a war. Mrs. Wallis adds, "Bau was never known to show so
much forbearance in any other affair. No-one could ever insult its haughty chiefs with impunity. But Rewa seemed determined to go on with the same conduct, which has resulted
in destruction" (Wallis, 1851:164). This in itself should
have been a warning to Rewa. Cakobau now took his party on
a trip to the Windward Islands, "with the professed intention
of enduring insult rather than fight" (Hunt *Journ. II:* 317).

During his absence the next blow fell on Tanoa and
left him a deeply offended and insulted man. His principal
wife, by birth a Rewan, left him and returned home, taking
with her all his concubines that were of Rewan birth. This,
in point of fact, deprived Tanoa of his best means of personal
defence in event of attack by Rewa, and as we shall see
shortly, Tui Dreketi himself played this as his last card.
It was, however, not their flight that grieved Tanoa, but
what Tui Dreketi did to them upon their arrival. He gave the
Queen of Bau to a Rewan and divided the others among the Rewan chiefs and people. Earlier when Tanoa had been driven
from Bau by a previous rebellion, this same lady had sought
refuge in Rewa and had obtained it at the same price. These
details provided by Hunt are confirmed by Mrs. Wallis (Wallis
1851:165). Hunt says furthermore that this more than anything

else sealed the fate of Rewa, for upon Cakobau's return Tanoa called his sons together and told them his mind. Cakobau took up the challenge. A messenger was sent to Rewa to
tatau (terminate friendly intercourse). The Rewans now pro-
posed to *soro*, but it was too late. Hunt's phrase is -
"Tanoa and Cakobau had crossed the Rubicon" *(Journ. II:* 318).

That is a good example of a combination of factors
which might well cause a serious war. For the time being let
us note it was engaged in with reluctance. Neither Tanoa nor
Cakobau feared skirmishes or finding excuses for causing
them; but 'a war of the chiefs' was quite a different matter.

The Manner in Which the War was Prosecuted

The war lasted for two years, and the casualties were
so great that the natives said the "ovens never grew cold"
(Waterhouse, 1866:112). Watsford at Viwa said, "Scarcely a
day passed without hearing the death drum" (Watsford, 1900:
57). Jaggar at Rewa said much the same thing - "The death
drums give us no quiet now" (Jaggar/LC 9/7/44). So many bodies were brought to Bau that they could not be used, and
corpses drifted over the sea and were washed up on Viwa (Wats-
ford/LC 6/10/46). All generous feelings were put aside. Relationship counted for nothing. Both parties considered they
were in the right - Bau smarted under the rejection of her
first atonement, the destruction of Suva and the despised
abuse of Tanoa's womenfolk. Rewa considered their offer of
atonement should have been accepted and should have covered
all they had done. Hunt says the Rewans never expected a
war of the chiefs - they expected a short war terminated by
an atonement as had happened before. But Bau, for once was
united, as no Bauan took the Rewan side, whereas the chiefly
family of Rewa was hopelessly divided by jealousy. Furthermore Hunt was extremely doubtful about the sincerity of the
Rewa atonement *(Journ. II:* 320). He knew that there had been
rumors in Rewa of war with Bau after the Suva affair, and Rewa was not unprepared (Jaggar/LC 29/5/43), although Bau had
not engaged in any large scale preparations as yet. But now
that communications were broken between the two places Bau
burst into feverish activity on a grand scale, men and arms
were prepared, and gods were supplicated. Action began almost immediately, and the first few towns fell quickly before
a spirited attack. It was Hunt's opinion afterwards that had
Cakobau pressed ahead with his movement on Rewa at the time
he could have terminated the war in 6 months. He says there

was one occasion when Rewa was practically in his hands, but
he returned to Bau to offer sacrifices of thanksgiving to the
god of war, and honour his heroes and make preparations for
another attack (*Journ. II*: 320).

An event of some major importance in the course of
the war took place after a few months of action. The youngest of the three Rewan brothers went over to the Bau side.
He was a man of influence and a warrior of some importance.
There never had been harmony between them and each brother
had a number of towns subject to him (*ibid*: 321). The Bauans
had encouraged the break by promising him the kingship of a
new and rebuilt Suva, but as the war went on it seemed he
would be rather the new king in Rewa itself. This had serious consequences for Rewa, because it enabled men and towns
to go over to the enemy without the stigma of disloyalty. It
is not strictly correct merely to say "these villages went
over to Bau". They remained loyal to Cokanauto, and thus
were taking part in a civil war between the Rewan chiefs.
This was a feature of Fijian warfare – to play one party of
the enemy off against another. This led to some frightful
scenes in Rewa, where for the following months the bitterness
against the followers of Cokanauto was intense, and prisoners
from his party were tortured unmercifully, as revealed by the
correspondence of Thomas Jaggar who lived at Nasali on the
other side of the river all that year (Jaggar/LC 9/7/44).

The successes, said Hunt, were mostly in favour of
the Bauans, but they were not entirely so, and the war was
expensive in men, food, property, arms and ammunition. Many
villages were destroyed and famine conditions prevailed
throughout the Rewa delta.

Tokatoka was one of the best defended towns of the
area, with a labyrinth of war-trenches that amazed seaman
Jackson at the time (Jackson, 1853:459), and made a noble
resistance against a strong Bauan attack, and was really not
taken at all, but wearied by continual watching and hunger
eventually joined the Bauans. Bau was a naval power, and
watched the coast, she had wealth and spies, and other means
besides normal war for winning allies, and in the face of
famine one by one villages went over to her (Hunt *Journ.II*:
320-321).

However, there is another side of the story. There
was in Bau a son of the chief by the Rewan lady, who also had
a strong body of supporters. He organized a plot for the
termination of the war in favour of Rewa, and with the

destruction of Bau from within. Hunt's judgement was that
the party had more spirit than ability, and that both leader
and supporters were the wrong kind of men for carrying out
so dangerous a venture. The plot was discovered and Tanoa
determined to wipe out everyone in Bau favouring Rewa. The
young chief was murdered, even though he was Tanoa's son,
and buried without ceremonies. He pleaded innocence, and
some said it was a plot against him, but Tanoa was taking no
risks. The fate was shared by the chief of Lasakau (*ibid*:
322-323).

Viewing the war from Viwa, Hunt said that the Bauan
plans succeeded whereas Rewan schemes failed. But no-one
can read the Jaggar correspondence, without realizing that
the record of casualties was a two-sided affair. The Bauans
had the advantage of isolation on their island fortress and
control of the sea; and the Rewans were more or less "bottled
up" within the river entrance. The war took place mainly
among the mangroves and the delta villages, and the losses
among the tributary states and allies were heavy on both
sides. The destruction of gardens and the fear of going outside the war-fence to garden led to famine, and the endless
prowling of Bauan parties made vigilance of paramount importance and the people grew weary of it. The Bauans had not
wanted to go to war in the first place, and had said so plainly
to the missionaries, with an explanation which seems to me
to ring true. They would gain nothing by it. The only fruit
of a war with Rewa was famine. War with Somosomo or Lakeba,
would make them rich, because of the plunder and the property
they would receive in tribute, but Rewa had nothing for Bau
to acquire that she did not have in abundance herself. There
is a ring of truth about it. There were no delta flats of
sugar cane in those days. Their life was insecure in every
way, their villages were destroyed time after time, were hard
to defend, and their trade was itself plunder. The places
they had subdued were remote and loosely held. Kadavu and
Beqa involved them in continual wars of subjugation, and were
continually at war among themselves. These wars continued
until the late sixties (Fison Correspondence). Jackson gives
an account of one of the Rewan visits of subjugation to Kadavu
(Jackson, 1853:472-473), and Cargill gives one of a similar
visit to Beqa (Cargill, 1841:269-271). Furthermore at the
time of the Bau-Rewa War under discussion, Beqa and Kadavu
were themselves at war. What sort of subject states were they
when Rewa was in a life and death struggle with Bau. This
accounts for the poverty of Rewan maratime forces in this particular war. Tanoa knew well enough the troubles of Rewa. To
conquer Rewa was to buy a bag of trouble for himself.   He

would much rather have turned his attention to Natewa or Somosomo, as he did immediately after the conclusion of the
1st Bau-Rewa War.

The dream of the significance of the title *Tui Viti*
was Cakobau's, not Tanoa's, and lies a few years ahead of
our period. Tanoa's policy had been to cement union with
Rewa by means of marriage and friendship. He was in their
debt regarding the restoration to his kingdom (Waterhouse,
1866:62), and the rebellion in the first place had been
largely on account of his Rewan sympathies (Wilkes, 1845:
199). Then Tui Dreketi insulted him before the whole land.
Long Tanoa had resisted his impulses, but when his resistance broke down we can quite understand the bitterness of
the war that followed.

Tanoa and Cakobau, knew the weaknesses of Rewa, and
they played upon them. They stopped the river mouth with
their canoes, and shut the Rewans up in the delta, destroyed
their gardens and sniped their stray gardeners, set ambushes
between villages, destroyed the normal communications between
villages and made it unsafe for going and coming except in
large parties. They had the best spy system in Fiji, and
traded on local quarrels and jealously, to encourage division
among the enemy, and did not hesitate to buy them over. On
the principle that a war is better fought in your neighbour's
yard than your own, Bau was devastating the Rewa delta.

We are therefore not surprised that the Rewa chiefs
made atonement, which Hunt called "the fatal step" (*Journ.
II:* 324).

In what followed we are able to observe the difference between the two Bauans - Tanoa madly consumed with bitter hatred, thirsting only for revenge now: Cakobau calm and
calculating, the rational mind behind the war effort. The
messenger had arrived from Rewa. Word passed round the town
that Rewa had soro'd. Tanoa could scarcely contain himself
and sent to Cakobau (who, let it be remembered, was fighting
the war on Tanoa's behalf) to send the Rewan messenger to him
that he might eat him. A *soro* was, of course, not enough.
Rewa must perish.

"No!" said Cakobau, "Had he been the son of the King
of Rewa, I would have allowed him to be eaten, but he is a
messenger to Bau, and messengers must not be killed." That
was the correct attitude for a sane Fijian to take. It

throws light on the difference between messengers and chiefs
the sacredness of one and the vulnerability of the other.
Cokonauto's party at Nukui, abused this sacredness of the
messenger, and Jaggar tells of the increased bitterness it
caused among the Rewa loyalists when the report came to hand
(Jaggar/LC 9/7/44).

The messenger was informed that there could be only
one end to the war - the end of Bau or of Rewa. He was to
return and communicate that information to the chiefs, and
also that when the Bauan army beseiged the town, that was
the time for them to soro. The meaning was plain enough. It
was not the first time such a message had been carried by an
unhappy messenger. The Rewan chiefs would understand that
it meant the firing of their town. Whether or not there
would be mercy or massacre would depend partly on the atonement offering, but more particularly on the mood of the con-
queror - which in this case was grim.

But Cakobau had a way with messengers. And had he
not already saved him from Tanoa? If he wanted to save his
life in the general destruction of Rewa there was, of course,
a way of doing so. He was to engage with some of his friends
within the town to set fire to the houses immediately the
Bauans appeared outside the town. He was to meet the Bauans
at a specified town near Rewa, which had gone over to Bau.
The messenger knew the "last hand" was being played, and he
had seen the "cards". During the night he removed the most
valuable of his private possessions to a secret place.   The
Bauans appeared at dawn outside the town and engaged in some
preliminary firing.

A Bauan messenger was sent into the town to call the
Queen of Rewa, who was a Bauan, and her Bauan attendants, and
before half the people were awake the town was in flames and
the general massacre had begun. The disaffected party within Rewa, no doubt to save their own lives, was foremost in
the killing of their fellow-villagers, and indeed, very few
knew who was friend and who was foe. Some were murdered for
the sake of the property with which they were trying to escape, and Hunt said that in a short time some 300 were dead,
many of them women and children (*Journ.II:* 324-325).   Later
estimates put the figure up to about 400. The Rewan warriors
or some of them, were not long in realizing there were trait-
ors among them and took to the bush, many living to fight
again in the second war.

With some interest we note the last card played by

Tui Dreketi. Cakobau anticipated it, and told the messenger
who was sent for the Bauan women, that the King was not to
accompany them, but was to perish with his town. The King
ignored this and went with the Queen to the river, to cross
to the other side where Cakobau's canoe lay waiting. It was
Hunt's opinion, and no doubt he talked the matter over with
those Bauan women, several of whom took refuge in Viwa shortlv
afterwards; that Tui Dreketi trusted in the high Bauan rank
of his wife to save his life, as it might have done had
the messenger not forstalled him by instructing him not to
accompany them. Cakobau, perceiving his action, called out
for him to return to his burning town. He continued to cross
the river. Cakobau sent a musket ball over his head. He
still came on, and as a result was killed in the presence of
his wife and family - an ignominious death (Hunt *Journ. II:*
326-327).

      Rewa was entirely consumed, a fate she experienced
three times in ten years. Qaraniqio was not in the town,
and took refuge inland.

      The final showdown was not an unexpected event, for
as we have seen, the Bauan intention was communicated to the
Rewan chiefs. In anticipation of these things the Mission
at Rewa had removed its valuable property, printing press
etc., to Viwa; but a Mission teacher and his family were
still there at the time and had a really remarkable escape,
which is an adventure in itself. Subsequently he and the
other Christians who had been able to escape took refuge in
Kaba.

      Rewa was destroyed on 1st December 1845 - the war
had lasted two years (*ibid:* 313-328). A few weeks later
Hunt made these notes from which I have drawn so heavily. It
is quite clear that he considered the war was over - at least
for the time being. He realized that with Qaraniqio still
at large there could be further trouble, and said that things
were in an unsettled state. Even so he anticipated the
younger brother would be made King of Rewa. "Rewa," he
writes, "as it formerly existed, is no more. The King is
dead and his family prisoners of war, and Qaraniqio in hid-
ing" (*ibid:* 329). The Queen and her son had become Christian and were at Viwa, and Hunt was about to start on one of
those long voyages about his area. Tanoa's humiliation had
been avenged. It had been a war of exhaustion, but as a
'war of the chiefs' could only end as it had - in the death
of Tanoa or Tui Dreketi.

Some Comments on the Nature of this War

One thing brought out by all the eye-witnesses who left journals and correspondence, is that all Fijian warfare was not definable as "petty skirmishes". This was malignant in spirit, heavy in casualties and completely destructive to the country. I press this because the point has been disputed. It is true there were few pitched battles of the 'classical' type, perhaps because there were no Plains of Marathon or Esdraelon or deserts of North Africa on which they could be fought. But the jungle warfare against Japan in the Pacific and the Communist bandits in Malaya, if I read the accounts correctly, have remarkable similarities. There were assaults and planned campaigns - both short and long campaigns, and in their own way they had quite a science of tactics, to which we will proceed in a moment.

In July 1844, Jaggar, cut off at Rewa, spoke of the spirit in which the war was being fought, he said the casualties were great and the end was not in sight. Looking at things from his end he felt Bau was gaining no ground, and neither were the Rewans. He felt the destruction of Rewa was a big task, and doubted Bau's ability to accomplish it - unless there was revolution within. He expressed this view after the departure of Cokanauto, and in spite of that event. Food was scarce, and the enemy (He speaks of Bau as the enemy, so apparently he viewed things from the Rewan angle.) had deliberately destroyed food supplies. He also speaks of the freedom of sailing possible to the Bauans, and the way in which the Rewans were confined in the river. He admits Bau was attacking all the time and Rewa mainly on the defence. At this juncture it seems from his letter that the Rewan offensive was more directed against the other Rewan villages which had followed Cokanauto; but there were more ambushes than open attacks. This form of warfare was continual and the casualties thereby were great on both sides. He comments on the number of heathen priests who had fallen among the Rewa people. (An interesting point - the priest was not normally present in the military manoeuvre.) Let us examine some of his references (*Journ.* 1844).

13th Jan. Some Rewan allies were lying in ambush awaiting the enemy, but were discovered and the enemy came upon them from behind and killed 30 of them.

22nd Jan. Chiefs and people of Rewa and some dependencies had gone to prepare a town for war by throwing up mounds and building fences. While at work they were attacked

by a tribe from among their allies, who had gone over to Bau.
The work party fled to cover, but 17 were killed. The Rewa
party (our party, Jaggar says) gathered together and burnt
the rebel town, but had to retreat speedily. It appears to
have been a plot to get certain chiefs exposed, but in this
it failed. However Jaggar admits the episode had a bad psy-
chological effect on the Rewa people, who were caught unprepared.

The first week of February saw a quantity of cannibal feasting visible from Jaggar's house.

On 15th February, a day of planned manoeuvers, when
several towns were burnt and there were heavy casualties on
both sides, action came so close to Rewa that Jaggar was
able to observe the firing from his house. This serves to
show not only how close the Bauans were to Rewa in the first
six months of the war, but also the vigilance required of
the Rewan watch. The tiring effect of continual watching
was one of their breaking points. On another occasion some
women were taken while fishing - which the Bauans considered
fair play as they were feeding the enemy (Jaggar/LC 9/7/44).
Even so the Fijian never viewed the killing of women in the
same light as we do. Women also took part in war in different ways, expecially in times of seige, in some places maintaining the internal organization of the fort, and feeding
the warriors with supplies, drink and ammunition; and in other places like Nadroga, for instance, the women went to war,
and in defence, their weapons were the bows and arrows (Jag-
gar/LC 29/5/43; Williams, 1860:57). In Malolo this also applied and even the children were used in action (Wilkes, 18-
45:248). Whether or not this applied in all parts of Fiji I
am unable to say, but if it did, and women and children were
the bow and arrow companies and major defence against assault of a town, we cannot wonder that they were not spared
in the massacres. But let us return to Jaggar's account of
the war from the Rewa end.

These women were taken in March. It was then that
he wrote, "The death drums give us no quiet now." He provides the gruesome details of many episodes, including the
torture of their prisoners. In May, a band of the followers
of the younger chief, who was then established at Nukui, on
the coast, with the sea and Bauan canoes behind him, and
therefore clear access to Cakobau's ammunition stores (which
according to Jackson were considerable [1853:455-456]) crept
into a town close to Rewa, murdering the watchmen, an example
of what happened when the watch fatigued. A few days later

a dozen were ambushed. Then a canoe was trapped near the mouth of the river and its travellers clubbed. This was a Rewa rebel canoe and the bodies were taken to Rewa. More often it was the other way round. A canoe bound for Rewa from Kadavu was captured near the mouth of the river and 30 bodies taken to Bau. One only escaped hidden in the jettisoned sail of the canoe and Jaggar had the story from him (Jaggar/LC 9/7/44).

Let us now return to Hunt's journal, and look at the same early months of the war from the other side. Rewa towns a little further beyond the observation of Jaggar were being badly hit. Between the first two events I mentioned above (the loss of the ambush and the party attacked while building fortifications, 30 and 17 respectively killed), between those events of 13th and 22nd January, Hunt tells us the Namata people took 39 in the destruction of a Rewa town and two other towns were similarly destroyed with great loss by the Naitasiri people - these all in favour of Bau. He also adds that everywhere the Bauans were successful (*Journ.* 15/1/44).

This is a valuable comparison because it helps us to get an over-all picture of what was happening. The whole delta was unsettled by ambushes and skirmishes, but further back from Naitasiri and Namata, a thorough and concentrated push was begun from near Nausori moving towards Rewa. The Namata attack was against Nadali. The push moved slowly, but one by one the key places in the delta were reduced, burnt, or came over to Bau - Tokatoka, Nakelo and others. The coast was Bau's. Slowly the Bauan claws closed in on Rewa; but not until the delta was thoroughly reduced, and all retreat was cut off, did they close. Hunt thought they should have closed after 6 months, but he was a missionary. Cakobau took two years. Only one single thing went wrong with the plan - when the claws eventually closed Qaraniqio was not in the town. I have no doubt whatever that the 1st Bau-Rewa War was as skilfully planned and excuted a campaign as took place in the Pacific before the 20th century. Clearly there were some Bauan reverses, but the general plan of the campaign was carried out, and by its very nature Cakobau if not Hunt, must have known it would take time.

On quite another point altogether it is interesting to set the opinions of Hunt and Jaggar side by side. Long before the war began Rewa made preparations for it. On 13th November, Jaggar having communicated this information to Hunt, Hunt talked of the possibility with Tanoa and learned

his mind was against war for reasons stated above.   Yet a
week later Hunt thought war was probable (*Journ.* 13/11/43;
20/11/43). A fortnight later it had begun. On 4th December
Hunt recorded the burning of Nadali (*ibid.* 4/12/43). On 25th
December he thought it would be a short war, as he felt the
people would soon want peace. He soon changed his mind.
This was a new kind of war to him.

We have seen that the Rewans made preparations in
event of war, thereby showing they were aware of their own
provocativeness. But there is reason to believe they did
not expect it to eventuate. Jaggar in another, earlier letter, written immediately after the Suva affair, makes an observation - his opinion, but no doubt the mind of the Rewan
chiefs among whom he was living at the time, and which may
account for much of their action. After the Suva affair
there were already rumors of war with Bau in Rewa, but he
did not expect it (so he wrote to England) because there was
war at Somosomo and Bau's mind was fixed on that. If Jaggar
and the Rewa chiefs thought that, it puts a different com-
plexion on the whole business of Rewa's attitude to Bau. So
Suva was destroyed, despite Cakobau's enquiries, 100 killed,[3]
mostly eaten, 30 bodies taken to Rewa, the hands of the victims smoked and dried for ornamenting the chief's house as
trophies,[4] and a festival of thanks made to their war-god for
their success against the Bauan town of Suva (Jaggar/LC 29/5/
43; Derrick, 1950:85 citing Wall).

So the Rewans thought the Somosomo situation, which
would offer far more profit to Bau, and possibly be considered
more urgent, would prevent her engaging in war with Rewa.
One can see then how these insults would only add venom to
the war when it did come.

War Between Somosomo and Vuna: 1840

Other historical issues also are involved in the
study of these documents. We have seen how Jaggar thought of
the Bau-Rewa situation in the light of events at Somosomo.
Let us then look at Somosomo, but before we examine the Natewa
trouble, of which Jaggar was speaking we must go back to the
preceding war against Vuna. Hunt was also an eyewitness of
much of this.

The period under study in this paper began with this
war in Taveuni. It can hardly be called a skirmish, and yet
it was not a war of the chiefs in the technical sense of the

term. At the same time it had in it the possibilities of
becoming a grim effort because of the political issues involved, both internal in Tui Cakau's kingdom, and because of
Bauan interest in it. In that it comprised a number of en-
gagements, it would, I suppose, be classed as a *campaign* over
a period of a couple of months.

Throughout this campaign, (the purpose of which was
to subjugate a rebellious subject state and restore it to
its place in the kingdom - not to annihilate it) various other
warrior states and allies came to Somosomo, performed their
reviews, and departed one by one to make their respective at-
temptsat reducing Vuna. These included the warriors of
Bouma, Wainikeli, Rabe, Macuata and Natewa, in addition to
those of Somosomo itself. In the final manoeuvre of the
campaign they were also joined by a contingent from Savusavu.
The campaign took place during September and October 1840.

The nature of this warfare was in some ways similar
to that already described - scouting parties, ambushes, attempts to entice the Vunans outside their fortifications,
and eventually a well-planned tactical seige. But the spirit
in which the war was fought was vastly different, and we must
not forget it was the suppression of a rebellion, not a war
to exterminate.

In comparison with the forces used the casualties
were very small, though in the end this was solely due to
the discipline and control of the Vunivalu, who against popular clamour prevented a massacre.

One by one the other states of the kingdom went to
Vuna, and all failed to bring the Vunans out into combat.
Here and there stragglers or providoring parties were picked
up, killed and eaten. An attack of combined forces, before
the arrival of the warriors of Natewa and Savusavu, failed,
and Vuna lost only 7 or 8 killed and one prisoner.   The
final assault was prepared with an army of 1200 to 1300.
Before we deal with the nature of their manoeuvres let us
note the political aspect.

In addressing the troops beforehand the King described the campaign as "a war of the whole kingdom". The
issue for him was wholly the internal state of his kingdom,
unity, loyalty, discipline, obedience and co-operation. Although Vuna itself boasted a king, he was a subject king -
and Somosomo disapproved of any subject state having independent political relationships with outside powers,particularly

with Bau, a sea power, and the most likely danger to his
kingdom.

Herein we see the great difference between Tui Cakau and Tui Dreketi. When Vuna was reduced and the trem-
bling Tui Vuna was brought before Tui Cakau, bringing his
atonement and his pretty daughter as an offering to the King,
he might well have been clubbed or tortured, but surprisingly
received but a severe rebuke for causing so much war.

"You have prepared your town to receive the Chief
of Bau," the rebuke began, "that he might come and destroy
me and my people; and why should you do this? You are not
a Bau man. You are a Ca'audrove man. I am a Bau man. My
mother was from Bau. Why should you assist a Bau chief to
destroy me?...." and so it went on, finishing, "Your town
shall be destroyed, that when the Bau chief comes he may
have an empty town" (Hunt *Journ. I:* 215).

There was in Somosomo, a genuine fear of Bau at
that time. And indeed the Bau canoes did come. The Bauans
landed and built themselves a fence, but discovering they
were too late left again without even calling at Somosomo or
paying their respects there. A short time before the King
had involved himself in a political marriage with a chiefly
lady of Bau, with the express purpose of preventing Bauan
interest in this war; and wisely so because many Bauans
lived in Somosomo. When it was discovered that the Bauan
canoes had come, and the warriors having built a fence, departed without reporting at Somosomo (which was not according to custom), there was much village chatter on the subject
which Hunt records thus:
Some say they are gone to bring more force, others
say, nay; some say, build a fence at Somosomo; others
say, our legs are our fence (*ibid.* 215).
Shortly afterwards there were further rumours at Somosomo
that Bau was out for a large scale war with them, and was
assembling warriors from Rewa, Verata and Koro, and that she
also had allies on Vanua Levu. Macuata was torn by civil
war and there was genuine fear in Somosomo.

Three canoes were now sent from Somosomo to Bau to
give them notice of a feast to be given shortly to a town of
Bau people, who lived near Somosomo, and for observation
purposes they were to call *en route* at Koro. They did so
and found warriors assembled there, and assuming the rumours
to be true, sailed in the direction of Bau and out of sight
of Koro turned back to Somosomo with all haste to make

report. Reports now came to hand of Bauan canoes off the
Vanua Levu coast near Bua. A few victims had been taken
and they moved on to Macuata. Somosomo sent out her scout-
canoes but they were afraid to beach and "slept at sea like
Englishmen" so they said. They reported evidence of a war
along the Macuata coast. Hunt himself was not convinced the
Bauan canoes were there at all, but whether they were or not,
his picture of the rumours and the fears of Somosomo in the
early forties, when he lived among them, makes interesting
reading, and throws light on the eagerness of Tui Cakau to
be on friendly terms with Bau.

It throws light on his reasons for concern about
any possible alliance between Bau and Vuna.

The Natewa Trouble

Vuna was not the only unsettled place in Tui Cakau's dominions. He was having precisely the same trouble
with Natewa, and it is reported in a letter written by Lyth
from Somosomo to Williams and Calvert, who were at Lakeba,
in October 1842, that the Somosomoans had gone to Vanua Levu
to deal with the Natewans (Cited in Williams, *Journ.* 22/12/
42).

In this they were not so successful as they had
been with Vuna, which was close at hand. Their subjugation
had been complete. Seaman Jackson observed shortly afterwards how they crawled before the Somosomoans (1853:421).
It soon became apparent that the subjugation of Natewa was
a different matter and after three months the whole affair
might well have ended disastrously for Tuikilakila, Tui
Cakau's son, who was prosecuting the war. On 21st January
he took canoes and men and went to a town which had professed
to have fallen to Somosomo. However the chief's party were
victims of a plot and ambushed. Most of the casualties
were high Somosomo chiefs and warriors. Tuikilakila then
realized that the subjugation of Natewa might well be beyond
his power and resources.

As a result of this disaster he sailed to Bau in
an attempt to win Bauan favour and support in this war. He
departed on 25th December 1842 to interview Tanoa and Seru
(Lyth/LC 10/1/43). Bau's mind was to join in that war, as
Rewan intelligence apparently knew, for it was but a couple
of months later that the Rewans sacked Suva, and Jaggar was
fairly confident that Bau would not war with Rewa on account

of her interest in Natewa affairs.

But the Bau-Rewa situation prevented any expedition
to Somosomo. Immediately after the fall of Rewa, Bau turned
to Natewa. In October 1843, when the war situation between
Bau and Rewa was getting tense, but still before war had
been declared, Macuata put reinforcements into Natewa and
further discomforted Somosomo (Williams *Journ.* 30/10/43).
Somosomo made huge sacrifices to her war-gods - 40 whales
teeth, about 10,000 yams, 30 turtles, 40 roots of *yaqona,*
150 clams, hundreds of native puddings, crabs, *dalo,* bananas,
water-melons and nuts (*ibid.* 24/2/44).

At the critical moment, when help was needed, a
Somosomoan eloped with a daughter of Tuikilakila, who was
betrothed to another who was *vasu* to Somosomo, and who, taking offence thereby went to Bau to lay complaints. This
could well have led to serious trouble and Tuikilakila went
to Bau immediately with two large canoes as an atonement
(*ibid.* 3-6/3/44). Incidents like this serve to show how
Somosomo courted Bau in those days, and perhaps support the
views expressed by Jaggar at Rewa.

Hunt wrote about 10 months before the Bau-Rewan
War ended -
     The (Somosomo) war with Natewa is still in progress,
     and perhaps not near its termination. It appears
     that the chiefs of Bau encourage the Natewa people to
     rebel against their chiefs, and are, in fact, using
     them to pay some of their old debts to the Somosomo
     chiefs. (And perhaps keep Somosomo occupied until
     their war with Rewa was over. ART.) When they think
     they have done enough they will go to Natewa with a
     large force, and pretend to conquer it, and Somosomo
     will have to pay the price, and bow its neck a little
     more willingly to the yoke of Bau (Hunt/LC 26/2/45).
What a remarkable insight this man Hunt possessed in native
behaviour for that was February 1845. The war with Rewa
ended in December. Six months later the review we are discussing took place. Within a month Natewa had been subdued,
and Williams, after spending some time with Cakobau himself
after his return, wrote in his journal -
     The war with Natewa must be looked upon as ended. The
     Somosomo people are greatly disappointed that nothing
     more has been effected. But Cakobau was determined
     before he left this place, and perhaps before he left
     home, to shed no more blood than necessary. Some six
     or eight empty towns were burnt and five or six men

slain on either side; but there seems to have been a
deal of arrangement in the affair. Tuikilakila may
look upon himself as 'done' (28/7/46).

Viewing things from the Somosomo end in 1843, Williams recorded in his journal his opinions -
The war between Bau and Rewa prevents Cakobau coming
in person to assist in the entire destruction of the
Natewa people..... To prolong the war between this
place and Natewa, without taking very active steps in
it, is politic on the part of Cakobau. The Natewa
people being on good terms with Bau, and having property to a considerable amount ready to present to its
chief, the Somosomo people find it needful to use
every means to gain and keep the assistance of Bau.
They have already taken a great quantity of cloth,
teeth and other articles to the capital, and the riches
scraped up from the windward islands will be cast into
the same place. It is not unlikely that, after all,
Cakobau will so bring matters about that Natewa will
soro to this king, and so the matter will end - like
a skilful man of the law, who after having well
drained the purses of plaintiff and defendant, dis-
misses the parties but little better for his inter-
ference.

That too, was a remarkable piece of insight, penned
at the commencement of the Bau-Rewa War, just as fighting
was about to begin (16/11/43).

Jaggar described the settlement thus -
The Natewa people begged pardon of the Bau chiefs,
and pardon being granted, the war ceased. It appears,
however, that the Somosomo chief and people were anything but pleased at the way in which it terminated.
They wished Cakobau to concede the pardon, and then
to slaughter the people...... They were therefore
chagrined and disappointed (Jaggar/LC 7/10/46).
However the political consequences were all in Cakobau's favour. Both Tuikilakila and Natewa were now in his debt, and
for the time being he need fear no trouble from them while
he turned his mind to dealing with Qaraniqio. This was
exactly as both Hunt and Williams has prophesied. We have
here a good example of the consequences of the division of
Fiji into numerous small kingdoms. A strong Chief had to
keep the others occupied so he did not himself have wars on
too many fronts at one time, or too lengthy lines of communications. There were seven wars reported at one time.

Some Manoeuvres of Fijian Warfare

Perhaps there may be some value in describing some
of the manoeuvres which featured these wars on which this
study is based. Apart from the many forms of trickery and
concealment attached to guerilla warfare, the killing of
fishing, gardening and provedoring parties, there were plots
leading to ambush, tactical seiges and attack.

A good example of a plot and ambush is that already
mentioned as trapping Tuikilakila. He received a message in
the normal way through approved persons, that the town of
Buca had fallen and captives had been taken and were ready
for removal to Somosomo if canoes were available. The circumstances were not unexpected and on the surface everything
seemed genuine. The town was situated a little inland, and
reached by means of a narrow river. Tuikilakila and part of
the party remained at the mouth of the river, and the others
followed up the river to the place of anchorage, and thence
they entered the town in the normal way, met and accompanied
by the normal officials. As they seated themselves on the
ground for the Fijian ceremony that accompanied such an action, the Natewa people who had been concealed all the time
rushed on them, killing a number before they regained their
feet, and those who did reach the canoe had to sail down the
river amid a shower of spears and arrows from those who
awaited them along the river banks. That is a good example
of a plot and ambush. One could give many others (Lyth/LC
10/1/43). Another type of ambush was that made possible by
obtaining beforehand information of the enemy's movements,
which involved the work of a kind of spy system, or the obtaining of information by torture from prisoners.

The point has been made more than once that the
Fijian was more expert at defensive warfare than offensive.
Perhaps this is so. The fortified town was a feature of his
defence. These comprised two types. One was an ordinary
village, protected by means of fences, mounds, moats and so
on. The others were properly established forts *(koro-ni-
valu)*, not just a *koro* with a *bai-ni-valu* (village with a
war-fence).

A fortified town was more commonly met with in the
lowlands and the river deltas. The trenches or moats were
filled with mud and water, or with bamboo spikes, so arranged
to do the utmost possible damage to the foot (Jackson,
1853:430), the fences were either stone or reed walls, or

both, with great strength, and sometimes apertures for shooting through. One of the best fortified towns of this type was Tokatoka, which put its trust in trenches (*ibid:* 459). This town was always fortified, as it was in an almost continual state of war with Nakelo (Bulu, 1871:21).

The fort, as distinct from the fortified town, was built on some rocky eminence, the very appearance of which would discourage the enemy. These *koro-ni-valu* were not normally inhabited, but were always kept in some state of repair. One does not meet them in the lowlands or river deltas, but they were the regular thing in the islands and where the villages lay on a narrow belt of land between the sea and the mountains. If the invasion showed any signs of size and strength, the village was often just abandoned without defence, everyone retreating to the fortress. Nearly all the villages of Kadavu, for example, have their old fort besides their village, maybe half a mile or more back. Mostly their attacks came from the sea. There were ways of delaying the enemy of course, which was done by the men while women and children retreated with food and drink. Most other things needed were already in the fortress. Many of these were never captured by an invader.

May I devote one paragraph to describing such a fort I visited on that island. It was known as Naborua and was the fort of the *yavusa,* Naikasovesi, resident at Daveqele. There are three long rocky arms or headlands which jut out to the south and west from Nabukelevu, the extinct volcano. They stand out like the buttress roots of great rain-forest trees. They are narrow with blunt ends and a precipice on each side. On the central ridge is perched this fort. Only from the back, i.e. along the mountain side by path, can the fortress be approached, and on all sides there is a death drop. Approach is by single file only. What better conditions for ambush? To storm it would be impossible. Even if an enemy did reach the top he had to pass four *keli-ni-valu* (war-pits), and a *sava* (spirit-land) perhaps feared as much. There one can still find a stone basin, the tree and other associations of the pagan war cults. The foundations of various buildings, including a temple remain. The place, they told me, had never been taken. I can well imagine that to be so.

Jackson described another at the top of a sugar-loaf mountain, at Male in Vanua Levu. There was only one path, very steep, and those on top rolled great stones down on any who attempted assault (1853:425).   He described

another at Natewa Matua, on top of an immense rock, with a
steep path that could be ascended only single file. The top
was flat and had some 50 houses, surrounded by a stone wall.
Each house had its bread pit and their preserved food supply
was thus enough for a 4-year seige (*ibid*. 429). These places
he found inhabited, but it was not by choice on their own
admission. The country was in an unsettled state in the
forties when Jackson visited it.

The same writer gives us a picture of how a moving
army feeds, living on the land, and using every sort of animal life and even grubs from rotten wood, and human bodies
(*ibid*. 423-424). In passing, he also confirms the fear of
Bau in Somosomo (*ibid*. 452).

The Seige of Vuna and Plans for Assault

The seige of Vuna is perhaps one of the best examples one could find of the Fijian tactical assault, and we
cannot pass it without comment.

The Vunans were in possession of their town, were
well supplied with everything needed for a long seige - arms,
food, water. Though the invaders numbered 1200, the chances
were that Vuna might still have withstood the attack.   The
persecuted Christians of Bau and Nadi withstood the best efforts of Tui Bua, when they had taken refuge in a fort, for
so long that he gave up, saying to the missionary, that his
prayers were stronger than the Bua armies (Williams *Journ*.
24/9/50 etc.). Vuna might well have resisted - yet she sur-
rended. Why?

The invaders knew the strength of the fortifications
and made their plans with care. They began by constructing
a path from their encampment to the position from which the
attack was to begin, and here they built a long wall. The
army now divided into three parts and each made a path, one
through the forest, the second by the sea-coast and the
third joining them. From Hunt's description I take it this
formed a triangular encirclement of the town. Each party
then turned to establishing its protective devices against
the Vuna muskets and spears, and each built three fences,
one within the other, making the inside one of earth and
stones, and again making communication paths between them.

It was now possible to launch three attacks simul-
taneously from different positions, and the parties took

their stand so. The three companies now grew restless and
wanted to storm the fort. To use their own phrase they wanted to "eat the town", but the Vunivalu held them back.   We
remember the purpose of this war.

Vuna was given three days. A high chief now went
forward and called to them to surrender, he addressed the
Tui Vuna and announced his own name, and added that refusal
meant complete destruction. He called for some time, then
retired. There was no answer.

Assuming this to be refusal there was some sharp
firing for a period. Its intention had been intimidation.
It failed.

At sunset another scheme was tried, and one might
almost imagine the Vunivalu had heard of the Bible story of
Gideon's army which terrified the Midianites by shouting,
"The sword of the Lord and of Gideon" and breaking their
pitchers during the night. All the warriors were instructed
at a given moment to shout their war-cries, and as they were
a combined army of some size from many places this would
mean quite a commotion, and as admitted later was far more
terrifying than much musketry. It left the Vuna people with
no shadow of doubt on quite a number of points. They knew
the size of the army arrayed against them. They knew they
were completely surrounded. They knew there were companies
situated on all the vantage points of the surrounding country. They had the night to think it over, and the army anticipated storming the town in the early morning as usual.

Before any action began however, the *mata-ni-vanua*
(herald) of the Tui Vuna came out of the town and presented
the whale's tooth and basket of earth to the King, Tui Cakau.
The *tabua* was the atonement of the town, the basket of earth
the symbol of complete submission, begging the life of the
people on the victor's terms - even slavery if he so determined. The offerings were accepted, and the second chief of
Somosomo took a body of men to protect the town, lest the
warriors should get out of control and commit outrages, which
they were more than anxious to do. It was then that the Tui
Vuna came with his personal offering and daughter, as I have
already described.

The town as determined by the King was to be destroyed,
and the Vuna people whould make the best speed they could out
of it. No sooner had they done this than the waiting warriors
fell on the town, plundering whatever they could,

and killing the few that had not escaped when the chance was
given them. The town was then burnt to the ground. It was
not often that such seiges ended in mercy, but there were
political reasons for this case. The warriors received their
payment in other ways and pledged themselves to further service, and partook of the feasts and dancing before they returned home (Hunt *Journ. I:* 207-212).

        That is a good statement of a Fijian seige because
it brings out a number of significant points. There were
generals in old Fiji who were able to plan tactical manoeuvres of a high order. There was care and forethought in these
plans, there was good use of the lay of the land, they were
thorough about their communications, they occupied all the
surrounding vantage points, and were effective in their efforts at intimidating those within. It was a perfect 'check
mate' and Tui Vuna knew it.

        There were other Fijian generals who had won blood-
less victories by strategy. There was an occasion when Na-
mosimalua and Varani of Viwa had beseiged a village, and by
a certain manoeuvre occupied their source of supply of drinking water, after which it was just a matter of awaiting surrender (Hunt *Journ. II:* 188).

        Regarding the defence of a fortified town which had
surrounded itself by means of ditches, the first part of the
defence would take place with the defenders outside the town,
making use of the ditches sometimes. Pitched battles were
uncommon, but they were not unknown. If things favoured the
defenders they could pursue the retreating enemy; if not,
then they could retire within the fence.

        A town on Malolo was prepared in the following way
for a pitched battle outside the town against the invader.
A moat surrounded the whole place, 12 feet wide and full of
mud and water. Within this was a palisade built of coconut
trunks, 4 to 5 feet apart joined by a fence of wicker-work
about 10 feet high. Inside this was a second ditch, the
excavated earth being thrown up to form a parapet about four
feet thick, and about the same height. So they awaited the
enemy, going out to meet him and only retiring behind these
defences when the attack grew too hot (Wilkes, 1845:247-248).

The Social Function of Fijian Warfare

        To this juncture I have mainly limited myself to
wars of some political consequences. There were other wars

of serious consequence and heavy loss of life that have yet
to be fully investigated by historical research, and though
I am tempted to deal with the struggle between Bua and Macuata, I must resist as one would have to use almost an entire
ly different data base. But though I leave the wars of Vanua Levu, and of Ba and Ra for some other study, they all
support my finding that all war in Fiji was not just mere
petty skirmishing, even though it may have been localized
in area.

Now, having made that qualification, let us turn to
these insignificant struggles that went on everywhere most
of the time during those years. One observer says they were
cowardly exhibitions, and another that they gained nothing
and so on. Nevertheless I venture to suggest, that though,
by our standards, they were cowardly and meaningless, that
they fulfilled an essential social function so the Fijian
society could continue to exist in its original form.   In
the remaining portion of this paper I shall give five examples of the numerous elements comprising the social function of war in old Fiji.

1.   *The Unity and Security of the Kingdom:*
When Hunt wrote in his journal that the war with
Vuna was of advantage to the King, because he had to keep
his people's minds occupied in order to keep unity, he
touched on this subject of the social function of war (*Journ.*
24/8/40). A chief might even have to make excuse for going
to war. Perhaps the first of those functions was the maintaining of unity throughout his dominions - I put it first
because perpetuity was a national security measure. Tui Cakau knew this and made war on Vuna to regain the unity that
was threatened. Tanoa knew it from past bitter experience
and killed his son rather than have Rewa sympathies within
Bau. It was not just jealousy. It was security and survival.
For the same reason Tui Dreketi made war on Beqa people,
on account of their insubordination for murdering Rewa people wrecked on their island. This was November 1839, and
this was another case of clemency after a seige had been
raised (Cargill, 1841:269). But what he demanded of Beqa he
was unable to achieve from his brothers, and that brought
about his downfall.

For the same reason Nadroga fought a war against
Malolo in the late forties, Malolo having treacherously received and then murdered Makutu, chief of Cuvu. But in this
case the spirit of revenge was also present (Lyth *Journ. V:*
22-23). The chief who by right should have followed Tui Bua

in office, gave his status to one brother and then to another because he knew that, being a Christian, he could not
maintain unity in his kingdom (Tippett, 1954:35). This was
also the fact which delayed the conversion of Cakobau for
so long. He had long pegged out his claim in Christianity
in several ways, and had allowed his wife and son join the
Church some years before, and though he himself fluctuated
between sympathy and persecution, his bursts of persecution
can usually be traced to periods following the conversion
of important warriors. He approved the Church at Viwa on
the whole, but it did create difficulty in his maintaining
unity throughout his domains.

Now petty warfare provided the chiefs with an opportunity of testing the strength of their forces, of discovering and weakening of loyalty, and noting the callibre
of the warriors *(bati)*.[5]

2. *The Training of Youth for Manhood:*
In the pre-Christian view of life the enculturative
stages by means of which a youth passed on to manhood were
most important social events. There were, of course, initia-
tory rites, which were often tied up in some way or other
with war - usually symbolic. But I do not mean that here.
Lawry said that war and strife are the noble employment of
men (1850: 124). Wilkes said that war was the principal
employment of males (1845: 204). Fijian life was geared for
war. It was the background of the games played by Fijian
boys. For example, a Kadavan chief told me that *veitiqa* was
a game which involved precisely the same muscular movements
as spear throwing, and was considered a physical training
for this kind of warfare.

After the destructive war at Verata, Seru had the
children of the vanquished taken to Bau and fastened to
trees, that the children of Bau might practise markmanship
on them, and thus learn to be warriors (Waterhouse, 1866:
86-87). This was apparently quite a general practice (Williams, 1860:53). Manhood was impossible until blood had
been spilt and without war of some sort there were few opportunities for such deeds of valour. It didn't matter so
much whose blood, or how it was done; but if accomplished
on some military exploit for the tribe there would be a
ceremony for the young man and for his fellow heroes.

Hunt gives the detail of such a ceremony (*Journ. I:*
200-203). The whole populace assembled in the market place
and the ceremony commenced with a chant -

> *Biusa! Biusa!*
> *Biusa! a ravuravu*
> *A tui me ravu a ravu*

Biusa is 'going to war'. Translation is difficult (This is
in dialect not in Bauan). It means that they are about to
attend to the ceremony of those who have killed enemies
after the King has been to war. And the King replied -

> *O cei? O cei?*
> *A 'oro a to'a leo*
> *Oi au leo*
> *Oi o cei leo?*
> *Sa biuciri va'avuso sai yacana o Serumana yala leo.*

He calls those who have been successful to receive a new
name. The song is vulgar. (The old name is cast away like
a foreskin.) They now all join in the chorus -

> *Buluta dre*
> *Buluta waiwai ni La'eba i.*
> *Wai yasa*
> *O 'atia, 'atia! a ta'ali, a ta'ali!*

The same allegory is retained. (Cover with a bandage, cover
with oil of Lakeba, scented (?) oil. Cut it. It has gone.)
The sound of conch shells is now heard, in short blasts, as
the time of a quick march.

> One shouts (or grunts): *Uh! Uh! Uh!*
> Another replies: *I! I! I!* (Long 'e').

Four or five persons each take a plantain leaf, making cups,
and water is poured into them. They hold them for a moment
and go through a brief movement, changing places and then
turning outwards to form a circle and pouring the water on
the ground, they call out -

> *Sova!*
> *A ratou motu va'aoti.*
> *Mana, i dina, e dina.*
> *E! I! I!*

(Pour it out. They are killed. *Mana!* It is true! [So may
it be]). And after this the young heroes are introduced.
Let it be noted that there is differentiation between the
hardened warriors and those who have shed blood for the
first time in war.

One who has killed his first victim in war comes
forward accompanied by a person carrying a new dress, and
others with mats. The mats are laid on the ground for him
to stand on, and one of the old men removes his old dress,
which is done quickly, and then puts on him the new one,
which is a work of time and patience. This is a large
piece of native cloth about a yard wide, folded lengthwise

once or twice and put three or four times around him, and so
tucked in as to form a large bunch on his back. We have all
seen these on the backs of Fijian club-dancers, but perhaps
we have not all realized their significance. Four parties
of young women then come from different parts of the area,
each with a small dish made from the stalk of a banana tree,
containing a preparation of oil and paint with which to an-
oint the heroes. Each party continues singing a song to the
end of the ceremony.

Other heroes who have previously killed in war, now
enter with clubs on their shoulders. As heroes whom the god
has blessed with power in battle they are thought to possess
mana. Many lesser persons now bring their clubs and other
weapons that these heroes may handle them and thus transfer
the *mana* to as many weapons as possible - some might thus
sanctify up to 20 weapons during the ceremony. The women
place their oils on the ground and retire. There is a division
of paint and the heroes are painted from head to foot. A further ceremony takes place at the waterfront and the singing
continues upon their return to the market-place.

Lyth, who quotes the whole of this description in
his own journal, having borrowed Hunt's account to copy,
adds something to this detail. The waterside ceremony he
asserts is to pay service to the sea god, Bureiwai, and each
man dips his foot into the water and throws a stone, saying,
"Me sili na 'alou!" (May the god bathe!) (*Journ. I:* 204).

The heroes, Hunt tells us (*Journ. I:* 204) must remain in the market-place four days, and a small shelter is
built for them there; but they must not lie down though they
apparently could sleep in other postures, but they could not
take their hands from their clubs or their clubs from their
shoulders. Lyth subsequently altered those notes a little,
thus - the first and second nights they could sit or recline,
but not lie down; the third they could lie down and drop the
left hand; and after the third their heads were anointed
with oil and black was painted on their bodies instead of
red. On the fourth morning they could bathe (*Journ. I:* 544).
Lyth remained in Somosomo after Hunt had removed to Viwa and
had further opportunity of witnessing the ceremonies. However as there were differences between the treatment of
initiates and hardened warriors, this may account for the
two versions.

The heroes had the freedom of the town, could take
what they pleased, and were inferior to none in rank, being

called *turaga le'ale'a* (i.e. short chiefs, or chiefs for a
short time). During this period it was *tabu* to beat a drum,
or make noises like hammering or chopping near them. This
lasted for four days, during which they were *tabu sara,* and
this - be it noted - is the most honourable payment for service to one's country in war (Hunt *Journ. I:* 204).

That may be contrasted with the less honourable
payment planned by Batinamu who gathered an equally large
army to make war on Ritova of Macuata, promising as payment
to his warriors, the Christian women and the plunder of the
Mission store at Tiliva (Bua) upon their return (Williams
Journ. 9,10,12,17 Oct. 1848), keeping only Mrs. Williams
the missionary's wife, for himself. However, Batinamu was
himself murdered before he had got far from his own village
(*ibid.* 17/10/48; Henderson, 1931:492-3). This was the new
mercenary spirit of paying for war services, in contrast
with the chiefly manner, I have described from Hunt's journal, at Somosomo.

Williams witnessed a similar ceremony at Somosomo
shortly afterwards. It varies at several points, though
none of them are serious. There may have been some variable
elements in the ceremony when the warrior was chiefly born,
and there certainly would be when he was *Koli, Visa* or *Waqa,*
killer of 10, 20 and 30 respectively, as distinct from *Koroi* (killer of one) (Fison, 1907:xxi). Williams' account
concerns a man who was chiefly born. He carried a pineapple
club, and in his left hand held a reed, which was taken by
the old chief and sent to the temple. Some of the mats and
tumeric were also sent to the temple. In his case the accompanying chiefs threw the stones into the sea, and he was
followed about the village by a number of youths similarly
painted. He was not allowed to enter a house where there
was a woman, for three weeks (Williams, 1860:55-57). The
ceremony was called *Buli Yaca,* (giving of the name) and this
Koroi was told to stand on a bale of cloth, or sometimes it
would be a body (Henderson, 1931: 347).

Putting the three accounts together the major difference is the incident of the reed, and it is unlikely Hunt
and Lyth, both good observers, would have overlooked it. The
use of such reeds was discussed by Lawry, and among other
things he said it was a symbol of a solemn pledge, a binding
promise (1850:127). In the light of this it seems to me that
this young chief, being a chief and a man of authority, and
being followed everywhere by the party of youths, a special
promise of loyalty to the paramount chief was extracted from

him upon his entrace into 'knighthood'. However, my point
here is that war provided the necessary opportunity for a
young knight to "win his spurs", as it were; and without it
there would have been no knights to fight when really serious
wars did come upon them.

Williams, I feel sure, would have protested, at my
comparisons of this with knighthood; for he had utter con-
tempt for Fijian warfare, and especially its cowardly acts
against defenceless persons, and he was a good observer and
left a valuable record. I think that most of us would have
agreed with him had we witnessed them as he did, they were
so very opposed to our standards. Yet as we look back after
a century and try to see things in perspective, we must at
least admit that they were acts which enabled society to
function as the Fijian knew it, and without them there must
shortly have been no survival at all.

Before leaving this aspect of the provision of
youths with the facilities for aspiring to manhood, I should
mention the custom of *sevu malumu* (first-fruits of the club)
which was associated with the cutting of clubs by young men
before going to their first war engagement away from the village. The function required a victim. We are told of a
group of such youths falling upon some innocent gardeners for
this purpose in Bua (Williams *Journ.* 3/4/48). These things
happened. Sometimes they brought retaliation on the basis of
"a chief for a chief" and "a commoner for a commoner". Sometimes an atonement was offered and all was well. Bodies were
required, just as they were for launching war-canoes, building temples, feasting visiting chiefs and many other aspects
of Fijian pre-Christian social life. Theirs was a course set
down by their fathers, a definite ritual, which involved costly
price in human life - but for them it was their way for young
men to rise to tribal honour for the glory of the state, the
security and pride of all.

3. *The Inter-relationship of War and the Priestly System:*
The social function of war is seen again in the manner in which it was so tied up with the priestly system - we
may say, they were interrelated. Some wars, at least, were
vital to the very existence of the tribe and there was no
punishment the gods could inflict that was more feared than
for them to become *kawaboko,* or extinct. Relationship with
the gods was a fearful thing, a wrongful approach could be
extremely dangerous, the priest class could not be done without, and costly sacrifices had to be made if the support of
their war gods was to be won. War-gods demanded human

sacrifice. I have already mentioned the size of the offering made by the Somosomo people when they advanced against
Natewa.

As the tribe could not do without the priest, the
converse was equally true. The priest had to live. If there
were no wars, there were no offerings, and the priests went
hungry. Priestly wealth was measured by the wars his tribe
fought.

A priest forgotten in a division of offering could
make things very unpleasant. Tuikilakila was once forced to
abandon a war project, because a more or less insignificant
little priest, whose ration had been but one Fijian pudding,
was dissatisfied and prophesied evil against the expedition
(Henderson, 1931:328).

"Before going to war" wrote Williams, "they study
to be right with the gods" (1860:43-44). This was done in
many ways. Temples were set in order, surroundings were
cleared and grass cut, offerings were presented, *Yaqona* poured out and drunk, and prayers offered. Usually the priest
became inspired and 'shook', prophesying victory, bodies for
the ovens and so on. On one occasion, before the troops
went to Vuna from Somosomo, the priest did not 'shake'. It
was sufficiently unusual for Hunt to make enquiries afterwards, and the reply he got was that the god did not enter
him on this occasion, for so eager he was to approve the project, that he had already gone to Vuna to entice the people
outside their war-fence (Hunt *Journ.* 7/9/40). We have many
descriptions of these inspirations in the early literature
left by mariners and missionaries. One good example is
Lawry's (1850:127).

But on this particular occasion at Somosomo when
there was no 'shaking', the King presented the offering to
the priest and addressed the god through him. He did not
mention the name of the god, only the title *'Turaga'* (Lord)
was used, and he stood up to pray - the priest sat and listened.
The King handed a *tabua* to the priest, together with a bunch
of nuts, which were accepted in the following manner.
The priest held the bunch of nuts in one hand, taking the
stems in the other, and then placing them also into the hand
which held the nuts. He made promises of which these stems
were the seal and sign, assuring them that Vuna should die,
and then swinging the bunch he shook it with all his might,
counting 1, 2, 3, 4 - the nuts flying in all directions.
Those who sat near where a nut happened to stop, took it up

and kissed it, believing to obtain *mana* thereby and be preserved from the spears, arrows and musket balls of the Vuna
people (Hunt *Journ.* 7/9/40).

That paragraph is capable of much expansion, but
the point is made - war and the priestly system were part
and parcel of each other; they were interdependent. Without war the priest class would have perished, without priests
the tribe would have perished, for there would have been
neither security nor confidence.[6]

4. *Social Intercourse in Community Ceremonial:*

We now pass on to the fourth element in which war
is seen to have a social function. For a moment I am at loss
to find a term that describes it, and for the want of a better one, I call it *community ceremonial,* by means of which
social intercourse is achieved, and the tribe realizes something of its own entity. By means of these community ceremonial, all the classes and tribal groups within the King's
dominion were brought together in a kind of fellowship.

I shall have to limit myself here to three kinds of
ceremonial of this nature, though there are others. Let us
examine *the offer of service in war (bolebole),* the *military
review (taqa)* and the *victory celebrations (cibi* and *wate),*
devoting a paragraph to each, though they might well be the
subject of a whole paper.

The *bolebole* is a ceremony performed by a subject
people or allies, who have been correctly approached in another ceremony and asked for assistance in war. The word
comes from the verb *bolea,* which is tamely put into English
by 'offer'. But *bolea* is a strong word; and when I *bolea,*
I "rise to an occasion", I am "inspired to undertake" the
project in question. The *bolebole* is the ceremony of such an
offer of service. The meaning, 'boasting', sometimes given
to this word, is a secondary meaning, because these ceremonies
were characterized by much boasting. When some 250 warriors
arrived at Somosomo from Bouma and Wainikeli, Hunt says
they came "with the full pomp of Fijian pride" (*Journ.* 24/8/
40). They began with an exercise outside the town, and when
the procession was about to enter several people ran to and
fro whirling large native fans, "emblem of despatch in war"
and a form of salute as in a march past. They presented
themselves at the King's house, and for a while he spoke to
them on the object of the war and then retired to a distance.
One by one they ran to where he stood, brandishing their clubs
and engaging in mock battle, smashing them on the ground

immediately before the King, with a promise of allegiance and a boast to deal with the enemy in that way. Examples of their boasting are given in Williams' *Fiji and the Fijians,* and these examples have been quoted by most subsequent writers on the subject (1860:46-48). After the *bolebole* the King presented *tabua*s and food.

The importance lay not so much in the boasting, but rather in the profession of loyalty before going to war. Often these warriors would have their own war cries, which they would use time and time again. May I give one example which does not come from *Fiji and the Fijians,* the shout of Naiceru -

> *A cava ko tagica, ko Raturakesa;*
> *Ai samu ga ni bunua ka vuka mai Tailevu oqoka.*
> Why do you cry, Raturakesa?
> This (the club he brandishes) shall be the smiter
> of this string of bats that has flown here from
> Tailevu.[7]

What, you may ask, was the value of such a ridiculous ceremony. Apart from its entertainment value for the populace, and there certainly was much laughter from the women at some of the boasting; there was also a social value in such a get-together, the bond that made them feel these visitors were one with them. At the same time it did give a chief about to go to war some idea of the nature and agility of his forces, their number, strength, arms and so on. And let us not forget it was an occasion on which he spoke to them formally as a body, and when they collectively assured him of their loyalty. After this there were visits to the temple and offerings to the gods, but the *bolebole* was itself a social gathering and a ceremonial pledge.

Of course, it was not without risks. For example Waqa Wai killed the Chief of Nakorovatu in this way, when he was treacherously performing the *bolebole* (Williams, 1860: 51). There was also another occasion during the 1st Bau-Rewa War, when the Chief of Toga, an ally of Rewa, was enlisting aid in this manner, and the people who were accepting his invitation to war were performing this ceremony before him, coming forward to him, one by one in war paint and full battle array. A warrior from a Bauan village slipped into the line and performed his antics before the chief, but instead of striking the ground he crashed his club down on the head of the Chief of Toga. This was the signal for the others of the Bauan party that had planted themselves about the village, (partly disguised by war paint, and no doubt

assumed by each group of local parties to be of the other)
to rush in and attack. The thing happened so suddenly and
unexpectedly, that the locals fled, not knowing the strength
of the enemy within their midst, and there was a general
massacre. This serves also to show the effectiveness of
Bauan espionage, for they must have had full details of
everything to be able to carry out such a daring scheme. At
the same time it is an exploit worthy of study by those who
think the Fijian warriors were cowards (Hunt *Journ.* 15/1/44).

Side by side with that we could place the exploit of
Tui Wainunu and his nephew, when separated from his army,
and discovering a great army enclosing him, determined to
act on his own, stole by night into the warriors quarters,
caught them unawares and slew 27 of them in quick succession
(Williams, 1860:58-59). It well compares with the daring of
some of David's exploits in the Old Testament. Cakobau also
was known to visit an enemy fortified town alone (Waterhouse,
1866:99). It takes a brave man to engage in such an under-
taking, but it could not have been really rare in old Fiji,
because the Fijians had a word for it. A man who went forth
to fight any sort of conflict, but went alone was *ravusebe;*
and the true meaning of the word *batikadi* is "one who sneaked
into a house of sleepers" (i.e. an enemy house) as Tui
Wainunu did. But it is a man who does the deed alone.   The
modern use of *batikadi* is a corruption.[8]

The second ceremony was the *taqa* or military review,
and again there are numerous examples given in the old literature on Fiji. The best description I have seen is that of
the review before Cakobau at Somosomo in 1846. It is a
classic example of old Fijian military display. It took 200
men several hours to stack the food for presentation, and
among other things this included nearly 40,000 yams, and a
wall of *yaqona* seven feet high and 35 feet in length, and
over 20 huge bales of native cloth, to name only some of the
things presented. Here again there was a demonstration of
fan waving, and then in came some 200 men carrying large
bundles of *masi* on their shoulders, two more with four large
masi hanging from a bamboo pole, and 100 more all with *masi.*
These men themselves attired in *masi* were then joined by another 250, similarly dressed. They sat on and about the
bales of cloth and other presented wealth *(ai yau).*

Then followed more fan waving, by two young chiefs,
and the army entered. It comprised 3000 warriors, armed with
clubs, spears, muskets and battle-axes, and formed in companies according to their arms. Henderson provides the full

detail in the editorial text of *The Journal of Thomas Williams* (1931: 347-351), and a reader of that long account will be able to see the difference between the *taqa* and the *bolebole* which were both performed together; each having its own prescribed ceremonial.

In passing let us note the quantity of *yau* or property that seems to have changed hands on this occasion, and with the forces Bau took it must have been extremely expensive to Somosomo to engage their help. It serves to support the view already expressed by Tanoa that there was far more profit from fighting in Vanua Levu or Lau than in Rewa. This was equally true whether he was fighting his own war there or on behalf of another. There are good reasons for believing that this expedition, as far as Cakobau was concerned, was political and acquisitive. As we have already seen, there is correspondence from Viwa to show that the missionaries thought this before the enterprise took place.

However, for our present purpose, my concern here has been more to observe the nature of a military review, and though the particular case I chose as my example had major political aspects, for the moment I want you to observe the social nature of the gathering, the organization, preparation, and fellowship. They were not often on such a large scale as this and more often concerned only a single kingdom. The *bolebole* and *taqa* were not always performed together, and there were other local variations in the ceremonies.

Before the Bouma people went to Vuna, they danced on the *rara* (village green), with bundles of coconuts on their backs, after the *bolebole*. Thence they advanced in formation to the temple enclosure and continued their dance, and heaped up the nuts for presentation (Hunt *Journ.* 7/9/40).

5. *The Ceremonial of Victory After War:*
The last matter for our examination concerns the ceremonial associated with the return from war, when excesses ran riot, with scenes, dances and songs of utmost vulgarity. Hunt, in his descriptions of the women going out to meet the returning warriors with songs and dances, described them as "savage and fiendish", the warriors answering back from their canoes, shrieking and beating the water with poles. He felt that there was something Jewish about the way the women went out singing, but the nature of those songs and dances were of an entirely different character - 'lewd' was the word he used to describe them (*Journ.* 14/9/40). Williams said almost the same thing, but though he admired the Hebrew hero songs

he felt the Fijian counterparts were "brutalized and abomin-
able". "The words of the women's song" he said, "may not be
translated; nor are the obscene gestures of their dance, in
which the young virgins are compelled to take part, or the
foul insults offered to the corpses of the slain, fit to be
described... On these occasions the ordinary social restrictions are destroyed, and the unbridled and indiscriminate
indulgence of every evil lust and passion completes the scene
of abomination" (Williams, 1860:53-54).

So we are left in no doubt about what Williams
thought of these ceremonies. These comprised the *cibi*
(death dance) and the *wate* or *dele* the song that was sung at
the time over the bodies of the slain (Fison MS., 1871:26). I
have a number of these songs, but I would not print them.
Let it suffice to say that the women greatly desire these
heroes, and their songs indicate that their exploits in sex
will be as great as they are in war. They are addressed by
such names as Ra Uti - Sir Penis. I shall leave the matter
there. In addition to this, the bodies of the slain, especially the genitals, are abused in various ways. Detail of an
example can be found in Jackson's narrative, if you want
some evidence from a non-missionary source (1853:438).

In a society which was polygamous, and where the high
chiefs had scores of wives, there was almost certain to be
some period of approved relief from social restrictions, as
far as the rank and file was concerned. It was thus looked
upon as a social occasion, the rewards of victory and valour",
as it were.[9] Whether moral or immoral, these dances served as
a social function in pre-Christian Fijian society. The tension of war was broken up with the physical satisfactions of
sex and rhythm.

Conclusion

In conclusion then let me summarize the major points
I have tried to make.

War is seen to have been of two types - one a bitter
and desparate struggle to the death, a 'war of the chiefs'
which could end only in the death of one of the leaders.
Though even these were local in area, they were major wars.

On the other hand there were seemingly insignificant
skirmishes, with great display and few casualties. Some of
these also had important political consequences, but mainly
their importance is seen to be social, for various reasons,

some of which I have outlined in this paper, although there may well have been others.

There are - 1. Wars to maintain internal unity and loyalty, without which there could be no sense of security for the tribe. 2. Without war there was no provision of facilities by means of which youths could graduate for manhood (as manhood was visualized in Fijian society). 3. War was the inter-relating link between the priestly class and the chiefs and people. Without priestly aid war could not be contemplated; without war priests were deprived of their livelihood. They were interdependent. 4. Community ceremonial bound the tribe in a sense of tribal glory and achievement, and satisfied their craving for display and exercise of the animal instincts.

In passing, several historical points are raised on which new light is now thrown, especially relative to motives, causes and events of the 1st Bau-Rewa War, and the Somosomo-Vuna War, the mystery of Rewa's attitude to Bau before the war began, the mind of the Somosomo people about Bau in the early forties, and Cakobau's intentions regarding Natewa. These factors, I think, have not been fully covered in any previous history.

Notes:

1   Paper read and discussed before the Fiji Society, September, 1954. The discussion was opened by Ratu Edward Cakobau.
2   I could produce dozens of references to 3-figure casualties, and there are some of 4-figure. For instance, I mention the way in which the Raviravi Chief fell on Goneseuseu and Dugawaqa, his challengers, near the beginning of the last century, and according to an eyewitness accounted for a thousand enemy casualties (Williams, 1860:50); and another example is the slaughter of delta tribes at Natogadravu, by Roko Tabaiwalu, one of the worst tyrants old Fiji knew, King of Rewa, cousin of Naulivou and Tanoa of Bau. He killed 1800 that day (Waterhouse, 1866:35). The former example was a pitched battle, the latter a treacherous massacre. This sort of thing accounts for the richness of the old Fijian language in words of extermination like - *dravutaki, kawayali, kawaboko, samulala, qeavu, yavu* etc. (Fison, 1871:46-7), and the tragic decline of population during the early part of the last century.

3   The figure of 400 casualties seems to come from a secon-
     dary source and I have seen no primary evidence for such
     a number (Jaggar/LC 29/5/43).

4   The smoking of hands for future jesting and mockery as
     a Rewan custom is confirmed by Joeli Bulu, who was sta-
     tioned at Nasali with Jaggar (Derrick, citing Wall, 1950:
     85).

5   Williams says the warriors were not a class in society,
     but that men of all classes had military obligations
     (1860:45). This universal obligation of all to fight is
     true, but there are different opinions about whether or
     not there was a warrior class. Lawry, who travelled
     round Fiji in the forties and fifties collected infor-
     mation from all the missionaries, and said they were a
     class (1850:119). So did Wilkes (1845:204). The solu-
     tion may surround the meaning of the word *bati*. Modern
     students have said it is from *bati* "edge", and that
     these are the border tribes, whose friendship was cul-
     tivated lest they change sides; but Cargill said these
     were the warrior tribes, from *bati* a "tooth" (1841: 326).
     Thomson (1908:88-89) takes the modern view. Others
     say 'border tribes' or 'allies', or as in the case of
     Lyth's journal we sometimes get the term 'fighting al-
     lies'(*Journ. V:* 22). Somewhere, I can't remember where,
     I have heard them spoken of as mercenaries. Waterhouse
     called them 'feudal soldiers' (1866:42).
         I personally, am not satisfied with any of these.
     Jackson spoke of the *Turaga Bati* as 'Chief of the
     Forces' (1853:459). I have met tribes *(yavusa)* inhab-
     itants of one village, where one clan in the village
     is *bati,* and members take their place beside the *tu-
     raga,* and *bete* and so forth. This makes them a class.
     In the little kingdoms this may be so. In other cases
     they are not a village, but a whole chain of villages
     widely separated - almost like a tribe in themselves.
     We still have a lot to learn about the *bati*.

6   One should perhaps qualify that statement by adding
     that there were other priests who attended to rain
     and sunshine, harvests and so on. But here also the
     security and life of the tribe is dependent on them.

7   This is a most interesting linguistic study, and also
     an interesting use of allegory. The string of bats
     hanging from a tree is called a *bunua*. This partici-
     pant of the *bolebole,* likens the Bauan invaders to a
     string of bats. He shall deal with the whole string of
     them by smashing the branch from which they hang, so
     they all fall. *Ai samu* from *samuta,* to beat or smite,
     is the instrument of the action. This also comes from
     Hunt, but through Hazlewood (1850:16).

8   *Bati kadi* is singular, not plural. If accompanied by
a party the word is *tataki* from the verb *tataka* "to
seek revenge". All these words are now obsolete, but
their existence throws light on the nature of this
sort of activity. The word was called back into use
for the guerilla warfare in the war with Japan. It was
the nearest term that could be found.

9   One can easily understand now the attitude of the missionaries to war and some kinds of dances, and had Professor Henderson and others who have criticized them
for this attitude, taken the trouble to investigate the
matter thoroughly, I feel sure they would have modified
their criticisms somewhat. The missionaries did not reject *all* dancing. They were quite discriminating.
They preserved many forms and their accompanying chant
patterns. But they did dispose of the *wate, dele* and
cibi.

References Cited:

Missionary Journals (Major Sources):
John Hunt: 1838-1848 in the Mitchell Library, Sydney
Thomas Williams: 1840-1853 with other papers in the
          Mitchell Library, Sydney (See also Hender-
          son, 1931)
Richard Lyth: 1835-1854 with many other papers, in the
          Mitchell Library, Sydney
Thomas Jaggar: Excerpts published in the *Wesleyan Maga-
          zine.* [The original has recently been placed
          in the Mitchell Library]

Missionary Correspondence:
Mostly to the London Committee of the Wesleyan Mission-
ary Society. Frequently published in the *Wesleyan
Magazine.*
          John Hunt
          Richard Lyth
          Thomas Jaggar
          Thomas Williams
          John Watsford
          Lorimer Fison (1860s)

Other Sources:

Bulu, Joel
  1871   *Joel Bulu: The Autobiography of a Native Min-
            ister in the South Seas.* (Translated by

Lorimer Fison) London, Wesleyan Mission House

Cargill. David
1841   *Memoirs of Margaret Cargill*, London, John
          Mason

Derrick, R.A.
1942   "Fijian Warfare," Fiji Society for Science &
          Industry *Trans. & Proc.*
1950   *A History of Fiji*, Suva, Government Printer

Erskine, J.E.
1853   *Journal of a Cruise among the Islands of the
          Western Pacific*, London, John Murray

Fison, Lorimer
1871   "The Fijian Judged by his Own Words" MS., in
          the "Fison Collection."
1907   *Tales from Old Fiji*, London, De La More Press

Hazlewood, David
1850   *Feejeean-English Dictionary*, Vewa, Wesleyan
          Mission Press

Henderson, G.C.
1931   *Journal of Thomas Williams 1840-1853*, Sydney,
          Angus & Robertson

Jackson
1853   *Jackson's Narrative*, App. in Erskine, 1853

Lawry, Walter
1850   *Visit to the Friendly and Feejee Islands*,
          London, O. Gilpin

Thomson, Basil
1908   *The Fijians: A Study in the Decay of Custom*,
          London, Wm. Heinemann

Tippett, A.R.
1954   *The Christian (Fiji 1835-67)*, Auckland,
          Institute Publishing Co.

Wall, Coleman
1919   "Sketches in Fijian History" *Trans. & Proc.
          Fijian Society*

Wallis, M.D.
1851   *Life in Feejee: or Five Years Among the Canni-
          bals*, Boston, Wm. Heath

Waterhouse, Joseph
1866   *The King and People of Fiji.....&c.....*
          London, Wesleyan Conference Office

Watsford, John
1900   *Glorious Gospel Triumphs as Seen in My Life
          and Work in Fiji and Australia*, London.
          C.H. Kelly

Wilkes, C.
1845   *Narrative of the United States Exploring
          Expedition* (One volume edition used)

4

AN INDIGENOUS POINT OF VIEW

Lady Nicotine

During the seventies and eighties tobacco was a hot topic in Fiji. The debate not only ran between the administrations of Church and State, but the Fijians themselves were "in the act" in fact the debate began with them. This brief discussion of the matter is assembled from Fijian material - tracts, written arguments and a song, correspondence and mission reports. It shows how a researcher, who keeps notes on a theme, as he works through records for some more significant purpose, may end up with something quite valuable. The value here is not in the subject of tobacco but in the way a Fijian structured an argument in the sixties and seventies, and in the environmental changes that came with Cession, and the new kind of encounter between Church and State that came with colonial rule. Thus a harmless but interesting subject becomes important evidence of more widely significant forces.

Tobacco: Pre-Contact and Acculturation Periods

Tobacco was known in Fiji long before the inhabitants learned to smoke it. In those days forest lore was important and almost every plant had some use or other. Tobacco was no exception. The ancient Fijian name for it was *Ai Vaka-mate ni Kutu* (Destroyer of Lice) which name explains its primary function - *ni sa kuvui e na kena kubou na ululevu, me mate kina na kutu* (for the large head of hair was smoked with it to kill the lice), (Tract:4).

It was not until the reign of the Bauan, Naulivou, that the Fijians took to the habit of smoking (Waterhouse, 1866:23), and then, we are told, it began on the island of Nairai. A vessel had been wrecked but somehow or other a party of the crew managed to escape to the island. Normally

81

they would have been killed for the ovens, as having salt-
water eyes but on this occasion they were preserved because
when the inhabitants rushed on them to claim their prizes
they observed smoke proceeding from their mouths and noses.
"Sa kalou bagi ko ira oqo!" (Surely these are gods!) they
exclaimed. Thus the lives of the mariners were saved, and
they lived to teach the Fijians to smoke (Tract:4).

        Nor was it long before the Fijian became a regular
slave to the habit, and indeed the Fijian minstrels were
composing their love songs to Lady Nicotine a century ago.
Ko Lewatagane, they called her, which means one who rules the
men, or one whom the men could not resist.
        You go to draw saltwater and return;
        Lewatagane runs after;
        "Is there no tobacco in the bag?"
        Maybe there is tobacco in the house
        Then devote the evening to it
        How is it the giving is so contemptible?
        Stir up the fire in the corner of the house.
        There dangles the lover's locks
        Dangles from the beams above.
        I hate the marriage of old people
        Mine is a young love
        My twist of tobacco (Waterhouse, 1866:425).
This poem, which I confess loses its rhythm in the translating was composed over a century ago in a Vanua Levu dialect,
and shows a form of personification quite equal to that of
our English poets. The minstrel finds his Lady Nicotine ir-
restible. He sees the long selected dry leaves of pandanus
or banana dangling from the rafters. He speaks of them as
tobe (lover's locks), which the maiden must remove if she
marries. He takes them to roll into his *suluka* with his tobacco, and spends the evening enjoying the company of his
ladylove. Thus smoking spread to every corner of Fiji and
was followed soon afterwards by Christianity.

        Now it is an interesting thing that for many years,
no matter how carefully one combs the archives of the Methodist Mission for the first thirty years, there is scarcely a
reference to the evils of smoking. In fact I cannot find any
really serious attack on the habit before 1868, and even this
was a private competition, or a game, not open propaganda.
It happened in this way.

The Fijian Anti-Smokers

        Two missionaries and a group of native ministers were
yarning *(veitalanoa)* together on a certain occasion and after

a time the conversation got around to the subject of smoking. One of these missionaries, I am told, was himself a smoker, and the native ministers (some Tongan and some Fijian) all spoke with one voice against the habit. The missionary smoker then said to them "Go each one of you back to his town. Take paper and write down the evils of tobacco and I will give a dollar to him who does it best." Whereupon the party broke up more quickly than usual, for a dollar was a lot of money to a Fijian in the 1860s (Fison/Symons, 1868). The dollar was eventually won by James Havea, who had come from Tonga to Fiji in the early days (Fison, 1868:29) and left a brief hand-written journal of some of his adventures. This in itself is of interest because the first articulated opposition to smoking in Fiji seems to have come from the Tongan teachers, and Havea was with Joeli Bulu and Paula Vea, among the most articulate. Two of the statements the missionary received in the competition were translated fairly literally by Lorimer Fison and recorded in his letter-book; one from James Havea, a Tongan, and the other by Kelepi Bai, a Fijian. Their arguments are set out below in full. They are good examples of Pacific islanders' logic and reasoning in the mid-sixties of the last century. At the same time they also show some evidential value of the influence of Tonga on Fiji through the Christian teachers.

James Havea's "Sixteen Evils of Tobacco" *(Translated from Fijian by Lorimer Fison.)*

1. One evil of tobacco I think to be this - that it is poisonous even as are strong waters, and thereby are men's bodies poisoned, and their souls darkened. I do not believe it to be the will of our Heavenly Father that we should take poisonous things into our mouths, but those things only which are not hurtful. This truly is a great evil of tobacco.

2. Here is another of its evils. It binds a man hand and foot. Thus in Tonga, where smoking is forbidden to those employed in The Work, not a few have wished to help therein, but not being able to give up smoking, they have been hindered from helping in that great and good work, because they have been held in slavery by tobacco, even as drunkards are held in slavery by drink.

3. Another evil of smoking among the Tongans and Fijians is that they swallow the poisonous smoke of tobacco, whereby they are made drunk and sick, and their bodies also are poinsoned. Now, if we swallow strong

waters, glass after glass, we are made drunk; whereas if we swallow tobacco smoke but once, it makes us
drunk: and hence is manifest its poisonous nature.

4.   Moreover it makes men lie. They lie when their tobacco is begged and they refuse it, saying that they
had none. Many local preachers also have lied about
it, saying that they would give it up, but not doing
so. I fear that many souls are thus lost because of
tobacco.

5.   Here again is one of its evils. Tobacco is a snake
of the Devil, whereby he entraps men to other and
greater evils, both in Tonga and in Fiji: and of these
evils I could tell you by word of mouth, but to write
them I am ashamed.

6.   Here is another evil. A father goes with his son to
the 'hearing of sermons'. The preacher's word pierces
the heart of the lad and he repents. When the service is over they go back to the house, where the
father stretches himself at full length on the mats,
while the lad sits down looking wistfully at him and
waiting for some good word of comfort. "Go!" says
the man, "Go and fetch me a fire-stick, that I may
smoke." Away goes the lad reasoning to himself as he
goes "So then tobacco is of greater mark than religion."
And so he leaves off thinking about his soul.

7.   Another evil of tobacco. There was a man of Namata
who smoked till he was both drunk and sick. Being a
member of the Society he was reported to our Weekly
Meeting, and we were not of one mind about the matter.
     "How would it be," said Tomasi Viomua, the Teacher,
"if we give him a sharp reproof, and let that suffice?"
     Then spake the Missionary, even Mr. Fordham, "And
who among you" said he, "can go and reprove him? Can
you, who are also a great smoker?"
     Great then was the shame of Tomasi, and as for me,
I saw the greatness of the evil - first in that members of the Society smoked till they were drunk and
sick, and secondly because the Teachers who smoked
could not reprove men for this evil and so were
ashamed.

8.   Another evil of smoking is that often are houses
burnt thereby, and clothes and mats and canoes.

9.   The ninth evil of tobacco is the spitting in the
midst of the house. O the filthiness of this tobacco
spitting! The utter filthiness!

10. Another evil is that our bodies are often burnt by
the tobacco fire-sticks - thus a child of mine burnt
its foot with one of them which was lying in my house.

Now if there had been no-one smoking, there would
have been no firestick, and if there had been no
firestick then would my child not have been burnt.
Alas for the evil of tobacco!

11. Yet again an evil. Smokers are lean of body and
ill-favoured. But let them turn from their evil ways
and leave off tobacco, then they will become fat and
well-looking.

12. Another evil is that it hinders work. When a smoker
craves tobacco, no matter what he is doing, whether
planting or reading, or whatever other work he may
be about, straightway he leaves it and goes seeking
his tobacco, thus leaving a useful thing for a thing
which is of no use.

13. Again smokers have evil smelling mouths.

14. Moreover a smoker's house is always in a litter,
with tobacco leavings and ashes, and bits of dried
banana leaf.

15. I fear that tobacco causes much disease; and if
this be so, it is indeed a great evil.

16. Yet one more evil thereof. A man said to me, "As
for my smoking, when I am about to lie down at night,
I smoke a great deal, and then a deep sleep falls
upon me, so that I rest well." Whence I judge that
he must be stupified by his tobacco, and how then
can he offer his nightly thanksgiving and prayer to
God.

And here is an end of my setting forth of the evils
of tobacco.
                    I, James Havea,
                        the Native Missionary (Fison, 1868:27-9).

Kelepi Bai was a Fijian, who stood in the same camp,
but whose arguments were expressed with more brevity and
point.

*Kelepi Bai's Twelve Reasons Against Smoking
(Translated from Fijian by Lorimer Fison.)*

1. In the days of my smoking, if a man begged tobacco
from me when I had but little, then I used to lie to
him, saying that I had none. This is one evil.

2. If, after I had refused him, there came another
begging tobacco, and I gave it to him, then was he
angry whom I had refused. This is the second evil
which I have seen.

3. Whenever I sat down to read it would not be long

before I wanted to smoke, and then would I throw
aside my book that I might make ready my tobacco.
This also is one of its evils.

4.   Here again is an evil. It causes heartburnings
between husband and wife; for, if a man cannot find
his tobacco when he is going forth in the morning,
then is he angry with his wife; and so too the woman,
alas, with her husband.

5.   Moreover men are often made drunk by it, and sick
even, as by strong waters. This also is an evil.

6.   Another evil. It makes a man late to chapel, if
he happen to be rolling up his *suluka* when the drum
begins to beat. A sad hindrance is tobacco.

7.   Again, when we are dressed in our best, often does
tobacco burn holes in our good clothes; and this indeed is a great evil.

8.   Here is another of its evils. When a man wakes and
sends his child for tobacco, he is angry if the child
refuses; or if the lad pretends to go for it, and
does not, then the father goes about cursing because
the child has deceived him.

9.   Yet again an evil. It makes a man short-winded.
Great smokers are soon out of breath.

10. Moreover it makes a man cold. Great smokers are
soon chilled. This also is an evil.

11. Here again is one of its evils. I think that like
the inside of a Fijian kitchen for blackness is the
inside of a great smoker.

12. Smokers waste their substance on tobacco.
And there are the evils of tobacco, which I have seen.
I, Kelepi Bai   (Fison, 1868:22-3).

It doesn't take much imagination to see what a lively
debate could develop when James Havea and Kelepi Bai, or others
of the same type, met in a house for the evening with the
minstrels who composed their love songs to the Maiden Tobacco,
whose willing slaves they were, and who could compose songs
about the hanging banana leaves as 'lovers locks'.

So as time went on the Fijian people fell into two
camps - one the heavy smokers and the other those who were
under a strict prohibition *(tabu sara)*. There were fewer and
fewer moderate smokers.

Social Disequilibrium After Cession

After Cession, with the rapid increase of population, the spirit of adventure and individualism led to a

heavy excess of drinking and smoking, so much so that the
missionaries, both European and native, felt they had to
move against the matter. This is historically interesting
because they had not done this aggressively during the earlier years of the mission. The Church became more and more
puritanical in the eighties - a characteristic which surviv-
ed until the Pacific War. In the eighties the evangelism
changed from an *invitation to heaven* to a *fear of hell,*
(which though present was not a strong feature of the period
of church planting in Fiji). This is strongly reflected in
the mission annual reports.

In 1880 William Weir Lindsay determined to establish
an Anti-Tobacco and Grog-drinking Society at Viwa, and
throughout his area. As to the reason, I shall let him speak
for himself -

> During the year we have been deeply impressed with the
> growing evils of tobacco-smoking and kava-drinking....
> The old men admit that these habits have grown with
> alarming rapidity within the last few years, until al-
> most every child smokes. These habits are evidently
> telling on the Fijian race, as they are no longer sat-
> isfied with the mild Fijian cigarette of former days,
> but now women and children as well as men, must have
> pipes and the strongest tobacco, which produce a state
> of semi-intoxication...(*A.R. Viwa* 1882).

Langham reported the same kind of thing in the Bau
Circuit but though he could persuade some 500 people to sign
the Total Abstinence Pledge, he could only get half that number to deny themselves smoking (*A.R. Bau,* 1882). In Kadavu,
missionary Jory was more successful (*A.R. Kadavu,* 1885).

In that Europeans had a hand in this new movement
it should be clearly stated that their motivation came from
the Fijian vital statistics, which were threatened by the
excesses of the first decade after Cession, and which were
such as had not been previously known in Fiji. The serious-
ness of the situation may be judged by the fact that approval
was given the puritanical social action, by Governor Des
Vouex, who was by no means an admirer of the mission theology
or politics, and held no brief for Wesleyanism. Even so, he
was so alarmed by the breakdown of social controls in this
first decade of colonial rule, that he pressed the Council of
Chiefs to approve the anti-smoking and grog-drinking policy
(*A.R. Bau,* 1883).

The Fijian ministers of the Kelepi Bai type threw

their weight into the movement, and went so far as to produce a pamphlet in Fijian for free distribution. The movement grew to some proportion by the eighties. The argument
of the pamphlet is much along the lines of James Havea's
sixteen points, and with some biblical augmentation. The
weight of argument however is on the physical effects of excess, so that we may assume that the Fijians responsible
were not unaware of the element which caused the European
missionaries' concern. Fijian population was falling rapidly, which Fison observed from his statistical records (Fison
Note Book). A most methodical person was Lorimer Fison. ·

The Mission and the Colonial Administration

This Wesleyan Fijian attitude towards tobacco led
them into strife with the civil authorities. For some reason or other the Colonial Administration officially decided
to exploit Fijian tobacco as a means of taxation revenue for
Fijians, and economic purposes. There was no point of time
in Fijian history before or since that such a bad decision
could have been made. The Fijians were alarmed at their
population decline. The Government had determined on a labour
program of indenture, and there had been many incidents between Fijians and introduced labour. The idea of tax was
being pushed with some difficulty. There had been a little
war in the interior, and considerable disillusionment about
penalties served out by the new administration. The Wesleyan Fijian and Tongan teachers felt that tobacco raised a
moral issue, and that cultivating it was as bad as smoking it.
At that point of time in history it was a foolish decision.
It could have been tea, or cotton, or cocoa, or hemp, or cane,
or copra, and only the idea of tax itself would have been involved. But the Church was already strong (one point the
new administration could not swallow), and immediately Church
and State came into collision.

I quote a letter of the Colonial Secretary to the
Chairman of the Methodist Mission -
It appears that one Levi and four others.... were
charged with refusing to assist in cultivating the
District Tobacco Crop, being under a vow to have nothing to do with tobacco. They were fined in the sum of
4/- or seven days hard labour.
At a Court subsequently held at Matailobau four leading members of the Wesleyan Church were prosecuted upon a similar charge. They pleaded conscientious scru-
ples with respect to the cultivation or use of tobacco.

They were fined 10/- each or in default fourteen days
imprisonment. They went to prison.

For many months past the Governor has anticipated
these events, a considerable number of natives having
been led to believe by Teachers, not understanding the
question, that smoking is a cardinal sin.

The Governor is well aware that you have urged the
natives to abstain from the use of tobacco and alcohol,
as also kava, and also that you have merely urged the
matter in the way of advice, the acceptance of which is
optional with the person addressed. But His Excellency
has good reason to think that your native agents are
gradually making it a question of doctrine on which
their zeal is carried to the verge of petty persecution.
After claiming that as another Mission provided excellent
tobacco and kava, and this variance of outlook caused mental
perplexity to the natives, the Chairman was asked to take
some steps "to correct the erroneous impression into which
the native members of your Church at Matailobau and else-
where have fallen" (Col. Sec./Langham, 1890).

This interesting letter touches one of the many matters where adjustments had to be made after Cession.   It
also shows how one Governor, observing the effect of excess
could support a movement, while his successor, whose mind
was on the matter of taxation could oppose it. The missionaries, on the other hand, were bound to support the right
of a man's conscience, and the dispute was no longer about
'tobacco' *per se*, but 'whether or not a man should be pun-
ished for refusing to work in a manner to which he had conscientious objection'. Surely the obvious way out would
have been to provide an alternative form of taxation, especially as copra, candlenuts, cotton and maize were also
used for taxation purposes in various parts of Fiji during
the eighties (Horne, 1881:188).

Anthropologically the primary function of tobacco,
as a destroyer of vermin in the hair fell out of use. In
time the devotees of Lady Nicotine came out on top in the
struggle with the Anti-tobacco Leagues, but not before some
equilibrium had been restored. There are still many Fijians
who are *tabu tavako*, but the smoke fills the house when the
yaqona bowl is in use, and *sulukas* are plentiful in the villages - although 'tailor-made' cigarettes are used in town.
A kind of co-existence exists. Before this equilibrium was
restored the Commission on the Decrease of Native Population
(1896) revealed the effect of smoking Fijian tobacco on the
milk of Fijian mothers and after the point had been scored

90

the public debate died down. So do seemingly minor matters
become reference points in the dynamics of cultural change.

References Cited:

Anonymous
   n/d   *"Ai Vola sa bale ki na Yaqona kei na Topako,"*
                Printed tract, (believed to have been edited
                by A.J. Small)
Colony of Fiji
   1896   *Report of Commission on the Decrease of
                Native Population,* Suva Government Printer
Fison, Lorimer
   1865-94   Reading Note Book
   1867-69   Letter Book - Outwards Correspondence
   1868   Letter to Symons 18/7/68
Horne, John
   1881   *A Year in Fiji* (An Inquiry into Botanical,
                Agricultural and Economic Resources of the
                Colony) London, H.M. Stationery Office
Methodist Mission Archives, Fiji
   1882   Annual Report, Viwa Circuit
   1882   Annual Report, Bau Circuit
   1883   Annual Report, Bau Circuit
   1885   Annual Report, Kadavu Circuit
   1890   Colonial Secretary to Langham - Letter 30/3/90
Waterhouse, Joseph
   1866   *The King and People of Fiji... &c.....*
                London, Wesleyan Conference Office

5

INDIGENOUS REPORTING

The Pig's Head[1]

The investiture of Laisenia Raboka into the office of Tunidau ni Bau makes relevant a discussion on the nature and significance of the ceremony performed at Bau on such occasions. The investiture of his predecessor, Tevita Naitini, was never actually performed, though he carried the responsibilities of the office. The last ceremony took place in 1909, so for 45 years neither Fijian nor European has witnessed this interesting ceremonial.[2]

My main informant for the compiling of this brief study is Etuate Sokiveta, who lives at Bau, and who is a mine of information on Fijian traditions for anyone who will engage in conversation with him. In this particular connection he remembers the ceremony of 45 years ago, having personally witnessed it, and he has given me copious notes on the points raised. Where these are used I have given the Fijian as he wrote it, beside my own translation of the same.

The importance of the ceremony is not confined to the customs involved, but also the reasons for their existence, and the real meaning of some of the names, like *Na Ulunivuaka* (The Pig's Head) which are often heard, but not so often understood today.

Na loma ni rara levu e Bau na yacana ko Naulunivuaka, ka sa nodrai tikotiko na kai Naulunivuaka e na gauna eliu, ka sa dua tale na yacadra - ko ira na kai Butoni.

A kenai Balebale na vosa oqo, Butoni, ko ira era tiko donu e loma ni vanua, se 'Buto ni Vanua.'

The name of the interior part of the village green at Bau is the Pig's Head, the dwelling place of the Pig's Head People in former times. They were also known as the Butoni People.

The word *Butoni* means those who dwell right in the inner part of the land.

91

*Ia sa nodra na kai Korolevu
na Delana, kai tikotiko ni
Lotu e Bau e na gauna oqo, ka
koro ni vuli, kai bulubulu
Vakaturaga e rua ka tu edaidai, ka sa wase tu vakarua na
kai Korolevu, e dua na yacana
na Manuku i cake, kei na Manuku i Ra, ka ra tu mai Levuka, Lakeba edaidai.   Era
veiwekani kei ira na kai Korolevu era tu mai Serua edaidai
ka vaka kina ko ira eso ka tu
mai Vuna, Taveuni; ka so e
Mataqali Tuina e tu edaidai,
era vakoro tu mai Nacamaki,
Koro, Lomaiviti, ka dua tale
nai tikotiko na yacana na kai
Nasaravi, nodrai tikotiko ko
Soso mai Bau. Era kau talega
mai na kai Lasakau me ra tiko
vata. Ia ka ra qai tiko e loma na kai Butoni se Butoni-
vanua. Sa tiko donu e loma
oqo na kenai balebale na kai
Butoni.*

*Na veimataqali tamata kece
oqo era sa kai wai se gonedau. Eso e gonedau ni soko.
Oqo ko ira na kai Naulunivuaka, se na kai Butoni. Eso
e gonedau ni ika, oqo ko ira
na kai Nasaravi se kai Rara
ko Soso. Ia ko ira na kai Lasakau era gonedau ni vala e
wai. Ko ira na kai Korolevu
se na kai Delai era gonedau
talega ni soko era lewai ga
vakadua vei Roko Tui Bau (na
Kalou Tamata). Era sa yali
edaidai e Korolevu se Bau, eso
na veimataqali tamata oqo era
sa vakasavi. Ia nodra yaca
buli kece na vei yavusa oqo
Tunidau ni Bau.*

The hilltop belonged to the
Korolevu People, and to this
day the   Bauan Mission Station, the school and two
chiefly burial grounds are
there. The Korolevu (Big
Town) People were divided in
two, named Upper and Lower
Manuku. Today they are at Levuka, Lakeba.   They are related
to other Big Town People, who
are now at Serua, and also to
others at Vuna, Taveuni; and
also with some of the tribe
of Tuina at the present time,
and who dwell at Nacamaki,
Koro, Lomaiviti and others,
the Nasaravi folk located
at Soso, Bau.   Some
Lasakau people were brought
to live with them, but the
Butoni People dwelt in the
interior part of the land,
and this is the element in
which we find the true meaning of the Butoni People.

All these people were sea
folk. Some were sailors.
These were the Pig's Head
People, or the Butoni People.
Others, like the Nasaravi
People from Soso, were fishermen, but the Lasakau People
represented the Navy.   The
Korolevu or Hilltop People
were also sailors, and were
directly subject to the Roko
Tui Bau (or *Kalou Tamata*).
Some of these people are no
longer resident in the Big
Town or Bau, some of these
tribes have been expelled. All
these tribes now come under
a new name - Tunidau ni Bau.

Visitors to Bau have a habit of asking why the Hilltop

People were expelled. This being part of the story, let us now turn to it.

Sa vuna ga na ika. E tukuni mai Kubuna me dua yani na ika me vaka na lewa sa vakatura mai ko Roko Tui Bau se ko koya na Kaloutamata. E tukuni yani e Korolevu (se Bau edaidai) ni sega na ika, ka sa mani malumu kina na yalo i koya na Turaga Roko Tui Bau, se Kaloutamata.

Ia e·rua na bui ni Delaikorolevu, erau lako tu ki Kubuna me kere Kuro. Ia ni rau tiko vakalailai mai Vale Levu sa qai tagi na makubuna e na nona via kana eqai. Tara mai na ketekete ko Buinigone e dua nai olo lewe ni ika.

E qai raici ka tarogi sara na bui oqo, a lewe ni ika cava oqori. E kaya na bui ni lewe ni dua na saqa levu ka rawa, Saka, vei ira na kai Korolevu, ka keimami kania Saka, ka sega ni rawa, ka'u mani ologa Saka mai, me kei na makubuqu, de tagi via kana me qai kania.

Ko dina sara ni rawa na ika levu oqo e na noa, e taroga na Turaga Roko Tui Bau. Io, Saka; e sauma na bui ni gone.

Vakaevei ni'u a tukuna me dua mai na ika, dou qai kaya ni sega. Drau lako tani sara. E sega na kuro. Drau la'ki tukuna noqu vosa. Mo dou lako tani vakadua na kai Delaikorolevu ki na vanua au sega ni kilai kina.

Fish was the cause of it. Word was sent from Kubuna requesting fish, by the order of Roko Tui Bau or Kalou-Tamata (Godman). It was then reported that there were no fish at Korolevu (or present-day Bau), and eventually the heart of Kaloutamata, the Roko Tui Bau was softened.

However two old women from the hilltop town chanced to go to Kubuna (the point of land opposite Bau. A.R.T.) to beg pots. But during their brief visit to the Chief House the grandchild of one cried of hunger, whereupon the old woman took from her basket a bundle of fish.

The old woman was seen and asked what fish it was. She replied, "It is some of a large *saqa*, Sir, which was caught by the Korolevu people and though we sat down to eat it, Sir, we could not finish it; whereupon I wrapped up some, Sir, for my grandchild, so that should she cry of hunger she might eat."

"Are you speaking the truth about the catching of so big a fish yesterday?" asked Roko Tui Bau, and the grandmother replied, "Yes, Sir."

"And what about my request for fish, and your reply that you had none. Go away at once. You shall have no pots. Go and tell my words: the Hilltop People shall go away, once and for all, to a place where I am unknown."

Era sa mani lako tani a kai Delaikorolevu ka yaco ki Lakeba, ka ra tiko kina ka yacova na gauna oqo, ka ra bulia nodra Turaga me yacana na Daulakeba ka sega ni Daubau se Tunidau ni Bau ka yacova tu edaidai.

Whereupon the Hilltop People departed to Lakeba, where they are still found to the present time, and they established their Chief with the title, Daulakeba instead of Daubau or Tunidau ni Bau, and it remains so unto this day.

Era sa mani lomani ira na wekadra ko ira na kai Butoni, se kai Ulu-ni-vuaka. Era sa biuta nodrai tikotiko na kai Butoni.

The Butoni or Pig's Head People were sympathetic with their friends and departed their dwelling-place also.

Au sa nanuma ni rairai tiko beka ena 350 na yabaki nodra biu vanua. Era sega ni bau vakasavi, era lako walega e na vuku ni nodra veilomani vaka-gonedau ni soko. E biu tu nodra veivale kei na nodra bure levu e katu 20 na yacana ko Na Ulu-ni-vuaka.

I believe it must have been 350 years ago when they departed. They were not expelled but went of their own volition and sailor-sympathy. They left their houses and among them a large sleeping-house measuring 20 fathoms, and named the Pig's Head.

I shall return shortly to some of the points raised in that account, when I have put further data before you. Meantime we should investigate the meaning of this word - *Na Ulu-ni-vuaka* or the Pig's Head. We have already met the Pig's Head, a piece of land; the Pig's Head, a large sleeping house; and the Pig's Head People. What then is its significance?

E dau nodrai votavota tu ga na veimataqali na ulu-ni-vuaka; ke dua na kedra magiti na yavusa ko Kubuna ena kedra ga na yavusa gonedau kece oqo na uluna.

Their (the Pig's Head People) portion is the pig's head. Whenever the tribe of Kubuna has a feast the seamen are entitled to the head of the pig.

Era dui kila tu ga na veiwasewase ni ulunivuaka e dui kedra.

They each know their respective portions of the pig's head.

Dua, e kena na cumusomo, oqo nodrai Liuliu, se nodra Tunidau Levu sa kena na cumusomo.   O koya e kena nona tabusiga ai karua vua na Turaga, koya e Soso. E kena na sila e ra koya e Muridua, ·e dua vei ira mai Lasakau. So e kena na nona dela-

The portion of the Great Tunidau is the snout, and the forehead is for the second chief, namely, him from Soso. He from Muridua (Lasakau) receives the lower jaw. The back of the neck and the ears are for the official heralds, who receive messages, report

*vuvu kei na daligana, ko ya ko
ira na dau rogo i tukutuku se
kau i tukutuku ni ca ko Manuku
i Cake kei Manuku i Ra, era tu
edaidai mai Nacamaki (Koro)
kei Vuna (Taveuni). Sa qai ma-
cala e nai talanoa oqo ni liu
duadua na kai Butoni se na
Ulunivuaka.*

evil tidings, namely those
from Upper and Lower Manuku,
at present resident at Nacamaki in Koro and Vuna in Taveuni. This explanation makes
it clear that the Butoni or
Pig's Head People held the
highest status among them.

How is it then, if these people were so bound together
by ties of sympathy and custom, that they are so widely distributed over the islands? If they left at one time and for
one cause one would expect them to have migrated to one place.

*Era dui waqawaqa vakamata-
qali, ka mani tabaki ira e dua
na loaloa ka mani dui veisese
yaki nodra mua. Eso e kele mai
Nairai. Oqo na waqa ni Mataqali Tunidau ni Bau kei na
Taurisau e tolu eratou mani
yali, ka kele mai Cicia na Baleinasinu, ka kele mai Vamaso,
Gau, na Mataqali na Sanisamu.
Ia nai kalima ni lakolako na
Vusaratavuto e kele mai Matavuralevu mai vei Tui Narocake
se Tui Vatuviti. Era sa mai
sota vata tale ka tawa ko Namacu, Koro, Lomaiviti.*

Each clan had its own canoes
but they were scattered in all
directions by a storm. Some
came to Nairai. This was the
canoe of the clan Tunidau ni
Bau, and the three Taurisau
were lost at sea, Baleinasinu
anchored at Cicia, and the
Sanisamu clan came to Vamaso,
Gau. Vusaratavuto, the fifth
group anchored at Matavuralevu
of Tui Narocake or Tui Vatuviti. Eventually they met together again and occupied Namacu, Koro, Lomaiviti.

*Nodratou yaco mai na Yavusa-
ratavuto kivei Tui Narocake,
se Tui Vatuviti, eratou tiko
kina e kea mai Natavo na kai
Nacawa, ka toka e Matavuralevu ko Tui Vatuviti ka ratou
sa Mataqali Vusaradave na kai
Nacawa, Nativa, Vatuviti; ka
vaka kina na kai Vusaratavuto,
ka lako yani e Bau, eratou kai
Vusaradave talega, ka qai tubu
nodra veilomani ka ra mai cakava vata eso nodra riri e na
ucuna ka cokotaka era vaka-
ravia eso na sasa ni niu, ka
mani yaca ni vanua se ucuna ko
ya Navakaravi, se ko Navaka-*

When the Yavusaratavuto
presented themselves to Tui
Narocake, or Tui Vatuviti,
then the Nacawa People were
dwelling at Natavo, and Tui
Vatuviti was at Matavuralevu.
Now it happened that the Nacawa People, at Natavo, Vatuviti and likewise the Vusaratavuto who had come from Bau
were all Vusaradave, and thus
a friendship sprang up between
them, and together they made
temporary houses by plaiting
coconut leaves on a certain
headland, which was thereafter
known as Navakaravi or Navaka-

*ravisasa me nodratou riri na
lewe ni Mataqali Vusaratavuto
ka ratou mani veilomani ka
soli kina na vanua se ucunako
Navakaravi me nodratou, ka
me veiyalayala kei ira na kai
Sicila e vakacokotaki oti.
Era sa qai lakovi na dui tu
e na veiyanuyanu ka ra qai
yaco vata mai ka yacova ni
cabe na Lotu, ka vakadabera
nai Talatala mai Mataisavai
ko Ratu Cakobau, ka qai tara
kina ko Nukumasia mei tikotiko ni Lotu.*

ravisasa (the method of build
ing the shelter. A.R.T.), as
temporary shelter for the
Vusaratavuto folk and the
friendship grew and they were
given the headland to be their
own, as a promise with the
folk of Sicila who had helped
establish them there. This
state of affairs continued
until the coming of Christianity, when Cakobau set up a
native minister at Mataisavai
and established Nukumasia as
his station.

Now although these people had departed from Bau, it has
already been pointed out that they did so of their own volition, and that they held the highest status in their group.
They had no desire to entirely sever connections with that
which had been their homeland.

*Era kerekere mai Bau me la-
ko mada yani ko Mata ki Butoni, se ko Mata ki Naulunivuaka ko Ratu Masau. Eratou
mai tukutuku na Taurisau,
koya ko iratou na Mata ki Bau
ka sa lako yani ko Masau ka
sa vakadonui me buli ko Tunidau ni Bau.*

*Ia na Mataqali oqo na Tau-
risau e tiko kina eso na vei-
yaca buli: e tiko kina na
Matasau, na Kadi, na Mata ki
Bau, nai Taka, ka sai iratou
oqo eratou dau gunu vata kei
Tunidau ni Bau.*

They begged of Bau that the
Herald to Butoni or Herald to
Pig's Head, Ratu Masau to go
there to seek permission for
the investiture of Tunidau ni
Bau. This was reported by the
heralds to Bau, and Masau
went and it was agreed to
have an investiture of a Tuni
dau ni Bau.
Among the Taurisau will be
found certain official titles,
the Matasau, the Kadi, the
Mata ki Bau, the Taka - these
are they who drink with Tunidau ni Bau (in the ceremonial
kava).

Let us now examine some of the ceremonial used in connection with the investiture of a Tunidau ni Bau.

*Era lako vata mai kei nai
yau ka ra mai taba vei Ratu
mai Moturiki, ka ra qai vaka-
uaqa buka tiko me raici yani
e Bau. Ni sa raici yani e Bau*

They come together with
their native property and pay
their respect first with Ratu
mai Moturiki, where they
light fires that will be vis-

*ka ra sa marau na Turaga ni
ra sa gole tale mai nai Liuliu ni gonedau era mani tara
e dua na tabua ka lesi e tau
yadua me la'ki cavu mai nai
kelekele ni kai Naulunivuaka
ka sa yaco tiko edaidai.*

*Ni ra yaco mai ka ra dau
sobu mai Muaidule ka kauti
ira ko Masau ki na bure ko
Naulunivuaka, era dau conaka
tu yani e na ibe na marama e
Bau, era yaco mai. Era cokia
ka maroroya me nodra, ka ra
tevuka eso na ibe era kauta
mai me nodra e Bau.*

*Sa lima na katuba vakayaca
mai Naulunivuaka. 1. Na Katuba ni Tunidau ni Bau. 2.
Na Katuba ni Yavusaratavuto.
3. Na Katuba ni Taurisau. 4.
Na Katuba ni Baleinasinu. 5.
Na Katuba ni Sanisamu. Sa
tabu e na kena lawa me dua e
curu e na katuba tani me ra
dui curu ga e na nodra katuba
me yacova ni ra solevu.*

*Era sa solevu oti, qai dui
curu e na dui nodra mataqali
me ra vakasobu kina, ko ya
me ra dui kauta nai yau era
dui digitaka voli mai, me ra
dui kauta vei ira na wekadra,
ka ra dui talaci e nai yau e
dui vakarautaki tu e na nodra
dui veivale e Bau.*

*Ia na lovo me kua ni mudu,
me ia tikoga ka yacova na
gauna ni lesu ki wai.*

*Ia ni sa mataka me ra lesu
sa qai vakarau na veibuli.
Era qarava na yaqona na Turaga e Bau, ka ra sa vakavodo
na turaga, marama kei na gone*

ible from Bau. When these are
seen at Bau the chiefs there
are pleased because of the
coming of the Chief of the
seamen. A whale's tooth is
presented and responsibilities
are allocated for the ceremonial reception of the Pig's
Head People who will arrive
this day.

Upon their arrival they come
ashore at Muaidule, and Masau
takes them to the house, the
Pig's Head, where the women of
Bau who have come have strewn
the floor with mats. They col-
lect these mats for themselves
and spread out in their place
others which they have brought
for the Bauans.

There are five named doors
of the Pig's Head - the Door
of Tunidau ni Bau, the Door of
Yavusaratavuto, the Door of
Taurisau, the Door of Baleinasinu and the Door of Sanisamu. It is strictly forbidden
for any to enter by other than
his own door up to the time of
the presentations.

This ceremonial presentation
over, they form up into their
clan groups for the group presentations, and each selects
property he fancies to take
away to his relatives and they
are farwelled thus with the
property prepared in the various households of Bau.

The ovens shall be kept in
use until the visitors return
to sea.

On the morning of departure,
preparations are made for the
investiture ceremony. The
chiefs of Bau attend to the
ceremonial kava. The men, women

*ni Naulunivuaka mai Muai-
dule. Era tiko mai Na Vata-
ni-tawake eso na kena turaga
ka qai caka na veibuli.*

*E sega ni meketaki na ya-
qona, e lose oti ga ka gunu.*

*Ena kacivaki se sauvaki ni
sa vakarau me gunu na Tunidau
ni Bau. Ena qai tabu sara me
dua me lako kosova na loma ni
rara ko Ulunivuaka. Ena sega
talega na veivosaki se na
vakasausau.
Era gunu oti ka qai tu cake
na Turaga Vunivalu ka kauta
mai e dua na masi ka bukia e
ligana (me vesa) ka tataunaki
Bau vua na Tunidau ka vosa
bubului ko Tunidau.*

and children of the Pig's
Head go on board at Muaidule
only some of their chiefs remaining at the *Vatanitawake*
where the investiture is to
take place.
    There is no traditional
chant with this *kava*, as on
other occasions. It is simply
mixed and drunk.
    It will be announced in the
village when the Tunidau ni
Bau is about to drink. It is
then forbidden for any-one to
cross the green, the Pig's
Head, and there shall be no
conversation or applause.
    After the drinking, the Bau-
an War Lord stands and takes
a piece of native cloth tying
it in a knot on the arm of
Tunidau ni Bau seeking his
support for Bau, upon which
the latter pledges himself.

    This latter part of the ceremony is highly significant,
for what better symbol or ritual could be found for the binding together of two tribal groups than the tying of a knot.
Originally this was done by the Roko Tui Bau - now by the War
Lord, or *Vunivalu*. The reason for the change is quite another story, and would be an intrusion here. The ceremonial
words used by the *Vunivalu* as he ties the knot are:
            *"Mo nanumi au, ka nanumi Bau
            Na kena magiti kei na kenai yau."*
            "Remember me, and remember Bau
            Its feasting and its property (gear)."

    The words of the Tunidau ni Bau's pledge to attend to
these matters are these:
            *"Au sa tiko mai Koro, Koro ni ka kecaga;
            Koro ni magiti, Koro ni yau.
            Au na colata na nomuni sau,
            Au na taqomaka na yaca ni Bau."*
            "I dwell at Koro, eminent in all things;
            Eminent in feasting, eminent in property.
            I shall carry your chiefly commission,
            I shall preserve the name of Bau."

These are the traditions that have been preserved to
this day by the Bauan and the Pig's Head People, and their
ceremonial functions and inter-relationships are by no means
infrequent.[3] The story is natural - it does not seem to be
enveloped in myth as so many Fijian migration tales. On the
surface it is an acceptable one.

On the other hand it is difficult to reconcile with the
tale told by the Hilltop People who went to Lau. There are
points in common but the Levuka tale is obviously definite
myth in many parts. Their tale was that Bau was their original land, they were of great numbers and divided into two,
the Butoni and themselves, the 'Dwellers on the Hill.' Then
a land tribe came from Viti Levu and fought them for many
days until they were exhausted and made peace offering *oro*
(cf. *soro*) and offered to become the servants of the lands-
men if their lives were spared. They were spared and informed that they would thereafter be the fishermen of Bau.
This task they performed and lived very happily with the
Bauans, joining them also in their subsequent wars, and
themselves enjoying something of the glory of their conquerors, who they admitted were of much greater stature than
themselves.

The story of the fish differs somewhat. It was a great
fish, such as had never been seen before, and no man knew
its name, and the people hid it, keeping silence that the
Bauans might not know of it. It was discovered when one of
the boys made a bow from the rib and went fishing on the
reef, and the Bau boys saw the bow, and the whole story came
out, and the Bauans determined to destroy the Hilltop People
and burn their town, and the people regretted their rashness.
However, just as the attack began there came in a great wave
from the sea, rising higher and higher, and stopping only
when they stopped. A god entered his priest then and said
that the people of Levuka and Butoni should not be killed,
only expelled from the island, and that was done.

The departure is tied up also with the discovery of a
beautiful girl, daughter of Tui Nayau at Kaba (which was un-
inhabited in those days). She had come there clinging to
the feathers of a giant sea bird, and at Lakeba they had
thought her dead. So the Hilltop chief hid her and fed her
in seclusion, saying the god was with them. Their popular
reception in Lakeba was accounted for by their taking back
his daughter to the Chief there. It is a long story in which
the seamen wearied as they journeyed from island to island,
and everywhere they left some of their number behind, thus

accounting for the widespread distribution of these people over the eastern islands. Lau and Bau were quite unknown to each other at the time.

The more we examine the story (full detail of which was gathered by Lorimer Fison nearly 90 years ago) the more we are confronted with a typical migration myth. No doubt their journey was a long one, and their numbers decreased as they went on. Perhaps they did take a daughter of the Lakeban chief back to her father and win his favour. It would seem also to confirm the departure of the Butoni People about the same time, but that they were expelled is extremely doubtful. The Levuka People rejected Bau thereafter, but the Butoni never did so, even though they left out of sympathy with the other sea people. The two traditions are at variance on this point - an important one. The survival of the investiture ceremony of the Tunidau ni Bau supports the Bau-Koro story.

Jesse Carey put the story in his *Kings of the Reefs*[4] like this:
> "Bau was not a regal city,
> But the home of serving fishers,
> Men who fished for men and fishes;
> Caught the women and the children
> As the mainland chiefs commanded.
> But there came a time of hunger,
> When the fishers, in their craving,
> Ate a fish by chiefs forbidden.
> Then the war drum broke its silence.
> King Nailatikau was angry,
> Rose in battle in his anger,
> Drove the fishers from their island.
> Came himself and lived upon it,
> Bringing with him many chieftains."

One thing however is quite apparent - those who rejected Bau, and those who were loyal and the Bauans themselves, all place the expulsion of the Hilltop People to an abuse of fishing responsibilities - or the responsibilities of the seamen groups to the overlords. And this is very important.

It was not just a matter of who was to rule, it was the whole question of social responsibility. This was one of the basic elements of primitive Fijian society, and the anger of the Bauans was not because of pride but because social responsibility was abused and loyalty among the fishermen was just as essential as among the warriors.

In 1955 Etuate set the date of this event, in his opinion,
at some 350 years ago. The Levuka myth puts it before the
inhabitancy of Kaba. The establishment of the Christian base
at Namacu was 100 years ago. Then, were their previous wan-
derings 250 years?

Now Epeli Rokowaqa in *Ai tukutuku kei Viti* attributes
this act of expulsion to Ratu Nailatikau I, and gives the
date at 1760, ten years after the establishment of Rewa and
Verata as Kingdoms. After another 10 years he died, and was
followed by Ratu Banuve in 1770. After Banuve had ruled for
30 years, bringing us to 1800, then was the beginning of the
period of intensive warfare. Banuve died in 1805 (probably
more likely 1902-3) and was followed by Ratu Naulivou Radomo-
domo Matanikutu - *Drau vakadrau nona vere* (his plotting numbered hundreds and hundreds). He achieved his position by
war within Bau and maintained it in the same way for 24 years.
He died in 1829 and was followed by Ratu Tanoa Visawaqa in
1830, who died in 1852 and was followed by Ratu Seru Cakobau.
Working inversely the Cakobau and Tanoa dates can be
verified by contemporary documents. Rokowaqa's dates follow
so closely the writing of Waterhouse, who lived in Bau in the
fifties as the first resident missionary, that we are almost
compelled to consider Waterhouse as the source of Epeli's
dates. However, whether or not this be so they certainly
form a reasonable time line, and seem to fit known facts. He
says Naulivou died in 1829, apparently by sorcery.

He had been installed into office about the time of the
dysentry epidemic which carried off his predecessor, Banuve.
The ancient poets have preserved a record that this was accompanied by a tidal wave and an eclipse of the sun - which
some believe to have been 7th September, 1802. Tradition has
it that he had reigned for something like 30 years, and on
the whole what scanty evidence exists seems to put it back
somewhere about 200 years from the present date. That would
reduce the 250 years wandering to 100, which is perhaps more
likely; but is it likely that Kaba was unoccupied at such a
recent date?

As to the loyalty of the Butoni People, we pick up references here and there to their fighting wars in the interests
of Bau in Natewa and other places. There are several such
references in the Journal of Thomas Williams in the middle of
the last century. Their loyalty also has extended to the
regular payment of tribute to Bau.

I think we must disagree with Derrick that the Butoni

and the Levuka People were the same in spite of the fact
that it is a current popular belief and is implied in the
title of Etuate's notes. There is century old documentary
evidence that these were two groups of sea-faring folk resident at what is now called Bau, and the traditions of both
people show them as distinct. In fact Waterhouse says that
the Hilltop People were of inferior rank to the Butoni.

Notes:

1   Originally written in 1955 and read before the Fiji Soc-
     iety, at Suva, June 13, 1955. The end notes have been
     added since.
2   As a resident of Bau I was able to be a participant ob-
     server (a silent one) in this ceremony.
3   On the other hand the actual performance as I observed
     it in 1954 departed from this in several ways, marking
     considerable acculturation. Neither the Tuinidau ni Bau's
     words, nor the Vunivalu's were rhythmic as I was led to
     expect. Functionally they were the same, and their mean-
     ing was identical but the form was contemporary and sec-
     ularized, even to the tune of one or two foreign idioms.
     This raises an interesting ethnohistorical question: was
     Etuate's poetic form deliberately created for purposes of
     traditional preservation only, or was it a case of tarri-
     ance of the originally politico-religious ceremony? I am
     inclined to think it was both. A few days afterwards I
     was sharing experiences *(veitalonoa)* with Fijians at Tai-
     kobau, subjects of Bau, and narrating the events which
     they had not witnessed. I was able to recite the appro-
     priate lines of the request and pledge in their poetic
     form. The listeners became visibly and audibly responsive
     when they recognized the rhythmic units: "It is true!
     It is true!" they interjected.
4.   A collection of oral traditions gathered in Fijian and
     translated into the rhythm of Longfellow's *Hiawatha*
     which is remarkably similar to the poetic Fijian form.
     His information was collected from the Fijians in the
     1860s.

References Cited:

Carey, Jesse
    1891   *The Kings of the Reefs,* Melbourne, Spectator
                Publishing Co.
Colony of Fiji
    1896   *Report of the Commission Appointed to Inquire
                into the Decrease of the Native Population,*
                Suva, Government Printer

Derrick, R.A.
  1950   *A History of Fiji*, Suva, Government Printer
Fison, Lorimer
  1907   *Tales of Old Fiji*, London, De La More Press
Henderson, G.C.
  1931   *The Journal of Thomas Williams*, 2 vols. Sydney,
          Angus & Robertson
Rokowaqa, Epeli
  n/d   *Ai Tukutuku kei Viti*, Suva, Methodist Mission
          Press
Sokiveta, Etuate
  1954   *"Kedrai Tukutuku na kai Naulunivuaka, se na kai
          Butoni,"* Manuscript in Fijian and the major source.
Waterhouse, Joseph
  1866   *The King and People of Fiji....&c.....* London,
          Wesleyan Conference Office
Williams, Thomas
  1860   *Fiji and the Fijians:* Vol. I *The Islands and
          their Inhabitants,* London, Alexander Heylin

AI VOLA SA BALE KI NA

YAQONA KEI NA TOPAKO.

Oi kemudou na veiwekani, sa volai nai vola oqo me sereki kina vei keda e dua nai tukutuku sa vakasamataki ena yaga vei keda sa wilika ka vakalewa vakatamatabula kina.

Sa dua na ca levu sa qai curu koso walega vei keda e Viti. E vinaka me da tukuna vakamatailalai na ca eso eda kila sa tubu e na noda daugunu yaqona kei na noda daukana topako. De sega beka ni yaco kece vei keda yadua na ka ca ena tukuni e nai vola oqo—de sa so ga sa tauva e dua, ka so tale e tauva e dua tani. Ia sa ka ca vei keda kevaka eda sa vakacacani keda vakatikina ga. E vinaka me sega na tikida e ca, me vinaka taucoko ruarua na yaloda kei na yagoda.

Na ka eso sa bale ki na Yaqona.

E dua na ka eda sa kila vei ira na noda qase e na gauna eliu; era sega ni gunu vakailoa na tamata, se mama vakailoa e dua. Era gunu ga ko ira na bete, kei ira talega na kena turaga dina, ka sa daucaka ga mai vale levu, kei na bure kalou. Ia ko ira sa daumama era vakatokai me "bati tabu," se "bati ni yaqona," era sai taukei dina ni vanua era sa lesi kina. Ia edaidai sa qai dua tani na kenai valavala ni sa caka e na veivale kece, ka ni ra sa qai gunu yaqona kece na tamata, na qase, na tamata bula, na cauravou, kei ira na gone. Eliu sa vakatabui vei ira na tamata bula, kei na cauravou, kei ira na qaqa e na gauna ni valu, de dua vei ira e tidara na yavana mai na kena masa ni yaqona, ka mani bale

6

A SYNCHRONIC ETHNOHISTORICAL RECONSTRUCTION[1]

One of the profitable dimensions of ethnohistory as a
research methodology is the reconstruction of the synchronic
ethnographic description at some precise point of time in
the past (Sturtevant, 1966:6-8). This is being explored
more and more since the breakdown of colonialism and the new
availability of historical documents from the old colonial
archives. The exploration in these new facilities by scholars
in the disciplines of history and anthropology has revealed
many hitherto untapped resources with tremendous potential.
From among these resources many personal documents - diaries,
journals and correspondence - have been brought to light.
The majority of these new resources are official, but one is
continually surprised at the discovery of important personal records created by planters, missionaries, traders
and slavers from Oceania, our present area of focus, all of
which give a different viewpoint from the official records.

A diary of this kind covering, say, a decade of history
in a remote island in the period of Pacific kidnapping permits a synchronic reconstruction. So much of the popular
Pacific 'history' has been *created* by historians and historical novelists, rather than *re-created* by historians capturing the relationships which give a diary its cohesive entity.
This distinction was articulated by the historian Gottschalk
(1945:9), who insisted that the historian's imagination be
directed to re-creation rather than creation.[2] We create,
for example, when we go to our sources to select evidence to
establish our hypotheses about historical events. We re-
create history when we take our primary sources whole and
struggle to discover their own implications.

I believe we have still much to learn about discovering
the wholeness of a journal or diary as a primary source. One
journal may be worth more than a hundred apt quotations. I
am reminded of Lord Acton's letter to the contributors to

the *Cambridge Modern History*, in which he spoke of the historian Froude consulting 100,000 papers in manuscript for his major work, and to which Acton added, "That is still the price to be paid for mastery" (Stern 1963:248). I would certainly agree that the price of relentless industry has to be paid, and I feel bad about one of my students imagining he has completed his thesis when there are still unexplored resources in our own library.   However I would rather have my manuscript confined to the analysis of a single journal and capture its cohesive implications and wholeness than be distinguished for its voluminous footnotes. I very much doubt that 100,000 papers can ever be adequately studied by a single person, if one has to project himself historically into another period of time, or ethnographically into another culture.

Before taking an actual journal for examination and discussion I need to make three comments about this kind of primary source material.

First, in the disciplines of both anthropology and missiology we are much concerned today with social or cultural change - terms which cover, among other things, the process of conversion from animism to Christianity. . Allied to this religious experience is the whole area of cultural dynamics including the how and why of the acceptance and rejection of new ideas or innovations.   In the history of the last century or two in the Pacific there are many gaps in our information just at this very point.   The phenomenological regularities in culture change (including religious change) have not always been noted.   Kluckhohn ascribed this shortcoming to paying "too little attention to the concrete individuals in whom the changes actually begin" (1945:136).   One main thesis of this paper is that the use of a missionary journal or an administrator's personal diary, when studied as a whole often makes it possible to rectify this shortcoming. In the Pacific area the sandalwooders, missionaries, whalers, planters, traders and escaped convicts were all agents of change - conscious or unconscious - and many of them kept journals of their experiences.   Such a primary source from any one of them is valuable, because we meet the author as a reacting personality in his real life context.

Second, much so-called history is far too simplistic with events frequently attributed, for example, to a single cause. Writers on Pacific missions in particular have time and time again interpreted conversion (especially group conversion) to a single cause. I devote an appendix to this

in *People Movements in Southern Polynesia* (1971:221-226) in
dealing with the case of the conversion of Tahiti. Behind a
conversion movement one usually discovers (1) a whole complex of specific events, (2) a significant number of key persons, and (3) a set of distinct and precise relationships
between them.   As Barzun says of the ways of culture history, there is -

> no short cut to arrive at an understanding of relation-
> ships ... cultural life is intricate and emotionally
> complex. One must be steeped in the trivia of a per-
> iod, one must be a virtual intimate with its principal
> figures (1963:394-395).

A personal document may thus not only fill in a gap in the
record of historical information, but also reveal something
of the situational complexity and the personal interactions
of the characters. Such discoveries are truly exciting.

Third, we have a concept from the historian, Renier
(1965:97-105), who takes the Latin word, *vestigium,* meaning
"the *trace* left by the sole of the foot and also the sole of
the foot itself". He speaks of documents, diaries, memoirs
and letters as *traces,* because either by direct statement
or by implication they are traces of the original writer's
desire to record events he had experienced for future reference. The fact that the word can be used for either the
footprint or the foot is employed to imply a fairly close
relationship between the footprint and the foot which made
it. Renier discusses historical method as *discovering
traces,* and then moving from the traces to the *events* which
caused their imprint, from the primary sources to the
events which stimulated the long since deceased writer to
record them in his life time.

After that rather long introductory preamble I now purpose taking such a personal document as I have been discussing theoretically, and examining its contents in some detail by means of a suggested research model. I shall try
to reconstruct a synchronic description at a precise point
of time, bringing out the social factors and personal rela-
sonships in a decade of culture change in a remote Pacific
island, and proceeding from the traces to the events.

The Methodological Tool

From some scores of possible personal documents I have
selected the *Journal of the Rev. John Geddie,* which comprises five exercise book volumes, located at the Latrobe

Library in Melbourne. The Journal covers the period from
July 29,1848 to December 11,1857 - a few months short of a
decade. Geddie was a minister of the Presbyterian Church of
Nova Scotia and planted the first Christian church in the
island of Aneiteum in the New Hebrides.

The Journal reveals a drama of cultural change being
played out in a dynamic struggle between three different
types of people with very different value systems - the
native animists of the island, the missionaries and a number
of white adventurers. In each group I could go on further
and break down the categories into personality types or
individuals, for the data is open to a more sophisticated
analysis than the length of this paper permits. We have
to be satisfied with the three basic groups, which are very
clear-cut. I am saying here that in this ethnographic synchronic reconstruction we find three clear-cut cultural
complexes *in a state of tension and interaction within a
cohesive whole*. In behavior, social values, morals and
religion the three complexes are quite distinct from each
other and clash at every point. Yet the very clash gives
a dynamic wholeness to the greater configuration which
the journal depicts.

Against this threefold encounter, which was the New
Hebridean world of 1848-1857, the Christian gospel was
offered, and a church was planted. It was a decade of culture change. Here is a study in microcosm of what was going
on in many parts of the Pacific. The key factors of the
forties and fifties converge and focus on Aneiteum, and here
is a record of it left by the man who planted the church in
that island.   But it is an equilibrium of tension and not
merely a biography that lies hidden in these five exercise
books.

To coordinate and present my material I shall use a
research model as a methodological tool. I call it the
triangle of personal relationships.
In the triangle NAM, N represents
the native animists, A the foreign
adventurers, and M the missionaries.
The sides of the triangle represent
the personal relationships between
the two parties represented by the
alphabetical symbols - NA, AM or MN

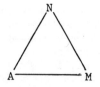

as the case may be. The perimeter of the triangle represents
the total configuration.[3] By using such a model I hope to
establish Barzun's claim that "in history no single element

is a prime mover, no single kind of clue an explanation of
everything else" (1963:392).   To this I want to add my own
claim that conversion does not result simply from the relationship MN, or that between the advocate and the acceptor
(using those terms anthropologically [Barnett,1953]), but
always takes place in the ramifications of a configuration
involving many persons and forces.

   At first I had it in mind to break down this paper into
three separate descriptions for NA, NM and AM, discussing
these relationships one at a time. But this I was unable to
do. The triangle is a useful tool. It does help one to ask
the right questions about the different relationships. But
it is theoretical. When you actually struggle with the data
and identify MN or MA you will never find them in isolation.
You are continually brought back, not to the side of the
triangle, but to the perimeter. Always to describe MN I
had to introduce both MA and NA. We are reminded that
analysis is always abstraction and, having served its purpose, in reality you are still left with the synthesis with
which you began; and there is something in the synthesis
which is more than the sum of its parts.

   Many missiologists say that because the Scriptures show
that M should establish an advocate relationship with N
(Matt. 28:20) that there is nothing more to say on the matter. But it is better argued on a basis of John 17, where
the emphasis is on the world to which the apostles are sent,
that the Christian mission takes place in a context not a
vacuum, and that there cannot be a MN relationship without
there also being an MA and an NA relationship.   For
purposes of study we break down our model into its parts,
but in reality it always remains a whole thing.

The Journal as a Cultural Complex

   John Geddie arrived at Aneiteum in the famous L.M.S.
vessel *John Williams,* taking with him teachers from Samoa.
Later he mentioned Rarotongans also. This lifted Geddie out
of his Nova Scotia Presbyterian background, and associated
him with the L.M.S. work of the southeastern and south-central Pacific, which had over fifty years of Pacific mission
experience before 1848, where the journal starts. These
Samoan and Rarotongan helpers were Polynesians. The people
of Aneiteum were Melanesians. Thus the assistants whom the
missionaries (and missionary historians) usually regarded
as "Pacific islanders" rather than precisely as Polynesians

were not differentiated from the Melanesians. Indeed the documents about the Melanesian blackbirding trade speak of these islanders as Polynesians. This imprecision of terminology led to much cultural confusion. Westerners did not realize that Polynesian missionaries to Melanesia were just as much *foreign* missionaries as they were themselves.[4]

The Samoans had been placed in Aneiteum before the arrival of Geddie, and were able to interpret for him while he was learning the language. Geddie accepted this as adequate for the start, but I should add that the early Polynesians themselves had trouble articulating some of the Melanesian sounds, and were not always good communicators once they went outside Polynesia.

Neither were they always particular about Melanesian custom. One of the first problems Geddie experienced in the NM relationship was due to the frequent offence taken by the local animists because of Samoan behavior with respect to their customs. For example, a taboo had been placed on a crop of nuts so that they would be preserved for an approaching feast. This is a normal practice all over Melanesia, and one is surprised that the Samoans ignored it. It put the missionaries in a bad position with the people. Geddie had to come to terms on behalf of the mission, apologize for his ignorance, and promise to observe these taboos *(itaup)* thereafter. This was not the only case. The teachers had taken coral from the reef to make lime for housebuilding (an art they had learned from other missionaries further east, and at which they were very skilled). Thus we see them as agents of change in the area of material culture as much as the white missionaries and traders. Apparently they collected the lime without ascertaining first that the reef was taboo. Eventually the Christians had to agree that after completing this project they would burn no more lime. A third incident concerned their "closing of the path to the sea," a religious obstruction, as indeed they all were. The fact that a number of such incidents appear in the early part of the first volume, and the accompanying fact that Geddie devoted so much space to recording them, shows up this relationship as a major problem of their initial contact which very much threatened the rapport of M with N.

For this relationship to be meaningful to the modern researcher he has to draw from other material in the journal that concerns the New Hebridean spirits *(natmasses)*. Geddie saw from the start that he "wrestled not against flesh and

blood". The shortage of nuts would not merely upset the
social organization for the feast - the spirits would be
angry. The burning of the lime would also make the spirits
angry. These spirits were supposed to live in a small hill
near the mission. They required a "path to the sea" but the
mission party had closed it off and the spirits were angry
again. When the spirits became angry they were disposed to
demonstrate it by causing sickness. Even if they did not
interfere with the foreigners, sickness and death would fall
on the local people. The missionaries had thus found themselves involved in an encounter of religious world views,
before they understood what they were up against, and as a
result the whole of the relationship MN was threatened.

Geddie was apparently a diplomat. He went to the chief
and people to arbitrate on behalf of his teachers. He found
the New Hebrideans reasonable. When they saw he wanted a
good relationship between them and was ready to listen to
them the chief was satisfied and made a ceremonial presentation of taro to terminate the disagreement. Let me quote
what Geddie wrote in his diary (Remember this was 1848 and
Geddie had received no training in anthropology. He was
learning it the hard way.)

> Missionaries among a heathen people ought, as
> far as possible, to guard against everything
> that would outrage their feelings. Our zeal
> in the cause of God must be tempered with prud-
> ence, or we are in danger of defeating our object
> in living among them.

Feast days were sacred. When a village was preparing
for a feast no stranger could enter, without enquiring first
and then doing so by a circuitous route. Failure to do this
would again anger the spirits. Although Geddie had paid
for the trees that surrounded his house, even so he aroused
anger when he cleared a space. No doubt there was an animist
ritual act for preventing offence to the spirit of the tree,
but Geddie did not know of it and thus angered the spirits
in general.

The spirits sometimes *possessed* people. The land and
sea spirits fought each other in a great battle. The sea
spirits were angry with the land spirits for allowing the
worship of the Christian God on their land, and determined
to destroy the people. This led to a communal demonstration
of spirit possession, which supposedly strengthened the
people to fight against the sea spirits. Geddie reported it
as a noisy business which left the possessed persons quite

exhausted. The ceremonial offerings which had to be presented at the gathering were considerable.

   The incident of the burning of the coral lime was explained in terms of the smell of burning which both interfered with fishing and angered the sea spirits whose domain
had been invaded. Although the missionaries had obtained
approval to complete the building project if they did not
offend again they had only won this approval on the basis
of a religious argument which the New Hebrideans could not
answer: God made the sea, the coral and the fish, and as
Creator he had control over them all. At this point one
might speculate that the chief, desiring no conflict with
an unknown God, was glad enough to compromise. This kind
of NM relationship runs through the first six months of the
journal.[5]

   Ramifying through all this are many kinds of radiations
from A - the white adventurers. When Geddie arrived he
found "no manifestations of kindly feelings" from the native
people, but a "distinctive coldness" which he subsequently
interpreted as due to their dealings with the white men,
who wanted no missionaries in their islands. So the missionaries' first obstruction was the white man image which
had preceded him. Some islanders were ready to fight all
white intruders, because as Geddie said:
        Their [native] lands had in some instances
        been seized, their wives and daughters stolen
        and their plantations robbed by men of
        Christian lands.
However, as one reads through the journal one has a feeling
that the island people soon began to distinguish between
sandalwood trader and missionary. Geddie felt the relationship changing steadily. He thought it might be partly due
to the presence of home life with missionary wives and
children. The Protestant home life stood out with its own
set of values, as different from that at the traders' posts
where they "saw firearms and other weapons of destruction
in abundance".[6]

   The improvement of NM relations was hindered also by a
visiting Tanna chief, who argued that all kinds of sickness
came upon them in Tanna with the presence of missionaries,
and that when the missionaries left the sickness departed
with them. The Tanna chief therefore advised the Aneiteum
people to leave Christianity well alone. 1849 began with
the arrival of the cutter, *Harriet* with the survivors of the
Revenge.   The latter had been driven ashore at Erromanga,

where the islanders had plundered the vessel. The crew had
escaped in the boat, but Geddie reported them as "very wick-
ed and hardened characters".

About a year after Geddie's arrival in Aneiteum the AM
relationships deteriorated considerably. The journal entry
for Oct. 20, 1849 reads:

> We begin to suffer much persecution from
> our own countrymen on this island. They
> begin to see that if we succeed, their
> wicked influence over the natives will be
> lost. Some of our enemies have urged the
> chiefs to drive us off the island and
> burn our houses. I know parties who have
> threatened more than this if we do not
> leave.

He goes on to describe "our efforts to arrest licentiousness."

> The conduct of the traders here is too
> abominable to be described. The poor
> women are chased by them and seized for
> their violent purposes. Females are bought
> from their husbands and parents to become
> the concubines of the white men, and the
> brutes sometimes purchase women from the
> chiefs, who sell them without the know-
> ledge or consent of their husbands. The
> house of one of my neighbours was entered
> by some white men and one of his wives
> forcibly carried off, and her husband
> threatened with instant death if he dared
> to resist. My house has often been an
> asylum for the poor women from their
> wicked pursuers. The opposition which we
> suffer is no new thing in the history of
> missions. Oh, what an impression it must
> make on the minds of the poor natives,
> when they see men from Christian lands far
> excelling themselves in wickedness! I have
> never seen manifestations of depravity as
> among the foreigners here. Little do we
> know the wickedness that is bound up in
> the hearts of our own countrymen. It is
> only when they are placed beyond the re-
> straints of civilization that we see many
> of them in their true colours.

It has been common for many scholars to reject this kind of
evidence as "typical missionary bias". On the contrary, in
that it does not emerge for twelve months this suggests it

was the result of growing disillusionment. In any case its
value lies in what it shows from the angle AMN, standing at
the missionary position, M, and looking at the relationships
MA and MN. Without this data our information of interper-
sonal relationships in the context would be deficient.

Exactly two months later the schooner *Rover's Bride*
arrived from Erromanga to report that a boat's crew of five
had been massacred by islanders and Geddie commented in his
journal -

> To those who are acquainted with the doings of
> the sandel[sic] wood men on these islands it
> is no matter of surprise that such occurences
> take place, the wonder is that they were not
> more frequent.

In this particular case the Erromanga chief had been badly
beaten on board the vessel, and an innocent native, who
happened to be on board when the five were killed in retaliation, was murdered there and then and thrown into the
sea.   On the first day of February the following year
Geddie was himself attacked by a seaman from a sandalwooder,
a Spaniard and "a son of the cross" and the mission house
was damaged. Again Geddie recorded that the sandalwooders
dislike the missionaries for their "exposure of the horrors
of the sandelwood trade".

By 1851 we enter into a period of struggle between the
missionaries and a certain Captain Paddon and Underwood his
boatbuilder. They blamed Geddie and his wife for protecting
native women from the white men. We have here a highly important series of journal entries, and a most needed corrective picture to the character of Captain Paddon. Paddon met
up with Bishop Selwyn and convinced him that his dealings
with the islanders were perfectly fair, and his understanding with them so good that he had maintained the sandalwood
trade for years to the satisfaction of all. Selwyn even
called Paddon his "tutor"(Fox, 1958:5). In *Solomon Islands
Christianity* (1967:355) I expressed doubt about this boast.
Belshaw (1954:17) also discusses Paddon's trade and movements.   The record of "Paddon at home" in Geddie's journal
is hard evidence which corrects a number of errors in the
supposed record of this man. In March 1851 he initiated a
raiding party against the Christian natives. "The sandelwood [sic] establishment" Geddie says tried to work through
the Anglican bishop to have Geddie removed, and listed a
number of frivolous charges made against the missionary.
The bishop had two interviews with Geddie and was not deceived. To Geddie he said, "Go on as you have been doing,

and by the blessing of God you will prosper." Geddie records
that the sandalwooders were just as abusive about the bishop
himself when it suited them to be so. Of Captain Paddon
Geddie wrote on Oct. 24 of that year:

> Captain Paddon ... has long been an avowed
> and bitter enemy and [Mr Underwood] is no
> less hostile. I heard a few days ago that
> Underwood offered a black man 10 gallons
> of rum to rid the island of me, and when
> he heard that a heathen had speared a cow
> belonging to me he said, 'I wish to ----
> that it had been himself.

On Nov.28 the mission house was set on fire but no lives
were lost. On the basis of evidence in the journal we may
assume that five natives had undertaken to burn the house
and church at the instigation of Captain Paddon. The incident had an interesting effect on the island people. The
incendiary involvement of Paddon and Underwood and their
general hostility to the missionaries divided the heathen
and Christian natives, and revealed that the strength of the
Christian community was growing rapidly. This indicates
another "thread of the story", which one finds running
through the pattern of events, and to which I shall return
shortly. The involved heathen confessed their complicity
in the incident with the sandalwooders.

1852 began with the report of the sandalwooder,*Deborah*.
On a nearby island the captain had argued bitterly with a
young chief. The latter was murdered and thrown overboard;
but his brother, who had also been there, escaped. On shore
some white men were seized for retaliation, and were saved
only by the intervention of some Christian teachers, who
negotiated a settlement. Even so, not to be outdone of
their "pound of flesh" the islanders swore revenge on the
first white man's vessel to come along.[7] It happened to be
the *Rover's Bride* (Paddon's) but the teachers sent a
warning ahead. Meantime Geddie wrote in his journal:

> If all the massacres which have of late
> years taken place in these islands were
> inquired into it would be found that in
> most cases white men were to blame for
> them. The sandel [sic] wood trade is a
> bloody business, and those who engage in
> it soon become more hardened than the
> natives themselves. The sooner the wood
> is exhausted the better for the cause of
> humanity and Christian missions.

Eventually Paddon saw the "writing on the wall" and departed.

Even so, the fourth volume began with the arrival of the
Black Dog, seeking a place to establish another sandalwood
station. Geddie also records his version of the murders of
the missionaries Williams and Harris at Erromanga, some time
before. These had been victims of the kidnapping or blackbirding trade. This is an important statement on one of the
major issues of Pacific history.

     Efforts to control these incidents from Australia and
New Zealand by the Royal Squadron had not been successful.[8]
In 1854 Geddie copied out in his journal Fitz Roy's "Proc-
lamation" on the purchase of native women, to cover Fiji and
other islands in terms of *slavery,* and to this he added the
following note:

>   The above proclamation was much needed. It
>   has been the custom of the sandelwood traders
>   to purchase females from their friends for
>   licentious purposes. Almost every white
>   man among them has his woman. These they
>   consider their special property and sell
>   them to one another. I am well acquainted
>   with a native woman on this island, who
>   was sold at auction and purchased by a
>   Tahitian with whom she still lives. All
>   the sandelwood vessels that I know are
>   floating brothels. (Entry July 4,1854)

     In the last volume of the journal we meet up with an-
other historical figure, Captain Towns, who figured in the
early development of Australia and introduced island labour
onto the stations. However his sandalwood establishment in
the New Hebrides suffered loss by fire, two houses being
destroyed with £1000 damage in January 1856.

     Sandalwooders were not the only adventurers in the
Pacific during the last century. Later in the same year
Geddie made the following entry of the whaler, *June*:

>   Oct.6 The whaler, *June,* of Sydney, Capt.
>   Waibrow, sailed today. We rejoice at her
>   departure. The conduct of her crew on this
>   island has been infamous. The men were per-
>   mitted to come on shore for licentious pur-
>   poses. One sabbath day they went 4 or 5
>   miles distant from the mission station and
>   offered payment all the way for women, but
>   were defeated in their object. They returned
>   d[is]appointed and enraged. The[y] said much
>   to the natives against the missionaries. They
>   also stole bananas and sugar-cane ....

Woven in between entries of this kind are references to a
growing Christian community. The MN relationship reflected
in a mood toward acceptance of the gospel on the part of the
islanders is seen to have a clear effect on the NA relationship as evidenced by their refusal to sell women, annoyance
at thefts of their food, involvement in brawls and murders,
and so forth.

An entry for April 28, 1857 tells of the *Lady Leigh,* a
whaler from Hobart Town, from which, after a brawl, eight
deserters were reported. These deserters were all dangerous
escaped convicts from Tasmania. Although both Geddie and
the chiefs objected to the Captain about leaving these men
on the island, they did so to no avail. This is the only
reference to convicts in this journal, but this type of
thing happened all over the Pacific, and escaped convicts
figure in many of the missionary journals. They were most
obstructive to the missionary cause even when they posed as
friends for their own profit, especially if they were there
first and knew more of the language than the missionaries.
One can imagine what eight convicts could do in such a situation. Of the whalers Geddie said:

> The Hobart Town whalers have an established
> character on these islands on account of the
> injuries which they inflict on the natives.
> The fewer that come this way the better.

Now let me back-track and take another look at the MN
relationship. In the first year the missionaries had come
into encounter with the Aneiteum spirits, or *natmasses,* the
indigenous taboos and spirit-possession. The customary way
of dealing with neighbors or strangers who created problems
within the terms of their world view or value system was to
fight and kill. The missionaries tried to demonstrate "a
better way", which required no weapons of war or magic. Today it would be called "the way of dialogue". In 1849 a
hurricane did much damage. Thinking within their own world
view, the islanders reasoned that this misfortune had been
the result of enemy manipulation, and by popular vote the
enemies who had supposedly caused it were to be exterminated.
The resultant war was effectively terminated by the missionaries through arbitration and reason. This gave them an
opportunity to press the interests of a new religion which
tabooed war and had a new set of values. Peace was made in
the ceremonial manner.

However traditional values were set against this kind
of success on the whole, and Christian missionaries and
teachers were frequently themselves blamed for natural

calamities. When persons and goods were shipwrecked the
islanders regarded the spoil as their peculiar property by
act of the spirits, and believed they could use them as they
wished. A chief's child died, and because of this two women
were strangled and the Christian teacher's house was burned.
Geddie and his party almost lost their lives at Ipece due to
an accident in which an unfaithful woman of that place went
to live with a chief in the locality where the missionaries
happened to live. The chief had rejected the husband's
messengers, and boasted that he would "make fish" of any
further messengers of reconciliation ("make fish"= kill and
eat). Geddie knowing nothing of this chanced to visit the
locality of the offenders. He and his party were immediately
regarded as "fish", and indeed were fortunate to escape with
their lives. This is a good example of how a chief may
regard a missionary who elects to live in the region of his
rival.

The missionaries had set their faces against a number
of practices they regarded as inhuman - cannibalism, live
burial and strangulation. In 1850 numerous cases of cannibalism were cited in the journal. Two years later the
matter was no longer taken for granted, but had become a
public issue - "cannibalism versus burial", and the growth
of Christian values over against the animist may be seen in
the following reference of January 1852:
> The parties who sought the body to bury it,
> would themselves have lately taken a part in
> this tragedy. What a change does the Gospel
> make! Christianity abolishes all former ano-
> mosities [sic] and old enemies become on[e]
> in Christ.

Strangling was a recognized form of human sacrifice.
We have seen that when a chief's child died two women were
strangled as a sacrifice. Sometimes the reference in the
journal merely reads - "Another strangling case " as if it
were quite commonplace. On December 28, 1849, a young man
and a girl were strangled to honour a woman who had committed suicide. Two weeks later a woman set out to strangle
herself; but was saved by some natives, who, though not
Christian, had been listening to Geddie on the subject. Such
cases were reported until well on into 1851 (Aug.15). However, before the end of the journal one reads for the date
March 17, 1857:
> The chiefs and people believe that
> strangulation is finished on Aneiteum.
The journal as a total thing reveals a process of change.

In March 1853 Geddie took a census of Aneiteum and he discovered more boys than girls, and proportionately many more adults than children. This disproportion led him to a "flash-back" on the subject of infanticide. He recorded that parents exposed their children in the bush or on the shore at low tide, so "the high tide takes them", and that this was especially done with females. Two years later (August 11, 1855) he entered information in his journal about a woman who had died in child-birth. Once the child would have been wrapped in a mat and buried with the mother, but "this time Christianity saved the child". Thus again the recording of simple daily facts in the journal reflect a major shift in social values over the decade.

The same may be said in the area of religion. I have already mentioned the place of spirits, of feast days, of taboos and spirit-possession in the first six months of Geddie's term on Aneiteum. The tendency was for the islanders to interpret all calamities as due to the anger of the spirits. When a Christian died that always told against Christianity. By February 4, 1852 - still less than four years after his arrival - Geddie was able to write:

> Heathenism is declining fast. The old objects
> of worship are being forsaken by the natives.
> Two celebrated disease-makers have recently
> joined us. They declare that they will no more
> serve the Devil and ruin their souls. As an
> evidence of their sincerity they sent me their
> charms for making sickness. These were done
> up in two native bags. I opened them in the
> presence of a number of natives who were amused
> at their contents. They contained some earth
> of a dark colour, leaves of a sacred plant
> chewed up, portions of human hair, fragments
> of women's dresses, sugar-cane chewings, &c.,
> &c. When a disease-maker wishes to cause
> sickness he endeavours to procure a portion of
> a person's hair or some fragment of his food.
> He then chews up a quantity of sacred leaf and
> puts the whole into his charming pot, which he
> sets on the fire. He then prays to his *natmas-*
> *ses* to inflict disease on the person whom he
> wishes to charm. The process is called *nara-*
> *gess,* and those who practise it are much feared
> by the people ... This class, however, is
> hated as well as feared.

In spite of the decline of the old religion these sorcerers remained actively opposed to Christianity, and used their arts to obstruct the conversion of individuals.

Turning now to the actual response of the people of Aneiteum to the gospel we find that by the end of the first year about ten islanders were attending the Christian fellowship group. A year later this had grown to 45. Missionaries from further east had reported to Geddie that the general pattern was that the people waited for their chief to become Christian before they actually took the step themselves. Geddie, on the other hand, found the women and young people more responsive. After the beginning of the third year about 80 persons were attending. Although the chief felt he gained prestige by having a resident missionary, and valued his medicine, nevertheless many of the other chiefs were obstructive.

In August 1851 Kapaio, brother of the chief, came to Geddie asking for Christian instruction. He confessed that he had regarded the missionaries as liars when they first came with the new teaching; but having observed that their living supported their teaching, he was now prepared to accept their word as true. That was on August 20. Five days later several chiefs and priests renounced the old religion. It was this movement to Christianity on the part of the leaders which stimulated Capt. Paddon to stir up the heathen islanders to fire the mission house, and thus accentuate the division of the islanders on a basis of their attitude toward Christianity.

At this time "the chief himself had a large piece of sacred ground cut down and cleared for a plantation",which Geddie claimed would have been the "precursor of death twelve months ago". So had times changed!

Walking with the chief, Nohoat, one day Geddie came upon a woman preparing food from a certain bark, an agreeable food, but one forbidden to chiefs and sacred men, and used only by commoners. Geddie asked if he could try a piece. The woman obliged and Geddie ate. The chief looked at him strangely, and then asked for a piece himself and ate of his own accord. Thus was a sacred food taboo broken.

Less than a month later (Dec. 20) Geddie described the process of religious secularization going on at the hands of the people themselves:

> In the district where I reside there has been a great destruction of sacred groves. The Christian natives are now cultivating these spots ...
> The sacred stones likewise, which were worshipped as gods, are despised by the natives.

The conversion of the two celebrated disease-makers followed
only a few weeks after this, and again Geddie reported that
in one village where the people had lost their faith in the
old religion, but had no substitute for it, they were afraid
to destroy the village *natmass*, a "piece of durable wood
which branched out" like "the horns of a deer" (showing the
term was used for both the spirit and the fetish).[9] They
authorized a Christian native to destroy it. He broke the
heavy sacred object, burned part of it in their presence
and carried the remainder home for some less dignified purpose than it had hitherto enjoyed. Shortly after this
event Geddie recorded the formation of a church (congregation) and reported another thirteen baptisms. Even the
heathen had accepted the notion of Christian prayer, and
some of them had asked native Christians to pray for them.
A visiting Tanna party expressed surprise at being able to
walk about Aneiteum without spears and clubs, and the chief
of the party broke down and wept at the idea of a community
existing without fighting.

October 27, 1852: The oldest man in the island, an
inland native, came ten miles to confirm the news of the
gospel which had reached his village. He accepted Christian instruction, sent his stone god to Geddie, and thereafter enjoyed a new lease of life - both physical and spirit-
ual. Two weeks later some distant islanders brought in
their sacred paraphernalia, including the skull of a high
chief. The pre-Christian practice was to bury the dead
chief in a shallow grave, leaving the head exposed, and to
present sacrifices there until the head separated from the
body. Then it was placed on a pole as an object of worship.
Now they brought the skull for burial, that the old form
of worship might be ceremonially terminated.

By 1854 the Christian community had been organized
with congregations, ordinances, school program and regular
itinerations. Work was going forward on New Testament
translation. In 1855 a printing press arrived with supplies.
The Christian effort was beginning to reach out to other
islands - Erromanga, Tanna and Futuna. Geddie began to discuss the notion of native laws and government with the
chiefs. He thought codified legislation should grow with
the people, and have its own indigenous authority - two
good anthropological principles. Many of the chiefs, especially Nohoat, were themselves good advocates of the gospel and witnessed to other chiefs. On the second day of 1857
the Gospel of Matthew came off the press, and here, most
appropriately, the journal of John Geddie ends.

Conclusions

I have by no means exhausted the subject matter or the valuable historical evidence on some critical points and anthropological issues, which still remain open. The journal narrates many episodes which concern Erskine of the *Havannah*, Bishop Selwyn of the Melanesian Mission, Walter Lawry the Wesleyan area secretary and other missionaries - among them Harris, Williams and Inglis, who figured in the labour trade controversy; also historically significant seamen like Paddon and Henry, and colonial figures like Towns; and a great wealth of material on the sandalwood trade. Quite apart from the value of this journal for its own sake, these references either confirm or challenge statements based on other documents, and therefore are an essential part of *a Pacific world of inter-relating documents.*

For my own immediate purpose in this presentation I have used a grossly oversimplified model, namely that of a *triangle of personal relationships,* the triangle being the simplest possible geometric figure by which I could demonstrate my claim that a conversion pattern requires more than just an advocate and an acceptor in a face to face dialogue. It has to be a complex or a configuration of some kind - a *multi-relational engagement.* There is always a context with social factors and usually with other persons. In reality the figure often has more points than a triangle. Thus, for example, the white adventurers,A, might have been treated as whalers, sandalwooders, sailors or convicts; the islanders or native people, N, might have represented those in the territory where the missionary lived, or those in the territory of the enemy; and the missionary, M, might have been Geddie, the Presbyterian, or the visiting bishop. Even more complicating would have been M, the renegade missionary mentioned in the journal, who because of the discouragement and early persecution lost his faith and turned to exploit the South Pacific for his own personal profit. He shifted from the point, M, to point A and did much mischief to the missionary program. In 1851, when Paddon and Underwood were stirring up opposition against the missionaries, a missionary named Archibald "joined the sandalwooders and disgraced the mission". On the other side of the account, however, Geddie had also spoken of a man, Henry, as a helpful sandalwooder,[10] "the only one". Was this perhaps the trader by that name, son of a Tahiti missionary? These sidelights show how grossly oversimplified my model is. Nevertheless it points up my general thesis that we are dealing with complex configurations when we consider conversion. The forces impinging on the decision-making process are truly multitudinous.

Finally, I believe these five exercise books, which I have treated as one whole primary source (They represent a unified account of one man's experience over a limited period of time in a single locality.), demonstrate the value of the personal document for filling the gaps in our historical knowledge by means of the *synchronic ethnohistorical reconstruction*. It is synchronic as it cuts across time for a single decade in the days of the Pacific sandalwood trade, and depicts a set of personal relationships in the lifetime of one missionary, from the original point of missionary contact to the production of a printed gospel for the Christian island community. It is more than a biography. It is a dynamic panorama of interacting people and events. Furthermore, in the archival repositories of the South Pacific scores of similar journals remain untapped. If this essay helps any Pacific scholars to undertake further research of this kind I shall feel more than rewarded.

Notes:

1   Presented first to the faculty of the School of World Mission, Pasadena as a basis for discussing the area of the discipline of *Missiology* where history, Christian missions and anthropology integrate.

2   Historical novelists have been particularly irresponsible at this point. James Michener's treatment of Hawaiian history is a good (or bad) example of *creation* where one might have expected to have found *re-creation*. Although he admits the book is a novel and the characters are fictitious, nevertheless he claims his writing to be "true to the spirit and history of Hawaii". Herman Melville, in an earlier period, manipulated what he saw. His claim of four months residence in Typee, by the logs of ships is found to be four weeks, which makes a great deal of difference for the validity of his anthropology.

3   The triangle is the simplest possible model for this kind of reconstruction. In reality one might require a multi-sided figure. The point is, however, that a simple MN relationship is never an adequate explanation for conversion. Furthermore, there is always at least one kind of A - maybe many. The motives of the sandalwooders, whalers, escaped convicts and blackbirders were never quite the same; but they can be grouped

because they all came into conflict with the missionaries and actively obstructed church planting. Their
social values were also similar.

4   For example, for some time the Indian indentured labour-
ers were treated as Pacific islanders in Fiji. The
first Fijian pastor appointed to minister to them was
selected because he had done overseas service in New
Britain.

5   The journal is a valuable repository of descriptive
material on pre-Christian Aneiteum animism, which was
never the same after the first six months of Geddie's
ministry.

6   This was Geddie's opinion. Perhaps the Christian natives had told him this, but he does not say so. One
would get a different point of view from, say, the
journal of a sandalwooder. In the same library as that
in which I found my source for this article I spent
some time on the photo-copy of the diary of a super-
cargo of a labour vessel, which traded in the same part
of the Pacific.

7   "Revenge on the first white man's ship that happened
to come" had awful consequences, evidenced by the record of a long list of murders of innocent men, many of
them missionaries. The record of Erromanga was the
worst of them all.

8   The Officers of the British Squadron could never win
a verdict against the blackbirders they caught, because
the colonial courts would not accept native evidence
against the word of a white man (Palmer, 1871).

9   This is an important anthropological observation, viz.
that the same term is used for both the spirit and the
'shrine' it inhabits. Many anthropological writers on
Melanesia have entirely missed this fact and thereby
misinterpreted their data. Note also that Geddie's
term for sorcerer is "disease-maker".

10   Samuel Henry had a good name among the missionaries
from Tahiti to Fiji, and figures in missionary records
as early as the thirties (Williams & Calvert, 1884:231).

References Cited:

Basic Source: "Journal of Rev. John Geddie, First Presby-
               terian Missionary in the New Hebrides" 5 vols.
               Manuscript. Latrobe Library, Melbourne,
               Refce. MS8774

Acton, Lord
–   "Letter to Contributors to the *Cambridge Modern History*" in Stern 1963:247-249

Barnett, H.G.
1953   *Innovation: The Basis of Cultural Change,* New York, McGraw-Hill Book Co

Barzun, Jacques
1963   "Cultural History as a Synthesis" in Stern 1963:387-402

Belshaw, Cyril S.
1954   *Changing Melanesia: Social Economics of Culture Contact,* Melbourne, Oxford University Press

Fox, C.E.
1958   *Lord of the Southern Isles,* London, A.R. Mowbray & Co

Gottschalk, Louis
1945   "The Historian and the Historical Document" in Gottschalk et al 1945:3-75

Gottschalk, Louis, C. Kluckhohn and R. Angell
1945   *The Use of Personal Documents in History, Anthropology and Sociology,* Social Science Research Council, New York, Bull.53

Kluckhohn, Clyde
1945   "The Personal Document in Anthropological Science" in Gottschalk et al 1945:79-173

Palmer, George
1871   *Kidnapping in the South Seas,* Edinburgh, Edmonson & Douglas

Renier, G.J.
1965   *History: Its Purpose and Method,* New York, Harper & Row

Stern, Fritz
1963   *The Varieties of History,* Cleveland, World Publishing Co

Sturtevant, Wm.C
1966   "Anthropology, History and Ethnohistory", *Ethnohistory,* v.13.1:1-51

Tippett, A.R.
1967   *Solomon Island Christianity,* London, Lutterworth Press
1971   *People Movements in Southern Polynesia,* Chicago, Moody Press

Williams, Thomas & James Calvert
1884   *Fiji and the Fijians,* London, Chas. H. Kelly (Originally published 1860)

44

from p. 38. ... & the dirtier it is the ...
it is considered to be. Whenever, as you
listen to a Fijian meke, ~~chancing forth~~ ...
~~remark~~ in at ~~waking~~ ... when you hear the bystanders
burst into a roar of inextinguishable laughter,
you may be sure that words of the ~~most~~ ...
...able filth have just been ~~sung~~. These occur
generally in the _dulena_, or chorus, which has
no connection whatever with the body of the
song. The song itself is generally ~~narrative~~.
~~but~~ the dulena being introduced at intervals &
consisting of dirt. Sometimes the words ~~are~~
~~nair~~ a double meaning; & one who is not
well acquainted with the language may
listen to them without a thought of their filthy
nature. Thus

    Sausau na taba ni Vivili
    Sa ua levu no na ba tiri
    ~~Sa~~ru sa bisi 'ani
    ~~Sa~~ru sa bisi 'ani

is innocent enough to those who do not
know ~~the~~ its double entendre. Its literal meaning,
is

   The shells of the cockles are making a
      clapping noise
   The tide has risen high along the fish fence made
        of mangrove sticks

   ~~You~~ & I are left behind
   We two are left behind

But its hidden meaning is too filthy to be
even hinted at. I often heard our ~~nurses~~
singing this song to my children, nor was it
till many months afterwards that an accident
revealed to me its true character.

A page from one of Lorimer Fison's notebooks. This
is a typical note on a sensual chorus. _Dulena_ is
not in the dictionary. One builds his ethnohistorical lexicon from such references. See pp. 7 & 194.

7

PRIVATE LETTERS
and
CROSS-CULTURAL VALUES[1]

In a significant paper presented about a decade ago, Jacob Gruber outlined the importance of personal documents in the reconstruction of the history of anthropology and discussed the intellectual breakthrough which resulted from personal encounters of scientific persons in specific situations. He argued that correspondence and private notebooks often indicate far more of the *moment of discovery* than do the works ultimately published, which are the tested and polished, final statement. He recognized that –

> Much more important – and, of course, much more difficult to come by – are the informal and fugitive products – letters, journals, and impressions. From these we can glimpse a science in the making (1966:25).

Then he goes on to discuss manuscripts of men like E.B. Tylor and Lewis Henry Morgan in known archival repositories.

In reality this is only a beginning of the subject. Search for this type of material leads one into private repositories the wide world over, for government and missionary reports are also finished products and seldom reflect the *moment of discovery* or the series of experiences which led the district officer or missionary to write that report. One valuable type of repository for these more personal letters and journals is the magazine which features such correspondence. The missionary magazines of the last century published scores of letters written at *moments of discovery and confrontation*. These are by no means travellers' tales, and on the whole are remarkably frank. Frequently they are the only material for reconstructing the pre-Christian rites of passage, magical procedures, cannibalism and other practices. In as much as I have been able to check a number against archival material, I have found virtually *no editing*; which cannot be said of the published books about missions of the same period. Quite apart from the history of missions, which is not our subject here, these letters are

127

an indispensable data-bank for any adequate diachronic or
synchronic study of social organization, political systems,
language, myth, and religion through culture change.   Here
you see the culture pattern at the point of culture contact.
Such documents become highly significant when they extend
the time sequence diachronically into an earlier generation
from that in which observations have been recorded.

Methodological Preamble

     In my own studies, concentrating on Polynesia and Mel-
anesia, I have identified a number of documentary corpora,
each of which has its own peculiar value. One, in particular, I want to discuss here. The Fijian people became
Christian over a period of about fifty years, beginning in
1835. One of the features of the missionary organization
was a printing program. There had been a press and printers
there from 1838 and at an early stage the converts were already literate and were encouraged in self-expression. In
the last decade of the century a small Fijian monthly newspaper began to circulate among the Fijians. *Ai Tukutuku
Vakalotu* had a remarkable number of indigenous Fijian contributors. About the same time the Fijian Church commenced
a missionary venture from British New Guinea (Papua).   It
already had one in German New Guinea (New Britain and New
Ireland) and was shortly to operate in the Western Solomons.
Fijian missionaries in all these fields contributed to the
Fijian paper by sending in letters and reports in the Fijian
language for their relatives and supporters at home to read.
Let me make that clear: the letters were written by Fijians
in their own language. These Fijians had a generation or
so of Christianity behind them, but had not completely forgotten their pre-Christian vocabulary and practices.   I
doubt if a present-day Fijian could write some of the descriptions in these letters. In contrast to their religious
and semantic change these Fijian writers had a style of life,
with subsistence and exchange economy, only slightly changed
by culture contact. It was similar to that of the people
they were describing in many ways. As their letters were
written for Fijians at home, they made comparisons in house-
building, gardening, canoe-construction and sailing, burial
customs and so on. Although in these comparisons one de-
tects the Fijian value-system as their criteria for comparison, it is only in religious values that this stands out in
highly contrasting colors.

     It has been popular to dismiss missionary documents on

the score of their *bias*. Yet normally this is no more than
the bias of any scientist who writes from the viewpoint and
theory of his own discipline. Any critical reader must establish the subjective viewpoint from which his reading material has been written.[2] In any case, if you are studying
a situation at, say, 1900 in Papua, and the missionary is
there as an agent of change, *he is part of the situation,* as
Malinowski pointed out (1965:xix), and a 1900 cultural reconstruction is incomplete without him.

However, much more difficult to evaluate than missionary bias, because they are latent rather than manifest, are
(1) the purpose of the writing and (2) the character of the
audience. These two may be related and they may be complicated. For example, a missionary writes a letter to his
board secretary, for personal reasons bearing on his service.
The secretary publishes it in the missionary journal for promotional purposes. Both the motive of the letter and the
character of the audience have been changed. Such documents
have historical and anthropological value *if* the researcher
can recognize these motivational rearrangements of the use
of the documents. The essential information for really critical testing is whether or not the editor edited or clipped
the letters.

In this case of the Fijian letter-writers from Papua,
the letters were written, not so much to the editor, as to
the Fijian community at home. The editor was merely the
'mechanism' by which their correspondence would be printed
and circulated. These letters were personal documents which
psychologically reinforced them in a foreign land by serving
as their link with home, friends and relations. If these
Fijians had any promotional motive it was rather to keep up
their numbers so that deaths and retirement would not de-
plete their ranks and their mission could be continued. The
editor had the same motive. The anthropological descriptions in the letters can be taken at their face value, as
what Fijians really observed.

This whole corpus of missionary letters, some of which
are quite long, comprises about a hundred, if we include a
few more formal reports that seem to belong with them. Those
relating to Papua (Dobu and Kiriwina), to which I shall now
turn, number forty-one. They are written in Fijian and most
of them are signed with localities identified.

A quantity of related documentation in English and Fijian also exists in the mission archives in Fiji and Sydney

and in the files of *The Spectator*, a Melbourne religious
newspaper. Names dates, places and the movement of Fijians
can be checked from these where the letters do not indicate
this. This means that the events, persons and cultural institutions described can be located in time and place, making them possible focal points for *diachronic reconstruction*,
and specially valuable where cultural institutions have become obsolete.

The value of these letters is not confined to the *descriptive reconstruction* of conditions and institutions at
the point of culture contact. We are also provided with
valuable data of the *dynamics* of that culture contact. This
is not another story of white missionaries, which we have in
abundance; but the encounter of Melanesian with Melanesian,
and within that encounter the differentiation between Christian Fijian and pagan Papuan values. In terms of the theory
of cultural dynamics, as worked out for example by Barnett
(1953), these letter-writers would be the *advocates*, their
purpose is religious *innovation*, and their letters are studies of how their advocacy met with *acceptance* and/or *rejection*. A whole study could be presented using the data in
the letters, to demonstrate Barnett's theory of innovation
and his recombination thesis.

The Papuan letters come from the archipelago at the extreme southeast of Papua - including Kiriwina and Dobu, the
happy hunting-grounds of Malinowski and Fortune - islands
of *kula ring* fame, and thus they push back anthropological
description to a greater time depth than the major ethnological studies of these two men.

Content of the Corpus

Now, let me turn to a few examples of the information
in these letters, and point up some of the cultural values
reflected in them.

1. Cannibalism:
Cannibalism is a recurrent theme. From J.T. Field's
contemporary account to Fison (*Spectator*: Aug: 12, '98) we
have a hard, gruesome, honest description of this ceremonial
'inhumanity' as he had met it face to face. He knew he confronted it daily. Two of his missionary colleagues perished
that way. He classified cannibalism, with *plunder* and *revenge*, as the three causes of war. The administration sought
to correct this 'offence' by punitive raids.

But these letters and reports show that *cannibalism was itself a result rather than a cause*. Papuan values went far beyond the feasting to the basic belief on which it rested to the acquisition of skulls and the build-up of mana-repositories, because of the Papuan conceptualization of *power-encounter* and *survival*.

A Christian party was beheaded, disembowelled, baked and eaten; the elder first, according to their pattern of protocol, in the presence of the others. The bodies were distributed over ten villages as gifts to be shared, but the skulls were preserved as highly desirable possessions. Whether of friend or enemy, the skull was valued, and its pedigree remembered. A man's power was measured by the skulls he owned. A punitive expedition, after killing 13 and wounding many others, burning both their war canoes and light-draft fishing canoes, discovered and fired two large men's communal houses, each 200 feet long and filled with skulls. This destruction of skulls was regarded as the height of their achievement. The two houses contained eleven hundred skulls (*T.V.* 45, 47: June, July '01).

Thus cannibalism is traced back to *a religious belief, the build-up of power for survival,* not merely a depraved taste. The flesh was given away, but not the skull. Indeed one letter tells how the Christian Fijians had to beware that human flesh was not sold to them as pork. It was the skull and not the flesh which had the 'soul-stuff'.

2. *The Nature of God:*

Different also were the Christian Fijian and pagan Papuan ideas of God, his nature, and the life of man after death. One origin story is recorded. The people of Dobu are said to have sprung from a female, named Kekewakei, who appeared from out of the earth, and gave birth to a child from whom the present race descended. One day the offspring went for water and returned to find the mother crazy. When the latter saw the child was afraid of her, she died and went to Buwebuweso, the abode of spirits (ghosts). This origin story links the Ancestor with the spirit world for the dead (*T.V.* 2. Mar. '94).

It had similarities with the old tribal relations between the living and dead, which the Fijians had themselves rejected in becoming Christian. They understood this kind of encounter between Ancestor Worship and Christianity. It was a problem they understood better than the white missionary. They knew they were dealing with ancestral spirits

rather than a high God and they were concerned with supernatural power *per se*. It was a world of *mana*. The idea, if
not the word was there, as in old Fiji.

Josua Mateinaniu described a prolonged series of dancing, day and night, and day after day, to stimulate and en-
tertain the ghosts of the dead, on the theological supposition that they were impoverished and hungry in the land of
the dead. He described the presentations of food and enter-
tainments and evaluated them in true Fijian style:

> There is nothing slapdash about the preparation of this
> feast. Each individual is responsible for the satis-
> faction of his own deceased relations, whether father,
> mother, uncle, nephew or neice, grand-parent, cross-
> cousin, elder brother, and so on. On the last night,
> before the conclusion of the ceremonies, after danc-
> ing all night until the crowing of the cock and the
> dawning of the day to the sound of the bamboo, the
> beating of the drum and the blowing of the conch-shell,
> they all run to the outskirts of the village, and send
> off the ghosts with the traditional farewell, "Go and
> sleep! Go and sleep!" (*T.V.* 19, Mar. '94)

Josua's concern, however, was not so much the futility of the
ceremony and the waste of food and human strength; (he could
appreciate the communal values of the entertainment) but that
the final stage clashed with Sunday and represented a "deliberate rejection of the better way" he believed he had to offer them. He had been only three years in this location and
was just beginning to get results. His motive was to show
the folk at home the need for the gospel, but in doing so he
left a nice anthropological description of how they prepared
their presentations and spread out a bed of leaves for the
ancestral ghosts to lie on for the entertainment. He also
left us an interesting picture of a conflict in Melanesian
religious values.

The same conflict also showed up with respect to the
moral nature of God. Setareki Tuicakau was much opposed by
an elder named Mabundi, but apparently Mabundi realized that
Setareki's God had too much *mana* for him, and that the best
way of coming to terms was to buy the god from its owner.
Fetishes, medicines and magical formulae were marketable com-
modities for the manipulation of the owner. Setareki had
been manifestly appraised as a fetishman. In his letter he
tells the friends at home of the position he took. His God
was not up for sale like a fetish or a charm. Neither was
he the owner of the god with power to sell it. He was trying to communicate that God was universally accessible to all

who believed, rich or poor, and had no material shrine or
vessel (*T.V.* 54, April '02).

A few months after this, Josua Mateinaniu wrote about a
strong gale which brought down many houses and fruit and destroyed the gardens. This was attributed to the missionary,
who, having seen the rapidly falling barometer had predicted
the coming wind. As none in the village had heard of a barometer, he was designated a big wind-maker. The people of
the district met at Boa, 25 miles from Dobu, and organized a
huge presentation for him, that he not again bring such a
wind upon them. Their request was that he "close his box of
wind, that they may live". The barometer was regarded as
his magical wind-making paraphernalia. There were repercus-
sions. The Fijian evangelist at Duau could find no-one to
row him to Dobu lest the missionary release the winds again.
The people, of course, were acting within their own conceptual framework. Did they not go to Bulitara, the pagan wind-
maker, with a presentation when they required a calm for
fishing? They were interpreting the foreigners by their own
Papuan values. Their attitude to the wind-maker was ambiva-
lent: fear of destruction, but readiness to draw on his resources (*T.V.* 59, Sept. '02; 62, Jan. '03).

Although this was a grave misunderstanding of Christian
Fijian values and motives; nevertheless it shows that the
people had recognized the Fijian presence, and were feeling
out towards the possibility of accepting it. Once they did
this, some kind of status and role had to be ascribed to them.

Pailato Silimi reported that their own great God, known
by different names in different localities, was far from a
loving deity. He was rather responsible for bringing sickness on all kinds of people. This he did by *possessing* them.
Correction of this possession-sickness required a priestly
exorcist, who soon grew rich with presentations. This did
not mystify the Fijians. There was an old pre-Christian
character about it and furthermore they had anticipated this
kind of encounter (Silimi/Fison, 11.17.91).

3. *War:*
The war descriptions are quite numerous. One is led to
believe that a serious war could commence with as small a
thing as an argument over a pig. Someone is hurt and there
is retaliation. Other villages are drawn in, fighting with
spears, stones and axes. In one such case of rapid diffusion 23 villages were soon involved. On such occasions the
Fijians frequently sought to become *peacemakers*. Josua Mateinaniu apparently won a reputation for this. He went out

in the midst of 900 to 1000 angry Papuans and called them
to see the foolishness of war and put in his 'plug' for Christianity. Many a time he at least restored law and order, and
even those who did not become Christian accepted his common
sense and arbitration (*T.V.* 25, '99; 33, '00).

  At other times war was premeditated and carefully planned. It began in the same manner as the wars of pre-Christian Fiji, the invaders surrounding a village by night and
attacking at dawn from all sides to the sound of conch-shells.
The older Fijians had lived through this and knew how to deal
with it. In any case the widespread destruction was always
the same. Setareki Tui wrote from Kiriwina:
  This land is at war. I went to see the warriors from
  my village (Emarakana) and sat in their midst. They were
  mourning their dead. I was unable to conceal my own
  tears at the tragedy. Eleven villages have been burned
  this week - the food, animals and possessions all destroyed (*T.V.* Feb. '00).
He went on to describe how the pagan rainmaker and his younger
brother had run to him on his return and wept. He described
the stench of the plunder of war and the decimation of the
coconuts (he uses a strong Fijian word for vicious and
deliberate destruction). He certainly identified with the
people with whom he lived. This time it cost him the house
he had built himself and everything he owned.   He went
through five villages on the Sunday to preach, but the biggest group he could gather was eleven. All had fled. Even
so, the preaching of a way of peace was not unacceptable
(*T.V.* Feb. '00).

4. *Funerary Rites:*
  The letters contain enough material on *the burial of the*
dead to have devoted a whole paper to this.   The accounts
demonstrate the cultural diversity of the various islands.
Juta Ranamalo reported from Dobu a burial in which the body
was leaned against the grave with the head up, and covered
by a pot shaped like a Fijian bowl. A few months later the
skull having become detached from the body, would be taken
away. Certain persons would sleep by the grave, and the
mourners would stay nearby for a month or so, heads shaven
and bodies blackened. A grave house was built over the grave,
and shelters for the mourners, whose responsibility it had
been to build the grave house. Mourning might go on for a
year, the mourners continually talking of the generosity of
the dead. On the day of the burial feast the relatives of
the deceased would mourn at the grave for the last time, and
when the widow ceased all would go to bathe (*T.V.* June '95).

A somewhat different account comes from Bwaidoga -
A chief dies. His younger brother and his sons weep in
the house. Other mourners refuse to enter the house
but sleep on the 'village green' outside. In the morning a grave is dug and a 'bed' of appropriate size is
set up. The extended family makes a presentation of
wealth - 2 pigs teeth, 2 orange trees, bracelets......
The body is brought out of the house and everyone mourns.
As the body is lowered into the grave they try to at-
tract the attention of the dead by burying food, drinking nuts, and tobacco with him. Eventually they bring
their weapons and fight with the spirits, until these
are all dead. Then those who have so fought will receive some reward (*T.V.* 56, June '02).

Still another account comes from Poate Ratu. It begins
as a typical Melanesian account would with kin orientation -
and more precise responsibility.
When an elder, either male or female, dies, the mother's
brother's son (F. *vasu*) or the mother's brother (F. *ga-
dinana* - could also mean father's sister's husband) at-
tends to the erection of a small grave house in the
midst of the 'burial place' with a 'bed' for the dead,
and a grave is dug beneath the small house. The body
is lain on the bed until the burial (*T.V.* 43, '91).
The report goes on to describe how another body is lain with
the dead as a cooked offering. The head man of the burial
feast probes the cooked body with the rib of a palm frond or
a fish bone so that some juice flows into the grave beneath
the burial house. As the bodies decay the head man of the
funerary rites takes any piece of rotten flesh which is about
to fall and wraps it up, placing it in the grave so it does
not fall there of its own accord. Eventually the remaining
bones are broken up and packaged in a mat and stored in the
burial house until the end of the mourning feast. After the
burial feast the skull is taken away. This is a very long
account in archaic Fijian and describes the yams, puddings,
fish and pigs used at the end of the mourning feast, which
might be delayed as long as 2 years. The food was supplied
by the village of the deceased. The party with the feast
moved to the house of the dead, where the last stage of the
mourning was going on with vigor - wailing, screaming, kick-
ing the wall, and making a song about the deeds of the dead.
Mourners displayed the hair they had cut off (heads, mous-
taches, eyebrows), so the ghost of the dead would feel he
was adequately remembered.

Now mourning was over. They bathed, oiled their bodies

and combed the new growths of hair. Taboo foods - pig, taro,
puddings and young coconuts could be eaten again (*T.V.*43,
Mar. '91).

This is a piece of objective description, but in another
letter from another area the same writer said -

In Fiji when our folk die we bury them with decorum,
and bring as funeral presents, rolls of native cloth,
mats, whale's teeth, sinnet, pigs and canoes. We strip
ourselves to honor the dead. These people wail more
than we do, but give little more than tears..... They
bury a few yams with the dead, that he may eat on the
way [to the spirit land]. They bury him in a sitting
posture in a hole lined with banana leaves like a
Fijian banana-bread silo. They even cry over their
war victims. They cry and sing a song called *Women,*
beat their drums and wail until they decide where they
will eat the bodies (*Spectator,*Feb. '92).

One speculates that even the ghosts of those eaten by cannibal conquerors can trouble the living if not mourned by
wailing. I think the Fijian account implies this, but it
does not say so directly. If we add to all this a description of a burial ground by missionary Field in a letter to
Lorimer Fison, we have a good body of data which predates
Malinowski by 20 years and fits the diagram in Fortune's
first chapter (1963:1).

5.   *Sorcery:*
I have already mentioned the "Owner of the Winds" and
the "Owner of the Rains" (F. *Taukei ni Cagi*. F. *Taukei ni
Uca*). These and a few other magical roles were normally
confined to males, but the references to sorcery usually concern females, and elderly ones at that. Apparently they were
a jealous breed.

Poate Ratu reported from Dobu in 1894 that of two elderly
sisters, the elder of the two had two children both of whom
died. The younger had five, all alive and married. The
elder one was infuriated that her younger sister was well
provided for by her offspring, while she had no-one to support her. She declared she would apply sorcery against her
sister, who immediately fell ill and died. Poate the Fijian,
buried her, for she had attended the Christian worship, but
by night the angry sister exhumed the body, took it into
the forest, cooked and ate it. When Poate heard of this
he went to the grave and found it empty but for the mat.
The civil authorities interfered and the sorceress was taken
to Samarai and hanged (*T.V.* 4, Sept. '94).

Shortly afterwards Ananaiasa Benu (*T.V.* 7, June '95),

told of two sorceresses who tried to prevent his converts
from joining the church by threatening that any who did so
would certainly die. Ananaiasa, the Fijian, countered by pro-
claiming that God had sent him to Papua to stop this kind of
work of the devil, and God would certainly deal with any who
tried to kill by sorcery. A week later the leader of the
two lay down and died. The Fijians believed the power of
sorcery could only be safely met in the name of the Christian God, whose power was described in the Bible. Here, phil-
osophically, Papuan and Fijian shared a common value - *mana*
working against one can only be overcome by a greater *mana*.

A 1904 report discusses the *Werebana*, old women sorceresses -

> When the moon is very red it is said that the sorceresses
> are eating it. The people say a sorceress has pierced
> it with a spear, so that it bleeds profusely and is
> therefore entirely red.
> These old women gather together in some quarter of the
> village for a lamentation, in which they mourn the moon's
> death, while it is being devoured. All these old women
> then discard their grass skirts; that is, their old,
> dirty skirts, and examine the inner cloth, [the Fijian
> term is *dau i taratara*, a method of detecting a guilty
> person by touch-divination]. When everything is discarded,
> the skirts are all burned, and then the sorceresses take
> a piece of mango wood and beat it while the grass skirts
> are burning. They continue weeping while they beat their
> drums, because of their love for the moon.

Then at the end of this quite objective reporting of popular
opinion comes the encounter of values - "Alas, this is certainly foolish, when Christianity is there for the acceptance" (*T.V.* 77. '04).

This is a typical closing comment.   In the same way,
Opetaia Muani (*T.V.* 62, Jan. '03) after discussing a polygamous wind-maker and a rain-maker, simply adds in closing,
"This kind of darkness is wide-spread." Other letters are
confined to their own positive values.   The inordinately
large number of obituaries shows the price they paid for
their missionary program in Papua. These are absolutely typical Fijian Christians. One letter of Josua Mateinaniu's
(*T.V.* 50, Nov. '01) about an infant almost drowned in the
sea, shows the Christian measure of health and hygiene. Several complained of the effect of liquor in the islands. One
blamed the white man's trade connections for hindering his
missionary work: this is not a Fijian reflection of missionary talk, it is the subsistence economy speaking against
"the enemy the Silini" (shilling).

6. Organizational Patterns:
Here and there throughout the letters one comes on references to social organization.

The Fijians were somewhat mystified by the ability of Papuan society to survive without a strong chieftaincy such as they knew in Fiji. Solomoni Tavatava told how the people who had become Christian in a certain village, worked to build a church. There was no head man in the village or in the Christian group and they had no preacher or lay leader - yet they put up a church building (*T.V.* 39, Sept. '00).

Poate Ratu also had commented on the absence of chieftaincy:
> These people have no real chiefs whose word all men follow, as we have in Fiji, and this is a bad thing (Ratu/ Fison, Feb. '92).

And again he wrote:
> They have a word for 'chief' which is *taubada,* but the trouble is they all call themselves chiefs, and every man is a chief in his own house. There are men who have a following, but there are no real chiefs.

In 1891 Bromilow the missionary, mentioned in a letter to Fison that a certain polygamist, Jikoro, had three wives but kept them in different villages. Poate Ratu, the Fijian, is very much more to the point, and shows this is not merely to keep them apart:
> If a *taubada* (chief) here has 5 wives, each of those women belongs to a different town, and he has to go to visit her and his offspring are not his children, but are counted to her town. Your own offspring go to other tribes, but your sister's children come to yours (*Spectator,* Feb. '92).

In a 1904 report, also from Kiriwina, surveying the decade, polygamy was discussed. It described how the woman's kin were responsible for building her house and yam houses which were quite stable structures, and supplying her with yams. The particular reference is to the chief Enamakala who had 22 wives.

One Fijian, who no doubt came from one of the sailing islands of Fiji has left us a description of Papuan sailing at Tubetube. We have also numerous other cultural institutions like peacemaking procedures and the transmission of obligations to relatives at the time of death. One could go on. There is more than this in the corpus of letters.

Throughout these years, the Fijian business was to bring about religious change. Where they met obstruction it was mainly resistance to their successes by those who were deprived of material advantage by the change - priests, magicmen, exorcists and elderly sorceresses. As Barnett points out (1953:381) acceptors are more likely to be dissidents than the satisfied. Conceptualization of Fijian Christians in some kind of priestly role opened the way for the acceptance of the new religion. Some demonstration of the power of the Christian God by his agents facilitated the decision-making. Although the religious innovation was considerable the indigenous culture was by no means destroyed. It remained an integrated thing.

The pattern of skull burial as an ocular demonstration of change of faith can be conceptualized in terms of Sherif's experiments as interpreted by Barnett as the reference point in a hitherto unstructured field (1953:116-117). The burial was the decision-making symbol. In August and September, 1891, Field saw them bury 57 skulls in three group ceremonials, after the presentation of his message of peacemaking (*Journ.* 11.6.91).

Some Evaluations

We have been told by Kaberry (Firth, 1964:83) that -
....for Malinowski an institution was multidimensional, having its personnel (social structure), its charter (or values), its norms, activities and material equipment. It was a construct, but it was a model closely linked to empirical reality, that is to social situations in which pairs or groups of individuals in defined relationships carried out activities in persuit of certain ends.
I certainly agree with this theoretical statement. However, to read Malinowski and Fortune in the light of the corpus of Fijian documents is to feel a stress on magical practice at the expense of religious belief. Nadel detected the same imbalance without access to the Fijian corpus in "Malinowski on Magic and Religion" (Firth, 1964:205).
Malinowski's account of magic is rigorously coherent and internally consistent; if you wish to quarrel with it you must quarrel with a systematic theory. Against this, the treatment of religion is loose and disjointed: there seem to be too many things incapable of conceptual integration.

Now I think it can be seriously postulated that both
Fortune and Malinowski, whose data-collecting was superb,ac-
tually failed to record what they saw - I mean the religious
dimension - because they regarded it as acculturation due to
mission influence. They were salvage anthropologists. Twenty
years later Malinowski saw the missionary as part of a "new
autonomous entity" (1965:xix). Meantime, better time depth
would have shown that *religion and magic do not change at the
same pace, or with the same rhythm.*

Malinowski's own objection to the manner of gathering
ethnological data from one dimensional accounts, that are incomplete because they ignore the social dimension (1948:240)
rebounds on him. This corpus of descriptive Fijian correspondence over a decade, written about the people of his own
research area and their social *and religious* patterns by persons from a somewhat similar Melanesian and insular world
could hardly be called one-dimensional. The letters form an
archival collection, a multidimensional entity - what I have
called a *corpus*. Indeed, I think that by throwing this corpus up against the writing of Fortune and Malinowski we are
able to add a *time dimension* which neither Malinowski nor
Fortune had.

The big difference is the disappearance of cannibalism,
which was mentioned in letter after letter in my data bank.
Fortune's references to cannibalism are either historic
cases (61,90,306) or described in the past tense (77,80) or
in oral tradition (302).

"Skull(s)" is not even in the index of any of the four
Papua volumes of Malinowski I examined, and cannibalism is
limited to references in the myths (Malinowski, 1961:321-2,
331) and by his only reference in *Coral Gardens* (1965a. I,
162), where he is discussing the possibility of endo-canni-
balism in time of severe famine, he is indeed a feeble wit-
ness. In view of the huge collection of Malinowski's data,
the absence of cannibalism and skulls shows the basic religious change which had taken place in the first decade of
this century. No better example could be found to illustrate the shortcommings of purely synchronic research.

Josefa Malumu (to Fison 11-13-91), Panieta, described
houses where the wall and end plates were entirely decorated
with skulls - friends and cannibal victims. Pailato Sili
(11-17-91) at Ekaroi reported to Fison a collection of 100
skulls from cannibal feasting.

When the Papuans were converted they buried the skulls.
Poate, the most fluent of the Fijian speakers of Dobuan, penetrated into the mountains of Normanby. As a result of his
efforts fifty skulls were buried in one village. Field
thought cannibalism had vanished in Tubetube by 1898 (*Spectator*, 11-4-98) despite the continuation of other non-Christian customs.

This must have meant a tremendous transformation in the
whole religious value system. This kind of change had already begun to operate in the values of the *kula ring* before
the arrival of Malinowski on the scene. Bromilow gave information on things like the secret gesture language, and
claimed a change of character in the trade over the period I
am discussing (Bromilow, 1929: 127-301).

The spirit land Bwebweso, is frequently mentioned in
Fortune, but he apparently did not explore mission archival
resources. He drew on the physical facilities and linguistic
work of the resident white missionaries and bracketed the
Mission and Government as agents of change, blaming them for
depopulation, but he refrains from mentioning the greatest
destructive agency of all, the recruiting and labour trade
which operated in the localities where he was working. The
mission is not a single discrete entity, as he would have
discovered if he had worked over the documents of the Fijian
missionaries as against those of the white missionaries.
Even the Pacific Island evangelists were not a discrete group,
being Fijians, Tongans and Samoans.

As Malinowski (1948) reported, the graves at Kiriwina
had been moved outside the village shortly before by Government intervention (257). One has the impression that the
Kiriwinans regarded their old beliefs about ghosts less seriously. The people were not afraid of the dark or the spirits
of the dead (152), and again the disrespectful removal of the
grave goods before the ultimate interment (156,258) suggests
the whole event was a *mock substitute* for the more-serious
pre-Christian proto-type described in my collection of letters, especially one account from Bwaidoga where the gifts
included weapons of war to fight with the spirits (*T.V.* 56,
June '02).

Fortune distinguished between witches and sorcerers as
female and male, making the point that the victims were *werebana* - mortal women (1963:150-153), but he did not give us a
great deal of information about their operations. He has a
single reference to *jealousy* as a possible cause, and this

is certainly supported in the letters, but the letters also
indicate the *werebana* applied pressure by *threat*. Apparently
a mere threat was enough to kill, and the Government, knowing this, treated it as murder (Ratu, *T.V.* 4, Sept. '94).
Bromilow recorded that the oldest chief of Dobu died through
a woman's sorcery (*Journ.* Jan. '92).

The terms *werebana* and *balau*, for the female and male
practitioners, were also used for the spirits which possessed
them (Field/Fison 9.7.'91; Silimi/Fison 11.17. '91), as with
kalou in some localities of early Fiji. Fortune held that
every disease was caused by an incantation of some kind (138),
but the Fijian material indicates some diseases as caused by
the spirit Werebana. In Kiriwina, Malinowski (1961:76) found
the *mulukwausi* and *bwaga'u* capable of causing sickness, and
the *tauva'u* non-human but anthropomorphic malignant spirits
who could cause death. What we have yet to establish, however, is whether the death by spirit-possession was due to
the spirit or initiated by a sorceress calling upon him for
power.

Fortune's description of a Dobuan burial (1963:193-200)
is mainly comprised of kin responsibilities and feast ex-
changes, with a number of details which could have been innovations after 1900 - i.e. *functional substitutes* for the
pagan features which had disappeared with the acceptance of
Christianity. I feel sure some features were *mocking substitutes*. The praises of the dead are retained, but in the
feasting rather than the wailing (199). However, the grim
associations of burial sacrifice, cannibalism, decomposition
of the corpse before burial, preservation of the skull as a
mana repository have no mention in Fortune, except for a few
references which, because of the bare reference with no treatment at depth, I suspect come from an informant or oral tradition rather than observation.

Ruth Benedict pointed out the importance of early case
study data for studying cultural process (1953:18) and used
Fortune on the Dobuans as her data base. Yet the society
she reconstructs was research at *a point of time only*. Malinowski, Fortune and Benedict, who leans on them (120-159),
all missed the point that the Fijian letters would have made
clear, namely, that *the Papuans had just passed through a
dramatic and rapid change of religious beliefs and values,
but the magical patterns, which are usually corrected by
slower educational processes had not yet been eliminated*.
When the Fijian corpus is set over against Malinowski and
Fortune and the passage of time is taken into consideration,

we are able to use the joint data diachronically. The analysis of Malinowski is synchronic. The description of the
letters is synchronic. But bring the two together so that
you introduce the diachronic dimension over the period of
more than a single generation and some of the problems which
Malinowski did not appreciate now become charged with new
meaning. Malinowski is not the only anthropologist who has
eliminated the religious dimension of an acculturated situation because of "mission influence", and the historical record of the process of cultural change is much the poorer because of these omissions. We have a great many gaps in our
knowledge of sequences. The hope is that many of these can
be investigated before it is too late. The living informants
are dead. Only the study of personal documents can help us
now; but the new availability of these throughout the Pacific
makes possible a diachronic reconstruction at many of these
broken sequences.

To return to Gruber's idea - these personal documents
record much valuable information of *moments of discovery and
confrontation* when major culture transitions began.

Notes:

1   Originally presented at the annual meeting of the Ameri-
     can Society for Ethnohistory, held at the University of
     Georgia, Athens (1971).
2   Bias and subjectivity should really be differentiated.
     Shafers' *A Guide to Historical Method* points out that the
     former is a judgement without really examining the data,
     the letter is an understanding in terms of personal val-
     ues (1969:149). If the missionary account is subjective
     this is evidence in the dimension of cultural values and
     important. If the missionary is really biased - i.e. re-
     fuses to face the facts - what he writes is still of evi-
     dential value, since he was himself playing a participant
     role in the situation.

Documentary Sources Used and Cited 1894-1905:

Collection of Letters and Reports from Kiriwina and Dobu
Circuits, Trobriand, D'Entrecastreaux and Louisiade Ar-
chipelagoes, from Fijian missionaries and written in the
Fijian language and printed in that language in Fiji for
their friends at home. 41 letters and reports.

A few similar letters sent to Lorimer Fison in Melbourne.

Material from the *Journals* of J.T. Field and W.E. Bromilow, also sent to Fison.

Contemporary newspapers:

Ai Tukutuku Vakalotu, Fiji   1894-1905
The Spectator, Melbourne   1891-1898

Books and Articles Cited:

Barnett, Homer G.
   1953   *Innovation: The Basis of Cultural Change,*
                 New York, McGraw-Hill Book Co.
Benedict, Ruth
   1953   *Patterns of Culture,* New York, Mentor Books
                 (First printed 1934).
Bromilow, W.E.
   1929   *Twenty Years Among Primitive Papuans,* London
                 Epworth Press.
Firth, Raymond (Ed.)
   1960   *Man and Culture: An Evaluation of the Work of
                 Bronislaw Malinowski,* New York, Harper & Row
                 (First published 1957).
Fortune, R.F.
   1963   *Sorcerers of Dobu,* New York, E.P. Dutton & Co.
                 (First published 1932).
Gruber, Jacob
   1966   "Biography as an Instrument for the History of
                 Anthropology," in Helm 1966:5-27
Helm, June (Ed.)
   1966   *Pioneers of American Anthropology: The Uses of
                 Biography,* Seattle, University of Washing-
                 ton Press
Kaberry, Phyllis
   1957   "Malinowski's Field-Work Methods," Firth,
                 1964:71-91
Malinowski, Bronislaw
   1948   *Magic, Science & Religion,* New York, Doubleday
                 & Co. (Essays published 1916-1926).
   1961   *Argonauts of the Western Pacific,* New York,
                 E.P. Dutton & Co. (First published 1922).
   1965a   *Coral Gardens & Their Magic,* 2 Vols., Blooming-
                 ton, Indiana University Press (First published
                 1935).
   1965b   "The Anthropology of Changing African Cultures"
                 Introduction to *Methods of Study of Culture
                 Contact in Africa,* London, Oxford University
                 Press (First Published 1938)

Nadel, S. F.
    1957   "Malinowski on Magic and Religion" Firth,
                    1964:189-208

Lorimer Fison's 'Doodling'
(See "Labour Trade" pp.165-166)

8

SKELETONS

IN THE LITERARY CLOSET

Of all the sub-disciplines of Anthropology none is more dependent on reliable historical reconstruction than the study of *Culture Contact* or *Culture Change*. Or to put it in the opposite way, no aspect of Anthropology has more to offer the historians researching the last century than the study of the dynamics of cultural change. This virtually makes it essential for any writer on the Pacific of the last century to be some kind of ethnohistorian. This applies to journalists, historical novelists, missiologists and economists as well as to professional anthropologists and historians.

One may spend a lifetime reading Pacific literature and a fortune collecting it, and still end up with a distorted view of the history, and a projection of his own twentieth century western values on its cultural dynamics, even though his library may contain a superb data base for accurate reconstruction. In this essay I purpose exposing some of the 'skeletons' in the literary cupboard; partly in the hope that such exposure will help us move towards a period of more responsible ethnohistorical reconstruction; and partly because the sources are far too valuable to be misused for a process of modern myth creation.

a. *Creativity and Responsibility:*
In any kind of literature - biography, travel description, promotional writing, as well as history and anthropology - the writer has to maintain a critical equilibrium. To communicate with his readers (and this is true for promotional writing or writing for a market) the writer needs *liberty* and *flexibility* with the use of his materials, and he needs *creativity* to maintain the reader's interest. Even in the most mechanical scientific treatise the writer

147

needs this freedom. However too much creativity may lead
to intellectual dishonesty; too much liberty may lead one
into a partisan position, in which he prejudges his sources;
and too much flexibility may lead to a confusion of fiction
and non-fiction, or apologetics and history.   The reader
should not be misguided about the kind of literature he is
reading, which would mean faulty communication between
writer and reader. This is not to say there is no place
for fiction or apologetics, but certainly they should not
be paraded as, or confused with history or anthropology.

Liberty, flexibility and creativity are as necessary to the writer as is electricity in a modern factory -
but unless controlled within certain insulated limits they
are about as dangerous. They call for *responsibility*.

In this paper I purpose exposing some of the more
common forms of irresponsibility in Pacific literature;
many of them by our best writers of literary prose, which
makes their irresponsible reconstruction even the more dangerous.

b.   *The Use of Documents:*
A document is a total thing. It should only be
dismemberd with extreme caution. If a piece of writing is
to be documented this means lifting quotations out of their
original matrices. We all do this - we cannot avoid it.
If we use the reference in a different context we are bound
to say so, so that the reader may know what we have done.
If we reduce a quotation, as we often must do, we are obligated to indicate the reduction by means of ellipses, and
also to be sure we have not eliminated any qualifiers of the
statement we want to quote.[1] Or on the other hand we may
reduce a long episode to a short paragraph, which is quite
legitimate as long as we do not so simplify the complex episode that we substitute a single cause of the event, say,
for the multiple causes. This is the most common distortion.
Both historians and anthropologists do it. For example, the
reason for the growth or non-growth of an island church is
often attributed to a single factor, the illustration cited
often actually having multiple factors within it. In *People
Movements in Southern Polynesia* I felt compelled to devote
an Appendix to this (1971:221-226). I cite the use of the
same episode by an anthropologist , a missionary historian
and a missionary theoretician, yet the readers would hardly
recognize them as the same. Each had a valid point to make;
but each had his own purpose and selected a single detail
to make his point, ignoring the others. The anthropologist,

concentrated on an historical accident and a cultural aspect, the missionary historian on the divine element and
the theoretician on a missiological problem. Each of them
alone was a distortion. Each needed the perspective of the
others. Yet they had all worked from the same data base.
Each had failed to explore his data fully, because each was
concerned with his own hypothesis only and was selective
with his primary source. The old classical method of posit-
ing a hypothesis and researching from this had serious
shortcomings, and by no means the least of these is the motivation it gives you that makes you excessively selective
with your supporting evidence and blind to the conflicting
data.

        As we saw with creativity that calls for responsi-
bility, so with documentation. The writer in being himself
must not force the material he borrows from his sources into his own mould.

c. *Distorted Stereotypes:*
        There is a third problem which plagues the ethno-
historian. What is the relationship between the historical
character and his public image?

        Is there any way in which we can speak of, say, a
missionary or civil servant stereotype? If so whence do we
derive the prototype for that stereotype? I should think
this ought to come from the *historical* character. It would
of course, be no more than a stereotype *for that period of
history;* and there may be a sense in which we may speak
collectively of missionaries or civil servants in any given
period. Unfortunately both historical novelists and anthropologists often project the stereotype of one historical
period on another - to the present-day, for example. This
is credible to the public because of the existence of what
Calverton (1931: 1-37) calls *cultural compulsives* (something false, but accepted because people want to believe
it). In the last century there was a missionary stereotype
of the whalers and sandalwood traders, and quite a different stereotype of the church supporters of missions in Britain and America. These have to be evaluated on their contemporary evidence. Both of the stereotypes may have been
false, but their reconstruction is valid historical research,
and the ethnohistorian has to set one over against the other.
In much historical fiction and anthropological writing sometimes one of these stereotypes is projected to missionaries
in general at any point of time.[2] Ethnohistorical research
must expose this kind of projection, because there are two

serious fallacies in it: one relating to the stereotype itself, and the other to the point of time to which it is applied.

An historical novel like *Hawaii*, with a distorted
stereotype (even for its historic period), especially in the
hands of a powerful writer like Michener, tends to transfer
the stereotype by *intrusive coalescence* to the present-day
missionary of real life; who is thereby victimized by the
untrue stereotype. Even in the last century Michener's
whaler-sandalwooder missionary stereotype needed the corrective of the missionary promotional stereotype (the documents for which were available had he chosen to use them),
but in any case *the mind-set of 1820 cannot be transferred
to the 1960s.*

Whether Michener intended it or not, his own distorted stereotpye was transferred by his reading audience to
the missionary as a person, and thus the distroted period
stereotype became a doubly distorted generalized stereotype.
This intrusive coalescence has done much injury to both the
missionary cause and the missionary image; as a personal en-
quiry of random informants recently showed - more young
Americans have transferred their allegiance from missions to
other cross-cultutal welfare services for this reason than
for any other. The most common reason given was that Michener had exposed the true missionary character.   Even persons employed by the churches on their mission boards have
been known to 'swallow' the Michener fiction "hook, line and
sinker".[3]

A similar distorted stereotype has been established
by the salvage anthropologists, who should have known better.
Alarmed by the disappearance of pre-Christian material culture, they have blamed the missionaries for the destruction
of material culture. Had they studied the conversion process
as culture change they would have discovered that the destruction of religious paraphernalia was usually performed
by the convert himself, and this because he himself demanded
this evidence of the religious change. The anthropological
error of the salvage anthropologist was ignorance of the
basic phenomenology of religion and his static view of society. Thus the missionaries became victims of the barbed
wit of many undergraduate lecture rooms, where some profess-
ors are still bedecked with the frills of an anthropological
garment that has now generally been discarded. The stereotype came from a passing phase of anthropology. The sub-
disciplines of acculturation and applied anthropology have

brought anthropology into a new day, but the missionary
stereotype continues because of cultural compulsives - people want to believe ill of the missionary. This study is
not intended to be a missionary defence: it is an ethnohistorical attempt to research out the truth. The truth will
not be an absolute. It will be the truth as seen by the
whaler, the truth as seen by the colonial administrator, the
truth as seen by the missionary, and the truth as seen by
the islander - a synthesis of viewpoints about the truth,
giving us the mind-sets of the period being researched. It is
opposed to generalized stereotypes, that spring from intrusive coalescence and present-day cultural compulsives.

. . . .

Let us now turn to examine some of the forms we meet
in the literature of the Pacific, which have been responsible for the creation of these distorted stereotypes, and
which call for correction by means of ethnohistorical (literary, historical and anthropological) criticism. We shall
consider them under the following heads: (1) Literary Criticism and the *Noble Savage*, (2) Philosophy or History, (3)
Protestant Fears and Catholic Apologies, (4) Newspaper Controversies, (5) The Historical Novel and its Film Version
and (6) The Fictional Sermon.

1 *Literary Criticism and the Noble Savage*

Herman Melville's *Typee* was published by John Murray of London on the assurance that it was factual ethnography.[4] The basic narrative - his desertion from his ship
with a fellow sailor, their journey overland, and brief residence in Typee Valley, his injury and eventful escape - is
all probably true.[5] The description of the scenery and the
people is also reliable. The ethnological material, however,
is mostly borrowed from travellers who had visited the place
before him - Stewart,[6] Porter[7] and Langsdorff.[8] Sometimes
he rewrote it to suit his literary purposes, sometimes he
never even put it in his own words. He prevaricated about
the length of his stay on the island.[9]

From the very beginning, Miller points out (1962:19)
the accuracy of *Typee-Omoo* was challenged, yet some of the
best biographers still accept its general reliability, Lewis
Mumford among them.[10] Missionaries who knew the Pacific
called *Typee* "fiction in the guise of a travel book" (Anderson, 1966: 180-181).[11]

One reason for the popularity of Melville's *Typee*, was the supposition that it supplied a living case of the theory of the *Noble Savage*. Those who identified with the Rousseau tradition which "assumed the superiority over civilized society" saw in *Typee* "an idyl, a relaxed description of instinctual society".[12] To them, says Miller (*ibid*: 24) -

Like a medieval romance portraying the hero's quest for the Holy Grail, *Typee-Omoo* dramatizes the protagonist's search for an innocant and untouched Garden of Eden.

The idea of the noble savage had a long history in English literature, and has always been attractive to those with a 'gripe' against civilization and established institutions. Students of this philosophical persuasion have classified its writings in types - romantic naturalism, pseudo-classical and so on.[13] However the question which Typee leaves unanswered is why did Melville, having sung the praise of his new-found Paradise, seek so aggressively to escape its imprisonment, and reject the readiness of the Typees to incorporate him into their society by tattooing him? If this life was so much happier and more virtuous than civilization, why did he so greatly desire to return to the latter?

Not only was the notion of the noble savage a myth, but so too was the idea that Marquesan society was primitive and undeveloped.[14] Melville's noble savages were splendid physical types of beauty - both male and female. But they were not so innocent. The arts by which their beauty was achieved were highly institutionalized. For the male - the physical exercises and contests and training for the warrior life: and for the female - by the use of cosmetics and artifacts for removing superfluous hairs. Rather sophisticated 'savages' these!

The picture of supposed patriarchal rule is much over-simplified, and by contrasting it with western monarchy Melville rather shows up his personal 'hang-ups' and disqualifies himself as an ethnological observer. Like his model, Langsdorff, he found no form of government; but of course in reality it was there all the time. Indeed the communal organization, with tribal land tenure vested in a chief whose authority[15] was restricted by communal mechanisms, could hardly be defined as 'savage'. Patriarchal communism, almost without stealing and killing, "springing from innate goodness", just will not hold - even on a basis of Melville's own story. As for the supposed paradise without legalism - the Marquesan *tapu* system was as highly institutionalized and diversified as most legal systems.

The impression that these people lived in the pre-contact state of noble savagery is undermined when the Typee go to war against the Hapa with muskets; quite apart from their own highly developed technical skills - weaving mats, manufacturing and ornamenting *tapa* cloth and polishing drinking pots, canoe-building, wood and stone carving, ornamenting weapons of war, private ownership of trees, and storage pits against famine.

When it becomes apparent from literary criticism that Melville used the reports of earlier travellers for his descriptions, the question arises as to why he was so selective. Why did he by-pass their descriptions of systematically laid-out villages, of cultivated plantations, canoe-building, stone and wood-carving, and sophisticated stone fortifications? Unless the literary critic is correct in suggesting that it was "because they indicated a higher degree of civilization than he cared to assign to his Noble Savages".[16] The same critic also pointed out that his ethnographic knowledge was "insufficient to warn him that he was appropriating incorrect information when he borrowed his account of tattooing from Langsdorff and his naive religious ceremonies from Porter and Stewart" (Anderson, 1966:459).[17] We recall of course, that to the publisher this was posing as ethnography, not as fiction.

Despite the accuracy of the local colour, *Typee* is a story in which the writer was torn between his personal philosophy with respects to the evil of civilization and the suspense situation required by his adventure story. His noble savage on the one hand, and his fear of cannibalism on the other, are in a continual state of tension, with the result that the ethnology will not hold together. The people were indeed cannibals. It was this inner conflict within the book which struck Nathaniel Hawthorne when he reviewed *Typee* for the *Salem Advertiser* in 1846 (for text of review, see Rountree, 1972: 13). He summed up the book as a contrast of "gentleness of disposition" and "traits of savage fierceness"; and as a "system of innocence and peace" and a "smoked human head and half-picked skeleton".

The simplicity of the sex life of Typee, just will not do.[18] Melville stumbles over the polyandry. In point of fact it was a system of secondary husbands and wives, and a complicated arrangement requiring the agreement of the original couple, and cohabitation with the second restricted

by a system of tapus. Furthermore the same rights were extended to fathers-, brothers-, mothers- and sisters-in-law.
It looked highly promiscuous, but it was systematically developed and regulated (Handy, 1923: 98-102).

All this leaves us with a picture of Melville's literary methods. One does not have to question his literary
skill, and the reality of his island descriptions. But his
method of borrowing from other writers,[19] and doing so selectively to suit his philosophical and literary purposes,
leaves us with a literary composition of which the ethnographic value is very slight - all the more unsatisfactory
in that it broke into print on the public assurance of its
validity at this very point.

This does not mean that *Typee* and *Omoo* have no historical value; but that value can only be perceived by the
ethnohistorian in the light of this revelation of how he collected his data and assembled his books. Allowance has to be
made for his grudge against both civilization and formal religion, for *Typee* and *Omoo* are not so much evidence of Polynesian values as of Melville's own. They are more important
in the history of ideas, than in the history of the Pacific.
ific.

The tragedy of it all is that before this exposure,
anthropologists like Sir James Frazer, Edward Westermarck
and Marshall Sahlins had used Melville as a valid source
for ethnological data, and sometimes on the very things
which he was most unreliable.[20]

2 *Philosophy or History*

When Toynbee wrote his ten volume work, and called
it *A Study of History,* he described it as a "synoptic view
of history". I shall not comment on the merit of that work,
but I have problems over the methodology, in particular his
selection of data to illustrate his presuppositions as if
they had already been proved. As a social anthropologist
and a would-be ethnohistorian I look at *A Study of History*
as a philosophy of history rather than a history. In some
respects it affects me in the same way as did *The Prince,*
when I first read Machiavelli many years ago. One can read
these books for profit and pleasure and beg to disagree at
this point or that: but I want something more than this from
history.

Ashley Montague's significant volume of critical reviews of *A Study of History* (1956) - thirty of them by historians, geographers, sociologists and literary critics -
reveals that my unrest about the methodology is shared by
all kinds of specialists. All appreciated the literary effort and the fund of information, but all had trouble with
the methodology.[21]

This kind of history may be useful and important -
I will not argue about that - but it makes cooperation with
the social sciences difficult, and this has serious consequences for *ethnohistory* in particular. Ethnohistory,is not
a discipline but a process and a *methodology* (Washburn, 1961:
45), and if there is to be a philosophy one would expect it
to be derived from the data rather than *vice versa*. If generalizations or universals are to be sought or established
they should not be presupposed, unless put forward as hypotheses for testing - and one would expect some data base even
for this. This does not deny Toynbee his right to a philosophy of history, or the right to advocate it, or even to use
it as a grid for his writing; but if ethnohistory is to be
team work of historians and social scientists the philosophy
must be credible when tested by *all* the data, not selected
data; and if the anthropologist is to be satisfied then a
universalistic philosopher has to come to satisfactory terms
somehow with ethnic diversity. Neither is it adequate for
Toynbee to dismiss the Polynesians and Nomads, as his critic
in the London *Horizon* put it "as arrested civilizations which
are pinned to the precipice, by a special kind of misjudge-
ment, in a state of life-in-death" (*ibid:* 23).

This is not just a disagreement which I have with
Dr. Toynbee over an interpretation, it is methodological.
It could be argued that these peoples had proved themselves
competent to survive for centuries in the most severe and
isolated environments of the world. This achievement, which
is as great in its own way as building temples or sky-scra-
pers, is not to be bypassed or dismissed. In any case when
a supposed law is stated, any exceptions need all the more
treatment and documentation, because the validity of the law
itself is at stake with every exception to it.

According to Montague's computation *A Study of History* has over three million words on 6,290 pages (averaging
40 lines) and 19,000 entries in 332 pages of index.   The
Polynesian race is disposed of (except for a short note on
Easter Island in another volume) with a microscopic fifteen
lines (Vol. III: 3). There is one single verifiable fact -

viz., that they were great navigators. Thirty percent of
the apparently begrudged fifteen lines is devoted to ana-
logies - Minoans, Vikings, Lotus-Eaters and Doasyoulikes,
Arctic hunters' seals and prairie hunters' bisons, all of
which imply unproved presuppositions and a set of equations
which are highly speculative to say the least. No data is
presented and no attempt is made at documentation. These
fifteen lines have no awareness of time, space, cultural
diversity or achievement and are unlikely to satisfy either
the Pacific ethnologist or historian.

        "Doasyoulikes" forsooth! Shades of the "noble sav-
age"! The place of individual freedom in Polynesian society,
its satisfactions opportunities and controls is highly institutionalized (Mead, 1961: 480ff; Grattan, 1948: 10-24;
Tippett, 1971: 152-154). It never was do-as-you-like. The
proficiency of navigation and length of the voyages, their
going and coming, even for trade into Melanesia (Tippett,
1968:8, 9,83-4, 103-4, 114, 179) through Fiji; the highly
developed political structures and architectural achieve-
ments which in some islands indicate two thousand years of
developing civilization (Suggs, 1961: 220-245); the skilled
craftsmanship, manifested in their pre-contact domestic
utensils of war; their oral traditions, music, chants, and
dances: all these things of which we have some surviving
evidence, mark the Polynesian civilization as one which en-
dured and is worthy of serious study. Under no circumstances can it be bypassed as "an arrested civilization"
which "degenerated into [an] incarnation of the Lotus-Eaters
and the Doasyoulikes" as we are told in *A Study of History*
(III.3). The Pacific (like the desert and the polar ice
cap) are limiting factors, which offer a laboratory-like
testing ground that calls for specific adaptive skills,
which are themselves a cultural achievement. In other words
I dispute the supposed validity of universals or generalizations or exceptions when the environments in which they are
tested, are themselves variables. The civilization that
developed navigational science in the West after the Renais-
sance and down to the XIXth Century technological changes,
had very little edge over those which developed without
iron, and with no more than the raw materials of the Pacific
itself. One of the greatest navigators of western history,
Captain James Cook, who proved himself in that same Pacific
'laboratory' in that amazing ship the *Endeavour*, had a craft
twenty feet shorter (Villiers, 1967: 84) than the Fijian
war canoe, *Rusa i Vanua*, which pioneer missionary Thomas
Williams measured (1860: 75). The *Thaddeus* (Judd, 1964: 7),
which transported the first American missionaries from

Boston to Hawaii in a voyage of 164 days was 33 feet shorter
than this Fijian war canoe. Such a canoe carried a crew of
fifty and up to 300 warriors if needed,[22] and Toynbee's
judgement of their inability to deal with the Pacific envi-
ronment "with any margin of security or ease" is completely
out of *historic sense*. The *Rusa i Vanua*, or the *Loba ki
Tonga* (which was fifteen inches longer than the *Endeavour*
(Williams, 1860: 75) and was built, as its name implies, for
service over the deep sea between Fiji and Tonga) were sailing the Pacific at the same time as the *Thaddeus*. They com-
peted well with sandalwooders, beche-de-mer traders and
whalers and operated on different scientific principles for
capturing the wind in their sails. If they required larger
crews to handle the giant sails, (the masts were sixty feet,
and the yards eighty to ninety) they produced greater speed
and were vastly superior in tacking. For hundreds of years
they mastered the winds and currents of the very much mis-
named Pacific, with as good a "margin of security and ease"
as the western ships of the same period.

Toynbee set me thinking about these things, but he
is typical of many other writers who in their search for
theoretical generalizations tend to dispose of significant
evidence of particular situations that don't quite fit their
generalizations. I do not wish to discuss his ten volumes
or his philosophy *per se* -nor am I competent to do so.   I
just feel bad about the Polynesian, the Esquimo and the No-
mad, particularly the former. Somehow I feel there is an
urgent function for ethnohistorical research here. From
archaeology, oral traditions and documents of the contact
period a reliable picture has to be reconstructed, and the
gullible western public has to see the Pacific of the contact
period in its historic sense. Furthermore it is a great pity
when such brilliant literary skill departs from historical
fact and ethnological values for purposes of a philosophical
presupposition. We have to allow for the relativity of space
and time, and we have to protest against the extremes to
which this abuse of ethnohistory can lead us, or we end with
monstrosities like James Michener's *Hawaii*, about which more
under the discussion of the historical novel.

3 *Protestant Fears and Catholic Apologies*

The narrative of the *Tahiti Affair* has been written
up by numerous scholars, and the chronology of incidents
from the 1790s to the 1860s is available in secondary
sources (Ward, 1948; Williamson, 1946; Langdon, 1968; Brooks,

1941; Rhodes,1937 &c.). The most important collection of
primary sources was assembled by George Pritchard, and by
itself is worth a book by an objective historian.[23]   The
French need for colonies after the Napoleonic period, and
also naval posts and coaling stations, over against the
British policy of minium intervention during the period of
missionary expansion settled the fate of British missions
in what ulitmately became French Polynesia. The best documented account is probably Ward (1948: 117-163). Without
going over this well-beaten ground again I merely want to
point up two aspects of the struggle between French Catholics and British Protestants, which bear on the interpretation of the documents. First I press for full recognition
of the fear, approaching panic, with which the Protestants
viewed "the Bishop's gunboat" and their suspicion of France,
which repeatedly shows up in Protestant inter-mission correspondence, and the bad relations which stemmed from the
Tahiti Affair. The second matter is the validity of Roman
Catholic writing about Protestant missions round the mid-
century. I want to take a hard look at their use of primary
sources and raise the question of whether this writing was
not historical at all but apologetical.

(a)   The Protestant Fear:
        Events in Tahiti moved rapidly to a head between
1838 and 1842 (Ward, 1948: 127-137). From the first action
of Commodore Dupetit-Thouars in 1838 to his establishment of
a provisional government and its ratification by France in
1843, Protestant missionary emotions were registered in private correspondence. On August 14, 1838 James Buller wrote
from New Zealand to his Society in London. A copy of the
letter is in his *Journal* at the Turnbull Library in Wellington. He discusses Roman Catholic attempts at edging the
Protestants out of their locations throughout the Pacific,
and names Tonga among other places. He writes about Bishop
Pompalier and his offsiders, and his fears for New Zealand.[24]

        On January 31, 1839 he raised the matter again. He
was upset about their dissemination of information in his
area that "they have a large ship coming, which is full of
clothing to be given to their proselytes" (underlining his).
On April 20, 1841 he recorded in his *Journal* that Father
Petit was said to have "told the natives whom he met with,
that the British Government will take away their land and
make slaves of them". This rumour was so wide-spread that
the Governor wrote a letter making a public statement of
denial. But the matter did not end there, for exactly three
months later Buller prepared a three-page report about his

dispute with Fr. Petit, and eventually he wrote a twelve-
page letter to his London Committee.

From Hawaii also we have the same feelings and there
are many sources which could be cited. The letters and
journal of Cochrane Forbes, for example, housed at the HMCS
Archives and Library in Honolulu. In 1837 he complained of
Jesuit priests being secretly landed (12) and a French merchant's intrigues (14), and in 1845 he was worrying about
the Tahiti Affair (197-198).

The Tahiti Affair became a kind of 'bad dream' for
Protestant missionaries and continued to be so for many
years. They believed it reflected the French policy at
large and the Roman Catholic method of infiltration, and
both of these beliefs still remain to be disproved. An interesting set of Waterhouse letters exists[25] - personal letters to relatives at home - which includes one written from
Tonga where Waterhouse stopped *en route* to Fiji. It is
dated Nov. 4, 1850 and describes the Roman Catholic priests
trying to establish a rival chief as King. King George took
the matter in hand and the priests said it was only a joke,
but the letter reflects the Protestant feelings. The system
of cutting in on another mission by supporting rival chiefs
was not unknown, and the Protestants regarded it as no joke.
Waterhouse, and I presume he echoed the Tongan missionaries
at the point, felt the priests were trying to embroil two
Tongan rivals in war so a French man-of-war might be called
in. Right or wrong, this was their fear.

In the same file of correspondence, another letter
dated Aug. 30, 1852 (Waterhouse/Padman) shows how the Tahiti
Affair still determined the thinking of Protestant missionaries after a decade, and how they irked under the refusal
of the British Government to take action in the Pacific, but
never gave up hope that they would do so.
The French are going to make another Tahiti Affair of
Feejee, we fear. The priests expect two ships-of-war
daily, and then the natives will be converted to the
Holy Church. The priests do not tabu war or scarcely
anything that is bad. What would the Adelaide Papists
say to this? They tell the most awful lies.
We hear that the British are going to take possession
of Feejee, and hope it is so. If the priests gain their
point our heads will be worth very little. I would sooner
trust ten cannibals than the Papists, but their conduct
makes me conclude them to be worse than any heathen I
ever met with or read of. The Lord Save us from Popery.

[This letter has to be read in the historic sense. It was
written under the extreme tension of an incident and its
bias is part of the evidence. Things at Levuka in 1852 and
indeed until the conversion of Cakobau, the cannibal King,
in 1854 were quite dynamic. As a personal letter to one not
involved, it is an important index of feeling.]

          One situation passed, only for another to emerge.
Cakobau became Protestant in 1854 and some of his old enemies became involved with Catholic action in one way or
another. New Caledonia had been annexed by the French in 1853
and the Fijians and missionaries knew the French war-ships
had a port just over the horizon. In Royce's *Journal*[26] (May
14, 1857) we find him disturbed by a Roman Catholic alliance
with the heathen Fijians at Solevu (an area on which Cakobau
always had to keep an eye). The Catholic priests were
threatening to send to New Caledonia for a French ship-of-
war. The fear of the French was not only with the missionaries. The Fijians also shared the feeling, otherwise no
persuasive powers would have produced enough Fijian unity to
bring about the offer of Cession to Britain in the late fifties.[27]

          About a month before the signing of the first offer
of Cession, Royce discussed the step in his *Journal* (Nov. 5).
His concern was protection from "French intrigue with its
Popish retinue". "Of this," he said "we shall be afraid and
look out for. We don't forget that New Caledonia is French,
and Tahiti is French, and if Feejee should be French, God
forbid the calamity." Six months after the Offer was formally signed, he wrote again in his *Journal* -
     Alarm is again entertained for Tonga. The French are
     once more annoying George Tubou. No doubt the priests
     are at the bottom of the affair, and perhaps it will
     terminate in a second Tahiti, but God forbid that such
     a tradegy be again enacted. We hear also that a French
     man-of-war is sent to the Loyalty Islands to interro-
     gate English missionaries there . . . .

          Among the WMS Papers in the Turnbull Library[28] is a
report written by Horsley as late as 1868 in which he be-
moans the opening of new Roman Catholic stations in Fiji and
the distribution of twelve Catholic missionaries. The same
fear continues -
     By threats of French men-of-war they endeavour to frighten
     the chiefs out of their profession of Protestantism into
     Popery; and by directing their efforts more particu-
     larly among our people rather than among the heathen

they hope to injure our work and strengthen their
own..... (5).
The fear is not so much Catholic expansion as penetration
into already won Protestant areas.

    Captain Hood of the *Fawn* was in Samoa in 1862 and
felt the tension with which people watched the French ship-
ping. Every boat from Tahiti was suspect (1863: 83, 93).
The chiefs feared a repetition of the Tahiti Affair (41) for
the same reasons. This captain had respect for both Catholic and Protestant missionaries (41, 167, 199-200, 207) and
contrasted them with the sandalwooders (204). He had seen
and approved the comity practised by the Protestant missions
and wondered why it could not include the Roman Catholics.
This may well have solved the problem. It was the loss of
Protestant converts to Catholicism which worried the Protestant missionaries.

(b) Apology or History:
    I had been reading Marshall's *Christian Missions:
Their Agents, Their Method and Their Result* (1862); more
particularly chapters 5 and 6 in the second volume, which
concern Australia, New Zealand and Oceania. I believe I was
looking for a standard Roman Catholic history of missions -
something like Piolet's cyclopedic series at the turn of the
century, but a little earlier and closer to the action. I
wanted to know what the Church did and how it spread, and to
see the vital church growth statistics. But these things I
did not find. I found instead the Protestant missionary under fire. How was one to interpret Marshall? I eventually
decided that, despite its historical format, it really was
not history at all. I believe it is an *apology*.

    The author was not structuring a reconstruction on a
basis of events and sequences, but writing to a theme and
arguing a case. He was not looking at whole events but se-
lecting cases to illustrate his points. Quite apart from
what one might think of the rightness or wrongness of his
case, the methodology is apologetical, not historical. The
hundred pages of chapter five, for example, actually have
very little history at all, no historical survey, no discussion of related issues, no historical context, and no evaluation of sources. It has a single apologetic theme - to
contrast Protestant and Catholic missions, condemning the
former, vindicating the latter - with the documentation very
discriminatingly selective in the sense that non-supporting
data is not even considered. I am not suggesting that this
book should never have been written; but simply that we see

it for what it really is, and not be misguided into thinking
it is history. Let us now examine the subject matter.

The theme is stated at the beginning of the chapter.
Australia and New Zealand and the islands represent that
part of the world where Protestantism preceded the old
Church; so let us see, the writer argues, what Protestant
mission does by its results. Thereafter the author combs
Protestant and secular literature for all the discouraging
references to indicate the bad state of the land and the
Church. There is fallacious presupposition here, namely,
that no allowance whatever is made for the multicausal
factors that arise in the program of settlement and coloni-
zation. Reformed Religion is judged on the basis of (1) the
land speculation of the missionaries, contrasting it with the
Roman Catholic doctrine of poverty, but ignoring the whole
question of the Roman Catholic Church as itself a land owner
(Marshall II, 1862: 100-118); (2) the civilizing and trading
approach of the Protestant missionary and his colonialism,[29]
but without reference to French colonialism and the British/
French struggle (*ibid:* 119-143) (which he could not have
avoided in a history); (3) the disruptive character of denominationalism,[30] (*ibid:* 144-149), without reference to the
fact that in the Pacific the disruption came with the later
arrival of the Roman Catholics; and (4) an attack on the
personal character of the Protestant missionary[31] in contrast with the holier Roman Catholic standards (*ibid:* 149-
163). Not one of these claims will stand up to historical
analysis. Not one is even a simple 'black and white issue'-
the causative variables are legion. Not one of these claims
can be generalized. There were good and bad, successes and
failures among all missionary groups. On some questions
like the acquisition of land, the missionaries themselves had
most divergent views. Of course we have here any amount of
raw material for critical historical analysis, but Marshall
does not use it that way. He argues a brief for the Roman
Catholics. No doubt he was convinced of the truth of his
case, but it will not bear historical analysis. Indeed it
is so manifestly ridiculous that one has to look round for
some reason to understand its credibility to any reading
public.

One is reminded of a most critical passage in Professor G.C. Henderson's *Fiji and the Fijians, 1838-1853,* in
which this historian takes a Roman Catholic writer to task
for precisely the same kind of writing under the guise of
history.[32] One must find a reason for this type of literary
fantasy. One recalls that the Roman Catholic Bishop once

made the observation that the Roman Catholics had arrived
in the Pacific just a little too late. It must have been a
strange experience for them to have found the Pacific a hot-
bed of dynamic change, with people-movements into Protestantism going on in one island after another (Tippett, 1971).
By the time Pope Gregory had signed the *Omium Gentium* under
which the Society of Mary was approved (1836) there had been
people movements in Tahiti, Paumotus, Tubuai, Rapa, Manahiki
and the Cook Islands, all the Tongan Islands, and movements
had begun in New Zealand and Samoa. Fr. Batallion, the
first Vicar Apostolic of Central Oceania landed on Wallis
Island in December 1836 (Rhodes, 1937: 286), and Bishop Pom-
pallier arrived at Hokianga with two priests in 1838 (*ibid:*
291-292), by which time the Maori movements were in 'full
swing' and another had begun in Fiji. The Roman Catholics
were indeed too late. We have seen how their cause became
tied up with French foreign policy and they never produced
the evangelistic thrust of the Protestants, and their gains
if not by French diplomacy were by penetration into Protestant areas by attachment to tribal politics. As the Protestants had won the chiefly systems this Catholic penetration was not so effective - only frightening.

    This must have created a great problem for Roman
Catholic promotion with her missionary supporters over the
world. How could the lack of Roman Catholic growth be accounted for in the face of Protestant expansion? This promotional problem called for an apologetic, lest the faith-
ful think there really must be something in Protestism after
all. The apologetic therefore is to argue the superiority
of Catholicism in spite of appearances, and to question the
depth and sincerity of the Protestant responses and missionaries. In presenting their brief they 'stacked' the evidence by selection as a lawyer argues his case. This is at
least a more charitable explanation of the uncomfortable
facts, which otherwise must be condemned as historical manipulation. The Question is still very much open, and my
suggestion is admittedly speculation, but every historian
working on the sources of this kind from the Pacific, from
the Tahiti Affair onwards for about 30 years, has to deal
with this literary problem, and decide whether or not his
material is reliable. And let me in fairness add, that this
is not a one-sided affair. There are a few almost forgotten
Protestant documents which come under the same scrutiny, but
they belonged to a later period.

    Neither am I speaking of only religious disagree-
ments. Wherever we are dealing with controversies, and one

side determines to defend itself by attacking the other by
evidential selection, we have to ask the question - is this
history or apologetics? And to answer that we have to (1)
determine the motive of the writer and (2) identify the
audience.

4 Newspaper Controversies

A great deal of Pacific history, especially of the
popular type, is reconstructed from newspaper reports and
controversies of the last century. Indeed many subjects
simply cannot be done by any other means. This calls for
some kind of critical appraisal of the reliability of this
kind of data base, and both the problems and the potential
have to be identified. When the writer did his master's
thesis on the South Pacific Labour Trade he used seven different secular Australian newspapers, one from New Zealand
and four from Fiji and three different British reviews quite
apart from religious journals. The data from these sources
provided a most important elaboration for that collected
from official reports, correspondence of public figures, and
both primary and secondary printed sources. Without the
newspaper sequences many important aspects would have been
missed and the economic background certainly could not have
been reconstructed. Lorimer Fison's Fiji news columns in
the Sydney Morning Herald, for example, contained much material available nowhere else. Nevertheless the use of newspaper material is not just 'plain sailing'.

Newspapers, like their contributors, have their sympathies and biases, which may be religious, political or
ethnic. They may be progressive or conservative. On a public issue one paper has to be set off against another. Thus,
for example, if you build your writing on editorials from a
newspaper known to favour a policy of, say, indentured labour for economic reasons, you are more or less obligated to
test it against, say, the reports of island depopulation due
to the trade as presented in a religious newspaper. Eventually you may come out on one side - for economic development or for social welfare - but at least you must recognize
that there are conflicting issues, and the contemporary primary sources may favour one or the other. This is easier
when the material is found in a controversy running through
a single newspaper, and when you have access to the full
series in a library - provided you do work through the whole
controversy. If the case against some missionary practice
in the islands, say, is presented in some free-thinker

publication and responded to in a missionary journal, one
simply must have the binary evidence to make an evaluation.
This applies not only to newspaper controversies, but also
to travel books which supply much of our anthropological
data of the contact period. Thus, for example, one should
never form a judgement with respect to Christianity in Tahiti
on Kotzebue alone, without setting him off against, let us
say, Charles Darwin.[33]

Now, this may seem all very obvious, and yet it has
to be stated again and again, because the majority of evidence of culture contact in the Pacific found in anthropological texts of a general nature, in anti-colonialist publications and in popular history and journalism are one-sided
statements of this kind. No body of people was more involved
in the controversies than the missionaries. No body of
people paid a greater price collectively for the cause they
fought. No body of people has been more maligned in printer's ink. Therefore it seems to me now, without arguing a
case for them, that we might take a look at some of those
controversies with which they became involved, for these men
were also very self-defensive and 'pulled no punches' themselves. When they attacked they received responding fire;
when they were slandered, sooner or later they responded
with spirit; yet historians and anthropologists have paid
scant attention to their defences. It has always seemed unfair to me, that present-day writers will cite adventurers,
travellers and blackbirding super-cargoes freely and yet
often dismiss the missionary as biased. Here we seem to
struggle again with the cultural compulsive - the will to
think ill of the missionary. I am not arguing a case for
the missionary, but simply an appeal that both sides be investigated. After all a controversy is not a report.

With their parishioners the missionaries had the pul-
pit; but in the outside world the only weapon they had was
the pen. They could not dispose of drunken whalers and sandalwooders with weapons of war, they could not employ the
mean tricks used against them, they had a high regard for
truth and morality and had no weapons for fighting lies and
prostitution (which was not always voluntary): their only
weapon was the pen and the evidence they have left is worth
consideration.

(a) Fison and the Labour Trade:
The British Naval officers failed in their attempts
at dealing with the labour trade, because (among other
things) the colonial courts would not accept the evidence of

a Pacific islander against that of a renegade white.[34]   Led
by Lorimer Fison, the missionaries formed their own network
for gathering information about the trade.   With the aid of
men like Langham, Codrington and Inglis[35] from all over the
Southwest Pacific, Fison launched his attack in the Australian press.   Before long the readers of the *Daily Telegraph*
and *The Age* saw some startling exposures.[36]   Fison was a
bush lawyer in a way.   He drew fire.   His opponents thought
to silence him by demanding facts.   He gave them more than
they wanted - the names of ships, captains and statistics
of those murdered during and after the kidnapping incidents.
The Australian public now heard of the *Carl*, the *Margaret
Chessell*, the *Kate Grant* and the *Flirt;* and of the names
Ross Lewin and Dr. Murray, and the case of Mount and Morris.
This will take the newspaper researcher into the kidnapping
trials, and all kinds of other historical issues, for instance, the murder of Bishop Patteson and the missionaries
of Erromanga.[37]   Much can be learned from the books on the
trade, but for the dynamics of the struggle, and government
tightening of recruiting regulations, the researcher has to
go to the Australian press and follow it from start to finish.   The narrative of the South Seas labour trade as Fison
reconstructed it at the time, published first under the nom
de plume *Outis* appeared in a series of nine long articles
in the *Daily Telegraph* in 1873.   Another aspect of the case
requires following a controversy in a rival paper, *The Age*
about the same time.   Ramifications were felt in the House
of Commons in the debate on the Cession on Fiji.   There are
also a number of journals left by recruiters for their side
of the story (e.g. Restieaux MSS in the Turnbull Library;
photo copies in Latrobe Library, Melbourne) and correspondence (Walker, 1878).   For the later recruiters, who operated
after the reforms due to Fison's campaign, some good published reminiscences are available (Wawn, 1893; Rannie,1912).

(b)   Ellis and Kotzebue:
          The controversy over the labour trade was one in
which the missionaries were taking the initiative.   More
often they were defending themselves.   Some of these defences were conducted in a masterly fashion.   I mean they took
the arguments of their critics and laid them bare, point by
point.   As I said above, this was their only weapon, and
they ceratinly knew how to use it.   The Rev. William Ellis,
for example, whose superior knowledge of Tahiti cannot be
questioned was manifestly infuriated by Otto von Kotzebue's
second travel series, with respect to his account of things
at Tahiti and his criticisms of the missionaries and Tahitian Christians.   The work was published first in German

but excerpts were translated into English and widely circulated. Eventually the whole book was translated and widely
noticed in the press. This was too much for Ellis. He responded with an entire volume of 163 pages, and a title almost as long - *A Vindication of the South Seas Missions
from the Misrepresentations of Otto von Kotzebue, Captain
of the Russian Navy, with an Appendix*. He begins with the
inaccuracy of Kotzebue's map of Matavai Bay and the mislo-
cation of places put to the east instead of the southwest,
then the errors of his nautical calculations, and a comment
on his failure to explore far from his ship. A true Calvinist of his period, he points out that there were no "black
wooden crosses" in the "church-yard at Matavai" or any other
crosses except one in another place left by a Spanish navi-
gator, or in Catholic locations. Then he starts to pull
apart Kotzebue's philology showing among other things that
he was designating the King "dog of all dogs." Thence he
turns to the Kotzebue version of the marriage pattern which
left him standing badly with Pomare's Queen. The Russian
had picked up an English seaman as his interpreter and the
communication was bad. By the tenth page the reader is left
in extreme doubt about the value of Kotzebue's scientific
work at all. Certainly no anthropologist could take the
Russian as a serious primary source for the period of culture contact without following all these points one by one.
Unconsciously perhaps by his very criticisms Ellis has fur-
nished us with a valuable analysis of a great many points of
ethnology and history, whether we bother about it as a missionary apology or not.

The 18-page appendix, by the way, is devoted not to
the Russian but to Captain Beechy's *Narrative of a Voyage...
&c...* which had appeared in the interim. Beechey had cited
Ellis, and Ellis had some further comments to make. Apparently
he used the occasion of demolishing Kotzebue to deal a little
more gently with a fellow Englishman. The 'spin-offs' of some
of these controversies can become highly valuable primary
sources.

(c) Dunn and Stuart:
In the earlier part of the last century the time
factor was a serious one. Sometimes a ship would visit an
island where the people had become Christian since its previous visit. The supply of women to meet the biological urges
of the crew having been thus cut off the captain might have
trouble with his men. Often this led to unpleasant press
copy when the ship returned to its home port. The argument would be a circumlocution of the truth - an anti-

missionary report of some kind. It might be a year before
the missionaries concerned saw the report and maybe nearly
as long again before the paper published their reply. Unless the newspaper file has some kind of index the researcher
may never find the reply, and so he cites the critic's evidence un-challenged. Sometimes these issues were highly
political and of international significance. Let me cite
an example. The *New York Herald* published a letter signed,
David Stuart, on Feb. 16, 1856, purporting to have been
written from 'Feejee' giving a long list of crimes committed
by the natives against whites and accusing the missionaries
of involvement in them. This ties up with a very important
open issue in Fijian history, normally spoken of as the
American Claims Case. It involves Consul Williams and Com-
mander Boutwell, and several other important U.S. personal-
ities; and deals with an encounter between the U.S. and a
native monarch, which had major consequences thereafter.

The reply did not appear until nine months later,
when it came from Captain Thomas Dunn of the barque *Dragon*
of Salem. He provided one of the most important letters in
Fijian history, including the correspondence between Boutwell
and the Chiefs, a letter to Williams, a protest from Cakobau
(witnessed by two Englishmen) and another letter from Capt.
Magruder of the U.S. Navy. This appeared in the *New York
Herald,* Nov. 9, 1856. This was reprinted as a 16-page pamphlet in England. By no means the least important thing
about this collection of highly significant facts is that
they were assembled by an American sea-captain. Some day
the American Claims Case will have to be properly investigated, and this newspaper controversy will have to figure
prominently in it.

(d) Cargill and Dillon:
One of the romantic but questionable figures of Pacific history was Chevalier Dillon, who breaks into Fijian
history with the notorious Charlie Savage, who organized the
Bauans in the art of western warfare with muskets.[38] Dillon
published a pamphlet in England in December 1841. I have not
seen this pamphlet but I know something of its contents from
a reply to it by David Cargill, who had returned to England
for a break about this time.[39] It is important that the researcher on the history of Tonga locate a copy of the pamphlet Dillon published, because it discusses the rebellion of
the heathen party against Tubou in 1837, and in which Dillon
accused the missionaries of being involved. On the contrary
Cargill's reply indicated that Dillon himself was involved,
which is more like the Dillon we know in history.

Cargill had lived for almost two years in Tonga before his removal to Fiji in 1835. He understood and spoke the Tongan language, being a linguist by training. His reply to the attack demanded a validation of Tubou's chieftaincy, and this is one of the most important cultural elements in the reply. It also has a few interesting references to Fijians in Tonga, in fact the King's rival had Fijian connections. Dillon having accused the Christians of involvement in the war, much of Cargill's reply concerns the nature of Tongan warfare and the Tongan method of prosecuting it. Cargill shows how Dillon was himself involved in arming the rebels. He also mentions the French and the rejection of the French Bishop's request to reside on the island. Although for perfect clarity the researcher needs to have the original pamphlet at hand for the reply to be perfectly meaningful, it does throw light on many points of wider concern in Pacific history and ethnology, by no means the least is the succession to the chieftaincy.

Apart from the need of seeing both sides of an argument, these controversies demonstrate the way in which the missionaries, in the process of serious defence recorded much material of great historical and ethnological value, that is worth researching for its own sake. The tendency of anthropologists to by-pass missionary documents has been to their own great loss.

5 *The Historical Novel*

There ought to be a set of rules about writing an historical novel. If Dorothy Sayers says it is not fair for the writer of a mystery story to put a trick of undisclosed evidence over the reader in the solution of the mystery, there ought to be some restrictions also on the liberty of the historical novelist. In my High School days I was developing a regular taste for historical novels, thanks to Alexandre Dumas, Stanley Weyman, Walter Scott and Charles Reade. But now I have come to believe that to make a living, and to produce a constant flow of novels the historical novelist is inevitably a sloppy historian - unless he limits his field of history. As Jane Aiken Hodge says - "If you betray your reader once, he will never trust you again" (1972:18). How true!

No novel ever betrayed the reader more than James Michener's interminable *Hawaii*, which by length, structure and discontinuity is really four or five novels, each one of

them requiring some years of research. The first part is
before its time. The archaeologists are only beginning to
get the picture of the life and structure of prehistoric
Polynesia. And the anthropologists have yet not adequately
penetrated the phenomenology of pre-Christian religion for
fertile minds to work it into novels. The depicting of pre-
Christian religion in *Hawaii*, like that of its Hawaiian Calvinism is a miserable failure. But I must confine myself to
the second section, "From the Farm of Bitterness" because I
have not the competence to discuss the whole book. From
page 142 to page 447 is enough anyway.

Opposite the Table of Contents is a neat trick. It
reads -
> This is a novel. It is true to the spirit and his-
> tory of Hawaii, but its characters, the families,
> the institutions and most of the events are imagin-
> ary......
I shall have no time or space to deal with more than that
literary trick in terms of the planting of Christianity in
Hawaii.

"Sooner or later" says Hester Burton (1972:18),
"the writer of historical fiction has to make quite clear to
himself where history ends and where fiction may legitimately
begin." Of course, the moment one does that he imprisons
himself. His freedom and creativity are confined within
those accepted limits. The second part of the novel *Hawaii*,
is confined within the following limits. It is a story
about a real place - Hawaii. It is set in a precise chronological position, commencing in the third decade of the
nineteenth century. It concerns a precise, named missionary
body - the American Board of Commissioners for Foreign Missions - who did establish a mission at that time and in that
place. The missionaries came from New England and were Cal-
vinists. Let that suffice for a start.

These limiting factors impose a regular straight-
jacket on the novelist. The moment he nominates the ABCFM
he has no free play with its structure and organization, and
if he brings in its recruitment officer - as he does - there
is no possible escape from the conclusion that Eliphalet
Thorn is Samuel Worcester, and immediately he is in trouble.
Worcester is a well-documented character. In his time he
created a great many archival records, left a book of sermons, has been researched by a biographer. Michener is in
trouble for putting a cad like Thorn in place of Worcester.

He is historically not true to type. The problem arises
from Michener's nomination of a real missionary body rather
than a fictitious one. He cannot argue that the institution
(ABCFM) is imaginary when the name is identical to the only
missionary society that moved into that land in that period
of history.

        He has aggravated his own problem by steering as
close to the wind as possible. The historic variations in
the details are so slight as to give the impression that
they are the real thing. The *Thaddeus* is the linguistically
and euphoniously similar *Thetis,* the tonnage 230 instead of
241, the length only six feet different, the fictional establishment of the mission is only one year varied from the
actual one, the fictional voyage was through the Straits of
Magellan instead of the Straits of Le Maire, otherwise the
same route: all just different enough to protect the novelist as fictional, but close enough to convince the reader it
is the real thing. One doesn't mind such fictionalizations
in a novel; but the more they give the air of historicity,
the more dangerous it becomes for the writer to depart from
actuality in events of historical importance. Michener has
a Hawaiian on board. Actually there were three. This Hawaiian becomes one of the key figures in the story. His prototype would seem to be Obookiah, but the real Obookiah died
in Connecticut. Well, you say, a story is just a story: so
what?

        A random sample shows many young Americans believe
the book is basically true, including the things which are
quite imaginary and quite unfair to the early missionaries.
The following are four of the fictions which are commonly
accepted by a large part of the American public today as a
result of this novel.
1.   It is believed that the missionaries were icono-
     clasts, destroying the religious places and para-
     phernalia, the taboos and the old religion. In
     point of fact this happened before they arrived,
     and the Hawaiians were a demoralized people with-
     out their old religious supports when the pioneers
     arrived, and the most rapid rate of population de-
     cline was between 1780 and 1820.[40]
2.   It is believed that Abner Hale was typical of the
     leader of the mission party. Many say this was
     Hiram Bingham. Abner Hale is the most unreal and
     phony thing in the whole book, yet he is absolute-
     ly credible to the anti-puritan and permissive peo-
     ple who have read the book or seen the film version.

3.   It is believed that the Hawaiian Mission was a
      failure and that the missionaries had no real re-
      sponse to their preaching. On the contrary Hiram
      Bingham used to preach to 2000 people at a time.
      Furthermore the indigenous church grew so well that
      the mission was no longer needed after 1863.

4.   It is believed that the Hawaiian pre-Christian
      religion and social life was a way of love. This
      is false as the early sources demonstrate. The
      positive gains from accepting Christianity are
      largely ignored.

Michener claims he wrote a novel, that the characters and institutions were fictional, but when he set the
limits of historicity in a true institution in a real country at a precise point of time, and tried to be true to what
he saw as "the spirit and history of Hawaii", he was asking
to be believed. And after five or six years of questioning
young Americans on what they believe about this book, and
being myself shocked at the audience reaction to the film
version of the story, I can only say how sorry I am that the
book was ever written. It is certainly taken as history,
whatever Michener himself intended. It is prescribed as a
text book in the schools and has a tremendous impact on public opinion and on missionary recruitment. Two factors contributed to it becoming a best seller:[41] (1) it appeared
about the time Hawaii became an American State, when the public suddenly realized its ignorance of the place, and (2) it
found a response in the current mood of American anti-puri-
tanism and permissiveness that have characterized the fiction
of the country in the sixties. People were reading back into history their feelings of today. It was no longer history
but an escape mechanism for their feelings - our cultural
compulsives again.

A few years ago I set out to make a thorough investigation of the problem of the historical novel, using
Hawaii as a case study. It left me shocked as an ethnohistorian, appalled as a human being, and completely disturbed
that a novel could be so believed at the points of its departure from historicity. I know no other kind of writing
which carries such grave responsibilities for the author. I
shall never again be able to read a historical novel with
pleasure or confidence.

6 *The Fictional Sermon*

The historical novelists and journalists have given

the early Calvinistic missionaries a bad name for their preaching. I have no doubt there were some bad preachers among them, but the real form and subject matter of their preaching has never been properly researched by these writers. It has always seemed right to me that a writer should get to know a social institution before he builds it into his story. This is specially so when it can be used as a literary device that is open for manipulation. The functional sermon is certainly open for abuse. A writer can implant all kinds of intellectual biases and presuppositions into it, and his sloppy research can be easily hidden in the narrative. An historical novelist has no justification in employing the fictional sermon unless he can document that such sermons were historical at the time about which he is writing. I do not deny a writer the right to use the fictional sermon: what I do deny him is the right to use it as a cover-up for sloppy research.

Most great sermons which have led to dramatic response have been preserved. The missionary sermons which led to the founding of the London Missionary Society and the American Board of Commissioners of Foreign Missions - the two Calvinist bodies that opened up the Pacific as a mission field - have been preserved in their full texts. In any case enough Calvinist sermons of the period exist to show their literary structure and hermeneutical patterns, and one would think the novelist would set out to master this pattern of communication technique before employing it as a tool for building up his story. The first thing that strikes one when he researches this kind of preaching is the great difference between the topical preaching of modern western Christianity, and the rigid consistency of formal structure and the organization of ideas in the sermons of the first half of the last century. I have yet to find a fictional sermon that sounds anything but phony, after having worked through some hundreds of Calvinist sermons of the period and having come to know the *feel* of them. The fictional preaching of the most powerful writers like Melville and Michener is just not credible.

Not only are the form and feel not credible, but neither is the subject matter. These writers used the fictional sermon to work out their own 'hang-ups' about Calvinism, missionaries and religion in general, or to advance the narrative along the line they want to follow. Thus the cultural institution is forced to serve the purpose of the novelist, and this, of course, is not the function of a sermon.

The missionary sermon in *Omoo*[42] is surely one of the most phony things in all Melville's writing. Not only is it devoid of the predictable structure and pattern of argument, but it is rendered in ungrammatical English which suggests the missionary used pidgin rather than either formal English or the vernacular. Furthermore, the subject matter is not credible. It is a political platform, a literary device for expressing the opinion of the author through the mouthpiece of the preacher. The fictional sermon is a mean and dishonest trick, the way Melville used it. If he ever went to the Papara church, he did not have the language to understand the sermon in any case.

A century later James Michener employed the same device in his novel *Hawaii*. Miss Albertine Loomis, one of the recognized historians in Honolulu, and author of a genuine account of the early missionary years (1966),[43] took exception to the fictional sermon in the novel -

Fictional sermons seem always to be threatening sinners with hellfire; those actually preached, as shown in the record, ran the gamut from warning to reassurance, from admonition to 'good news' of salvation, with the emphasis on the latter (1967:3).

It was because I found these fictional sermons incredible that I set out to research the matter in the archives of Hawaii and in the U.S.[44] I did find and work over much material-manuscript sermons in full, and fully developed outlines and preaching logs, together with the scripture texts and so forth. I went through the preaching records of Titus Coan over 22 years (1835-57). Of 335 sermons, it seemed to me that 65 (19%) had a sin orientation. This is not to say they were hellfire, but the texts at least had a warning character. 110 (33%) referred to praise, or to some aspect of the moral or holy life, including a number on the Beatitudes. 160 (48%) had a definite salvation orientation. A sermon book (1841-3), belonging to an unidentified missionary, listed 24 sermons. Sixteen were New Testament themes, and the Old Testament themes were either topics based on the Wisdom Literature or prophetic salvation passages. A box containing sermons in Hawaiian were on moral subjects and Christian responsibility, the need for watchfulness and a vindication of the character of God.

A box of missionary Damon's sermons contained eight New Testament and six Old Testament themes - praise and temperance, (the latter for the benefit of sailors in port), and some apologetic sermons. All these were intended for

Christian people on the way. A sermon on divine guidance
which had brought the Hawaiians to that point in history was
preached in Hawaii to Hawaiians, but prescribed a view diametrically opposite to that in Michner's book.

The truth which came through clearly in this research was that, though each preacher had his own style and
system, none had a great deal of hellfire. The note of
judgement was stronger in Titus Coan than anyone else, but
he served for many years at the Seamen's Chapel. Sometimes
he dealt with the theme of the Christian mission itself, and
why they were there in the islands. One such sermon from
another missionary (Stewart) is reported in Levi Chamberlain's *Journal* (1822-1826). It was preached at the time
when the missionaries were having trouble with the crews of
certain ships, and preached to the seamen in English. This
is an interesting journal.[45] It reports the effective
preaching of Ellis the English missionary from Tahiti whose
Tahitian was understood by the Hawaiians. His preaching met
their felt needs, and responses came without any hellfire.

Chamberlain describes Bingham preaching to a congregation of 2000 at the central place, and visiting small
groups of 75 or so on his itinerations near at hand.   The
texts from which he preached are given. They were positive
and relevant preaching themes and were apparently acceptable.
This is all so diametrically opposite to the picture of the
defeated Abner Hale in the novel *Hawaii,* and the film version, both in the character of the preaching and the response
it received. In 34 sermons recorded, 26 of them were clear-
cut salvation themes.

Sometimes a warning was given first and then the
sermon came to focus on "decision for Christ". Miss Loomis
insists that there was very little *predestination* and *total
depravity* as we sometimes think of Calvinism. They still
believed in the sovereignty of God, but that He held men ac-
countable for their deeds. They preached *free grace* and
stressed *love* and *redemption* rather than *vengeance* (1967: 3).

Another character in Michener's novel is Eliphalet
Thorn, the corresponding secretary of the A.B.C.F.M., who is
theologically "tarred with the same brush" as the missionaries. Seeing Michener himself nominated the Board and the
official we have only one option for his prototype.[46]   I
have read through more than sixty sermons by this man. They
have a style of their own but conform to type. His normal
preaching was devotional and evangelistic.   When he became

aggressively doctrinal it was for some situation on the American front. Early in 1800 he preached on *eternal punishment*
for three Sundays, and a series of six on *judgement*.   But
this was not his normal style. He was dealing with a particular body of universalists who were attacking the idea of
Christian mission. He was then a young man just out of sem-
inary.

        The standard structure followed these lines: first
the exposition of a biblical passage, and second, arising
from this, a development of the biblical theme, spoken of as
reflections, improvement or *inferences*. The preaching was
not sectarian, but doctrinal arising from biblical exegesis.
There was theological repetition, but it always stemmed from
the goodness of God and the response of repentance.   His
texts were taken from all over the Bible, but when they came
from the Old Testament they dealt with the goodness of God
and moved to New Testament expectations. The sermons were
humble, and it is absolutely impossible to equate this historical figure with his fictional counterpart in Michener's
novel.

        On the whole I must agree with Miss Loomis.   The
fictional sermon in *Hawaii* is very sloppy research. Michener
has Abner Hale preaching on Zech. 2:11 - "The Lord will be
terrible unto them: for He shall famish all the gods of the
earth, etc...." - in a two-hour sermon in which -
    He described the terribleness of Jehovah when his
    anger was aroused, and he lingered over floods, pes-
    tilences, thunder and lightning, famines, and the
    tortures of hell.... Abner next turned to the specific
    gods of Lahaina, whom the new God was determined to
    destroy.... If you try to hide these evil gods in your
    hearts, you will be destroyed, and you will burn in
    hell for ever and ever (1959: 324-325).
I have never heard such an unmitigated distortion of what
the Hawaiian archival records show us of the character of
Calvinist missionary preaching. The research was either
very, very shoddy, or the manipulation was deliberate.

        Miss Loomis also takes Michener to task for suggest-
ing that Abner Hale had 100 sermons and 200 hymns on the destruction of idols (*ibid:* 324-5, 398), and disposes of the
fiction with the simple statement - "The record, including
the 1823 Hawaiian hymnbook, tells a different story" (1967:
3).

        It is not my purpose here to write a criticism of

the book, *Hawaii*, which after all claims to be a novel; but merely to say that in an *historical* novel, which claims on a fly-leaf to be "true to the spirit and history of Hawaii", with a country, a period of history and a missionary company precisely nominated by the author; I would expect the social institutions through which the story is transmitted to conform to their models.[47] If they do not do so then they are either badly researched or deliberately manipulated.

Notes:

1 Even trained historians betray us. Henderson a severe historical critic reduced several quotes in annotating Williams' Journal, thereby changing the meaning, stressing his point at the expense of the qualification.

2 A good (or bad) example of stereotype projection from a group of anthropologists, who should have known better, was seen recently in a report issued by a *Barbados Consultation*. These persons projected the image of the Roman Catholic missionary in Latin America in the days of colonial power, on to all present-day missionaries in Latin America, with some disastrous conclusions. They appear to have been motivated by present-day political cultural compulsives.

3 Hilton (Civil Rights writer) wrote after this fashion in a Methodist journal for women - "Should Missions Stop at U.S. Borders?" *Response*, Jan. 1970. He called *Hawaii* a "grim picture, based on fact".

4 Gansevoort, Melville's brother, who placed the book for publication with Murray in London, guaranteed its "entire veracity" as ethnology. The book first appeared as *Melville's Marquesas* (Weaver, 1921: 206-7).

5 Melville signed up on the *Acushnet*, Jan. 3, 1841, and sailed from Fairhaven, New Bedford for the South Pacific (Arvin, 1950). The vessel was at Nukahiva, Marquesas by July the following year. Anderson (1966:52, 113) sets his desertion after July 9. For evidence of this we have Captain Pearce's affidavit. Toby's confirmation of Melville's narrative would cover the desertion, the journey to Typee Valley and some 10 days in July. Arvin says this should not be taken too literally (1950:84). The Sydney whaler, *Lucy Ann* (*Julia* in the story) was short-handed and did seek him (Anderson, 1966: 194).

6 C.S. Stewart wrote the record of the visit of the U.S. ship *Vincennes* some twelve years earlier. He was the chaplain of the expedition, and one of Melville's major sources, but one which Melville used selectively.

7   Captain David Porter's *Cruise of the Essex,* which Mel-
     ville cites and says he "never happened to meet with".
     This was untrue. It was his most used source, and often
     is appropriated word for word.
8   G.H. von Langsdorff was the naturalist on the von Kru-
     senstern Expedition. Langsdorff's *Voyages and Travels*
     was another of Melville's major sources.
9   The publishers and a large part of the public accepted
     Melville's word for his having resided in the Typee Val-
     ley for four months, and this in turn validated it as
     ethnography. Literary critic, Anderson (1966), the major
     critical source on Melville, has identified the shipping
     documents and demonstrated that Melville escaped from the
     valley about August 15, which would give him a maximum of
     37 days on the island probably four weeks in the valley.
     See also Sturtevant (1966: 16).
         Historians' methods for the criticism of sources are
         also relevant to ethnohistory. Anthropologists per-
         sist in citing Herman Melville's *Typee* as a primary
         source on Marquesan culture, despite the fact that
         historical detective work has shown that Melville was
         in the Marquesas for four weeks rather than the four
         months he claimed, and that the ethnographic detail
         he presents was drawn from earlier published sources.
     Normally the best anthropological observation requires at
     least 12 months to cover the full agricultural and annual
     cycle of religious events.
10   Mumford knows the falsity of the claims of four months
     residence (29) but accepts Toby's testimony (probably
     for more than it was meant to cover), and a letter from
     M. Chasles, translated (not quite accurately) from the
     French. It refers to a rough journal which Melville kept,
     although in the Preface of *Omoo* Melville denies he kept
     a journal. So this evidence is questionable (Mumford,
     1962: 46-47; cf. Anderson, 1966:188-189 for the French).
11   The critical reviews of *Typee* found fault either on the
     score of the morals, the attacks on the missionaries, or
     for Melville's literary dishonesty. Though many reviews
     were favourable, those from Honolulu were particularly
     critical (Weaver, 1921:207-208, 255-256; Anderson, 1966:
     180-183). The critics also raised numerous other forms
     of exaggeration and freedom with the facts. Titus Coan
     visited Nukuhiva in 1867 and found Typee Valley only four
     hours climb from Melville's starting point, and the Hapa
     Valley but another three hours; so that in point of fact
     Melville was never more than four or five miles from the
     point where he deserted the ship (Coan, 1882:199-200).
         One of the severe critics of Herman Melville from the

island world itself at the time was a Tahiti merchant
author of *Rovings in the Pacific from 1837 to 1849*,
whom I believe to have been a Mr. Lucett. Of *Typee*
and *Omoo* he said -

> His sketches are amusing and skillfully drawn, but
> bear as much relation to truth as a farthing does
> in value to a sovereign. It is as if the said
> Herman Melville had burnished and guilded the farth-
> ing and circulated it as the gold coin (Lucett,
> 1851:293).

and again -

> Herman Melville.... has grossly scandalized by name
> some worthy men living at Tahiti who very probably
> have done more good, gratuitously, to their fellows
> since their residence there, than Herman Melville
> has done during his whole existence... (*ibid:* 293-
> 294).

He describes Melville as the instigator of the mutiny
which landed him in the calliboose, and identifies him
as the American who tried to knife him (Lucett). He
also identified the plagiarism in Melville's writing
(*ibid:* 296).

12   Weaver, Melville's biographer puts it like this -

> When Rousseau taught the world the art of reverie,
> he taught it also an easy vagabondage into the vir-
> gin forest and into the pure heart of the natural man

Rousseau's savage, he goes on again -

> attached to no place, having no prescribed task,
> obeying no-one, having no other law than his own
> will, was, of course, a wilful backward glance to
> the vanished paradise of childhood, not a finding
> of ethnology...... (1921:204-205).

13   This has been traced through the various periods by
Fairchild (1928), who places man conceptually in the
sequences of unilinear evolution and points out that
the recurring 'savage', is indeed a noble barbarian -
a Moor, an Inca, a Polynesian (*ibid:* 29, 33, 93).

14   Irving Goldman in *Ancient Polynesian Society*, the
most recent work on the subject, mentions Melville
was there but uses none of his data. Goldman claims
that the Marquesas was a major centre of Polynesian
stonework, that the status system and rivalry patterns
were highly developed, and speaks of the still more
sophisticated character of the whole conceptual construct of sancity and *tapu*, the labour organization,
warfare, wealth and politics, the descent group organization and social segmentation. He is speaking here
of Melville's period from 1790 A.D. on into the

nineteenth century (1970:131-148).

15   According to Suggs any lack of chiefly authority would
be due to his sharing it with the tribal high priest,
usually his younger brother, who became the "mouthpiece of God" when in a state of possession. Decision-
making was achieved in times of war by a council of
war-chiefs, and in normal social affairs by a council
of elders (Suggs, 1966: 14). This is far from the sim-
plified patriarch we find in *Typee*.

16   Melville dismissed the megalithic remains on a basis
of Korikori's statement that they were coeval with
creation, as being the work of some forgotten race.
However archaeological research rather suggests that
they were in construction at the contact period, and
indeed in their classic period (Suggs, 1962:198-201).
Frazer took Melville's account at its face value,
and the only qualification he raised was Melville's
not knowing the language.

17   Religion in Marquesan society was highly complex and
significant, and transmitted through the processes of
enculturation by the priestly unit of the community,
through myths, chants and genealogies, magical rites,
healing and divination (Suggs, 1966: 15).

18   The simple romance of man and maid in *Typee* only
demonstrates the superficiality of Melville's observations of both religion and sex. Sexual activity was
a "religious propitiatory technique" (ibid: 181) related
to fertility and ancestral rites, bearing on the life
crises and rites of passages of certain individuals,
and for the whole community at times of war, harvest
and stone construction-work (*ibid*:163-166).

19   This was his regular method. In *Moby Dick* he draws
from Beale's *Natural History of the Sperm Whale;* and
the fate of the *Pequod* comes from a newspaper article
describing a similar remarkable event of a ship being
pulled down in the vortex. Many of the concepts and
phrases in *Encantadas* are borrowed from Darwin and
Fitzroy - "Pandemonium, antedelivian and Cyclopean
scenes, where Vulcan might have worked!", "Plutonian
sight", etc. Information about cannibalism seems to
have come from Olmsted's *Incidents of a Whaling Voyage*.
Melville refused to use Stewart's religious interpretations but used his data sometimes for humourous
scenes. Stewart saw Marquesan religion as in a state
of decay. Melville just scoffed at religion.
Melville's indebtedness to his major sources may be
judged from the table of comparisons set out on the
following page, which is merely a sample.

SUBJECT	TYPEE	STEWART	LANGSDROFF	PORTER	ELLIS
Shaman Rite on Leg	106-7	1.270			
Funeral Ceremony	260-1	1.287-90	1.154-5		
Heads of Enemies	261-2,311-2			11.118	
Tattooing	104,111,181-2		1.122	11.14-5	1.207
Food Preparation	96,151-6	1.289	1.124-5	11.56-8	1.45-7
Oro	288-9			1.141	1.53-7
Fauna	283-6,290-1			11.130-3	
Making Tapa Cloth	197-9			11.125-6	1.145-9
Government	269-70,272-3		1.92-95	11.60-2	
Island Delights	16-8				

20   Although Frazer questioned Melville's evaluation of
religion because he had no knowledge of the language
(1922,II:330,373), nevertheless he accepted the supposed four months residence as factual, and used Typee
as a major source for chapter vi (Marquesas) and quoted
descriptive passages at length. He accepted his description of polyandry as a confirmation of Stewart
(338), apparently without suspecting that it was borrowed from that source.
     For Westermarck's use of Melville see *History of Human
Marriage*, III, 57, 146-148, 168. Sahlins cited Melville
in *Social Stratification in Polynesia* on the patterning
of the distribution of fish and on the authority of a
local chief. Subsequently he discovered how Melville
had collected his material and felt obliged to append an
apologetic footnote (1958: 74-75, 111).
21   One criticised his use of theoretical construction as
if it were an established datam (56), and another its
unverifiable presuppositions (112). Another raised the
question of whether or not his method was determined by
his theology (134). Still another saw it as "cultural
reductionism" (137), and a sociologist called it a
"creative theodicy". Several objected to his generalizations when it applied at certain points in their field
of specialization. A geographer (290) argued that his
philosophy, though claiming to be empirical has an *a
priori* aspect, and another objected to his selection of
data (306-7).
22   Further east Captain Cook had met another type of canoe
even larger than these and operated by oarsmen, which
meant a larger crew and fewer warriors: 144 of the former
and 39 of the latter. The length of the vessel was 130
feet (Loursin, 1964: 35). I cannot locate this reference in the original. The Tahitian canoes would run up
to 70 feet usually, and those that went into the deep

sea were double with a platform. The *pahie* might be out
for a month and up to 20 days at sea, and this was limited only because that was all the food and water that
could be carried. The advantage these craft had over
western ships was their proficiency in landing and putting off in the surf (*Account of Voyage....1768-1771...
by James Cook:* Hawkesworth's edn. v. 1:218-224).

23 This fine collection of documents is at the Turnbull
Library, Wellington. All the statements and agreements
have accompanying translations.

24 When James Buller published his reminiscenes after 40
years in New Zealand in 1878, he devoted a short chapter
to Bishop Pompalier and his twenty French priests, in
which he recognized their energy and service (294-5),
nevertheless he insisted still that –

> It is to be regretted that the agents of that Society
> are more zealous in treading in the steps of Protes-
> tant missionaries than in breaking up new ground in
> purely heathen lands (293).

He says they tried to undermine Protestant work by carrying about a picture of a chronological tree, showing
the Protestant branches lopped off for burning (295).

25 A typescript set of this correspondence is found in a
Wesleyan Mission Collection at the Turnbull Library.
Items cover events in Fiji in the 1850s. The originals
of these letters are in the M.O.M. Collection at the
Mitchell Library, Sydney. Turnbull reference # MS Pa-
pers 203 3 folders 1848-76.

26 The *Journal* of James Royce is in the M.O.M. Collection at
the Mitchell Library, Sydney. It covers the period
Nov. 1855 – Ap. 1862.

27 The first offer of Cession to Britain was signed by 26
Fijian chiefs, and witnessed by bilingual Europeans.
The deed was printed in English and Fijian.

28 Horsley's Report of the Wesleyan Mission was published
for the AWMS in 1968 for private circulation. A copy of
it is in the WMS Papers at the Turnbull Library.

29 Not all Protestant policy was based on civilizing. The
debate between this process and the evangelistic thrust
ran through the century and is a real historical problem
(Tippett, 1971:177-196). Civilizing and poverty cannot
be set over against each other for Roman Catholic missions in the Pacific are as commercialized as any – the
"Sacred Heart Co." kind of arrangement. These matters
call for objective or at least sympathetic treatment.

30 The anti-English and anti-Reformation innuendoes injure
the argument. We would not justify the divisions of

denominationalism in the Church, but writing so soon
after the Tahiti Affair, Marshall is obviously not speaking to any audience but a strongly Catholic one, and
apologetically not historically.

31   The butt of this attack is Bishop Selwyn, which is ludi-
crous and tragically simplistic. This purports to be
based on Protestant sources. It probes the inner disagreements of the missions, and selects the cases of
failures or men who came up for discipline. The Catholic record is no better than the Protestant in this.
Like the New Testament Church, each mission had its
Demas. As a good example of how this data is used,
Marshall takes the case of Vason, a lay missionary left
by the *Duff* at Tonga, who found himself the last sur-
vivor, and lived as a native (even to the tattooing).
Marshall has extracted the appropriate (or inappropri-
ate) incidents to use this man as a type for the Protestant missionary. On the contrary, this is just what
he was not. But worse than this, Vason's book, written after his return to civilization, was a confession
of a backslider repenting and a testimony to the grace
of God. Marshall does not mention this. He leaves him
as a renegade and extracts him out of his context. The
book finishes with a warning to all backsliders. How
can such a use of source material possibly be called
history (Vason, 1810)?

32   Professor G.C. Henderson, a historian at the Adelaide
University when he wrote, devoted a chapter in one of
his books on Fiji (1931) to the disagreements between
the Roman Catholics and Methodists (Wesleyans). Several pages are given to disposing of the writings of
Monseigneur Joseph Blanc, which "purports to be a history of religion". He says that were it not for the
important position held by Blanc in Oceania, he would
have regarded it as "almost beneath the dignity of historical criticism to take any notice of such a publication (1931:207-211).

33   Otto von Kotzebue made two visits to the South Pacific
and published accounts of his experiences 1815-8 (3
vols.) in 1826, and 1823 (2 vols.) in 1830. Darwin had
read Ellis, Beechey and Kotzebue before visiting Tahiti.
He found them very different points of view, and advo-
cated setting one off against the other. Quite apart
from this he took Kotzebue to task for claiming that
"the Tahitians had become a gloomy race, and lived in
fear of the missionaries". He says this is "decidedly
incorrect" and goes on for nearly a page. "There are
many who attack, even more acrimoniously than Kotzebue,

both the missionaries, their system, and the effects
produced by it. Such reasoners never compare the present state with that of the island only 20 years ago...
(*The Voyage of the Beagle*, [paperback edn. 1958]:357-8).
For more on Kotzebue see *infra*.

34 The legal problems involved in getting a conviction are
seen in the cases of the *Daphne* and the *Carl* (See Tippett, 1956: 90-100)

35 In 1872 Inglis himself edited a book of select documents on the Labour Trade as he saw it in the New Hebrides.

36 I have outlined the press campaign waged by Fison, with
heavy documentation in my master's degree thesis (1956:
101-119).

37 Patteson himself had said some strong things about the
labour trade. Like the Erromanga martyrs he died as a
direct victim of the trade, reprisals for murders committed by white men - either sandalwooders or recruiters.
Fison's public address on the murder of Bishop Patteson was published in the Sydney press in full.

38 Dillon frequently appears in the early mission records,
invariably with a bad name. He has left the record of
Savage's death in a skirmish they were both involved in,
in Vanua Levu (Wallis, 1950)

39 Cargill returned to England after the death of his wife,
but soon returned to Fiji.

40 The writer attended the Sesquicentennial of the Arrival
of the First Missionaries in Hawaii and heard Dr. Abra-
ham Akaka, the scheduled speaker for the occasion say
these words -
> When a people loses the foundations by which they
> determine what is right and wrong, just and unjust,
> they are on their deathbed and ready to die. Unless
> there comes a new way they cannot live. The mission-
> aries brought that new foundation.

The title of the address was - "Why I Am Glad They Came"
and he pointed out that the old religion had been destroyed and none had yet taken its place. *Time Magazine*
computation has a population drop from 400,000 to 150,
000 in fifty years, but gives the impression it is due
to the arrival of Christianity. What was false was that
this population drop in the 50 years came *before* the
missionaries arrived - the result of acculturation without mission.

41 The book ran 18 printings of the first edition, 1959-
65; 19 printings of the first paperback, 1961-6; and
I used 11th printing of the 2nd paperback (1968).

42 The book *Omoo* is hard to find, but the sermon is

included in Langdon's *Tahiti: Island of Love*, 152-153. Langdon accepts the fiction that Melville was four months in Typee (151), but knows he escaped in the *Lucy Ann*. He evaluates *Omoo* as a "half-factual, half-fictional novel."

43 Albertine Loomis, in addition to *Grapes of Canaan*, which covers the first seven years of the ABCFM mission in Hawaii, has written a general history of the Hawaiian Conference, *To All People* - an important work.

44 One of the best archival repositories for this kind of documentary material is the H.M.C.S. Archives in Honolulu, but the LMS and ABCFM printed sermons are found in the Research Library at UCLA, at the Missionary Research Library (New York) and at Yale and Hartford.

45 Six volumes of typescript bound together in a 469 page volume. Levi Chamberlain went to Hawaii with the second company. He was single, a teacher, and the missionary Agent. He married a woman from the third company and recorded his many itinerations, and the sermons he heard in the journal.

46 The life and work of Dr. Samuel Worcester is well documented, his reports, sermons and travel diary are preserved. Many of these are found in the *Missionary Herald*. A volume of his sermons was published very soon after his death.

47 My view is that a sermon is a technical instrument with a structure and a pattern. If you use, say, a radio broadcast or a computer as a device in your story for communicating information to the reader, one would expect the writer to understand at least how a radio broadcast or computer is organized. Yet apparently the novelist thinks anybody can use a sermon without worrying about what it is, how it is structured and how it has to be presented to the congregation for acceptance. The credibility of a sermon lies in the training of the preacher and in the receptive psychology of the congregation. Melville and Michener have shifted it to the gullibility of the reading public, that wants to scoff at Calvinist Christianity. This is a subtle but unpleasant form of persecution, to which ethnohistory must object.

References Cited:

Anderson, Charles Roberts
1966   *Melville in the South Seas*, New York, Dover Publishers

Arvin, Newton
    1950   *Herman Melville*, Wm. Sloane Associates   n/a
Brookes, Jean Ingram
    1941   *International Rivalry in the Pacific Islands:*
                  1800-1875, Berkeley, University of California
                  Press
Buller, James
    1878   *Forty Years in New Zealand &c....* London,
                  Hodder & Stoughton
Burton, Hester
    1972   "Where History Ends and Fiction Begins," *The*
                  Writer, June. 18
Calverton, V.F.
    1931   "Modern Anthropology and the Theory of Cultur-
                  al Compulsives," in *The Making of Man: An Out-*
                  line of Anthropology, (ed. C.V. Calverton).
                  New York, The Modern Library, 1-37
Cargill, David
    1842   *A Refutation of Chevalier Dillon's Slanderous*
                  Attacks on the Wesleyan Missionaries in the
                  Friendly Islands, London, James Nichols,
                  (Copy in Gregg Sinclair Library, Honolulu)
Chamberlain, Levi
    1822-6   *Journals*,- Vols. 1-6. Bound H.M.C.S. Library
                  and Archives, Hawaii
Coan, Titus
    1882   *Life in Hawaii, Mission Life and Labours,*
                  1835-81, New York, Randolph
    1839-52   Note Book with record of preaching. H.M.C.S.
                  MSS.
Cook, James Capt.
    1821   *An Account of a Voyage Round the World in the*
                  Years 1768, 1769, 1770, and 1771, by Lieuten-
                  ant James Cook,   Seven Volumes, (Dr. Hawkes-
                  worth's Edition). London, Longman, Hurst, Rees,
                  Orme & Brown
Damon, S.
    n/d   Box of Sermons, H.M.C.S. Archives, Honolulu
Darwin, Charles
    1958   *The Voyage of the Beagle*, (Paperback reprint)
                  New York, Bantam Books
Dunn, Thomas C.
    1856   *A Refutation of Charges Against the Wesleyan*
                  Missionaries in the Feejee Islands, reprinted
                  from the *New York Herald*
Ellis, Wm.
    1829   *Polynesian Researches During the Residence of*
                  Nearly Eight Years in the Society and Sandwich

Islands, London, Fisher & Jackson 2 Vols.
1831   *A Vindication of the South Seas Missions from
            the Misrepresentations of Otto von Kotzebue,
            Captain in the Russian Navy, with an Appendix.*
            London, Fredrick Westley & A.H. Davis (Copy
            in Bishop Museum Library, Honolulu)
Fairchild, Hoxie Neale
1928   *The Noble Savage: A Study in Romantic Natural-
            ism,* New York, Russell & Russell
Fison, Lorimer (nom de plume Outis)
1873   "The South Seas Labour Traffic," *Daily Tele-
            graph,* Series of nine articles
Forbes, Cochran
1832-47   *Cochran Forbes' Letters and Journal, 1832-47*
            Honolulu, H.M.C.S. Library
Frazer, J.G.
1922   *Belief in Immortality and the Worship of the
            Dead,* Vol. II Polynesia. London Macmillan
            & Co.
Goldman, Irving
1970   *Ancient Polynesian Society,* Chicago, The Uni-
            versity Press
Grattan, F.J.H.
1948   *An Introduction to Samoan Custom,* Apia,
            Samoa Printing & Publishing Co.
Handy, E.S.C.
1923   *Native Culture in the Marquesas,* Honolulu,
            Bishop Museum Press
Hawthorne, Nathaniel
1846   Review of *Typee* in the *Salem Advertiser* in
            Critics on Melville, Coral Gables, University
            of Miami Press, T.J. Rountree (Editor)
Henderson, G.C.
1931   *Fiji and the Fijians: 1835-56,* Sydney, Angus
            & Robertson
Hilton, Bruce
1970   "Should Missions Stop at U.S.?" *Response,*
            Jan.
Hodge, Jane Aitken
1972   "Writing Historical Novels," *The Writer,*
            June 15-18
Hood, Capt. T.H.
1863   *Notes of a Cruise in H.M.S. Fawn in the West-
            ern Pacific in the Year 1862.* Edinburgh,
            Edmonston & Douglas
Horsley, John F.
1868   *Report on the Wesleyan Mission in the Fiji
            District,* Sydney, Jos, Cook & Co. for

Australasian Wesleyan Missionary Society (Private circulation). In Turnbull Library, Wellington, # Pam. 0/1868

Judd, A.F. (Ed.)
1969   *Missionary Album: Sesquicentennial Edition, 1820-1970,* Honolulu, Hawaiian Mission Children's Society

Kotzebue, Otto von
1830   *A New Voyage Around the World in the Years 1823-1826,* London, H. Colburn & R. Bentley

Langdon, Robert
1968   *Tahiti: Island of Love,* Sydney, Pacific Publications

Langsdorff, Georg H. von
1813   *Voyages and Travels in Various Parts of the World..... 1803-1807,* 2 Vols. London, H. Colburn

Linton, Ralph
1925   *Archaeology in the Marquesas Islands,* Honolulu, Bishop Museum Press

Loomis, Albertine
1966   *Grapes of Canaan: Hawaii 1820,* Honolulu, H.M.C.S.
1967   *Hawaii: Fact and Fiction,* Honolulu, H.M.C.S.

Loursin, Jean-Marie
1964   *Tahiti,* London, Vista Books (Trans. by R.H. Dean)

Lucett, Edward
1851   See "A Merchant at Tahiti," (nom de plume)

Marshall, T.W.M.
1862   *Christian Missions: Their Agents, Their Methods and Their Results,* Vol. 2. Chapters V, VI: 80-285, Brussels, H. Goemaere

Mead, Margaret (Ed.)
1961   *Cooperation and Competition Among Primitive Peoples,* Boston, Boston Press

Melville, Herman
1846   *Typee* (Melville's Marquesas) London, John Murray
1847   *Omoo: A Narrative of Adventures in the South Seas,* London, John Murray
1967   *Typee,* Paperback edition, Washington Square Press

Merchant at Tahiti, A (M. Lucett)
1851   *Rovings in the Pacific from 1837 to 1849....* London, Brown, Green and Longmans, 2 Vols.

Michener, James
1959   *Hawaii,* New York, Random House, Paperback

                    edition, 1968. Bantam Books
Miller, James E.J.
  1962   *A Reader's Guide to Herman Melville,* New
                York, The Noonday Press
Montague, M.F. Ashley
  1956   *Toynbee and History: Critical Essays and Re-
                views,* Boston, Porter Sargent
Mumford, Lewis
  1962   *Herman Melville: A Study of His Life and Vis-
                ion,* London, Secker & Warburg
Olmsted, Francis Allyn
  1841   *Incidents of a Whaling Voyage.....&c.....*
                Rutland, Chas. E. Tuttle Co. (Facsmile 1969)
Porter, David
  1815   *Journal of a Cruise Made to the Pacific Ocean
                in the U.S. Frigate Essex in the Years 1812,
                1813 and 1814,* 2 Vols. Philadelphia,
                Bradford & Inskeep
Prichard, George
  n/d   "The Aggressions of the French at Tahiti and
                Other Islands in the Pacific," Collection
                of documents, statements and agreements with
                translations, etc. In Turnbull Library,
                Wellington, # 9 MS/184/p
Rannie, Douglas
  1912   *My Adventures Among South Sea Cannibals,* Lon-
                don, Seeley Service. (Rannie was a Govt. re-
                cruiting agent.)
Restieaux, Alfred
  n/d   Manuscripts 183pp. photo prints. Melbourne,
                La Trobe Library, Refce. M.S. 6935 (Origin-
                als in bad condition Turnbull Library, Well-
                ington).
Rhodes, Capt. F.
  1937   *Pageant of the Pacific: Being a Maratime
                History of Australasia,* Sydney, F.J. Thwaites
                Pty. Ltd.
Rountree, T.J.
  1972   *Critics on Melville: Readings in Literary
                Criticism,* Coral Gables, University of Miami
                Press
Royce, James S.
                Journal, November 1855 - April 1862. In M.O.M.
                Collection, Mitchell Library, Sydney.
                Meth. Ch/OM/135
Sahlins, Marshall D.
  1958   *Social Stratification in Polynesia,* Seattle,
                University of Washington Press

Smyth, Col. W.J.
  1861   Col. Smyth's "Report" and "Covering Letter,"
                App. in Mrs Smyth's *Ten Months in the Fiji
                Islands,* Oxford, John Henry & James Parker
                1864   197-210
Stewart, C.S.
  1831   *A Visit to the South Seas in the U.S. Ship
                Vincennes... 1829-30,* 2 Vols. New York,
                John P. Haven (Facsmile)
Sturtevant, Wm. C.
  1966   "Anthropology. History and Ethnohistory"
                Ethnohistory, 13, 1:1-51
Suggs, Robt. Carl
  1961   *Archaeology of Nuku Hiva, Marquesas Islands,*
                New York, American Museum of Natural History
  1962   *The Hidden Worlds of Polynesia,* New York,
                Harcourt, Brace & World Inc.
  1966   *Marquesan Sexual Behavior: An Anthropological
                study of Polynesian Practices,* New York,
                Harcourt, Brace & World Inc.
Tippett, A.R.
  1968   *Fijian Material Culture: A Study of Cultural
                Context, Function and Change,* (B.M. Bulletin
                232) Honolulu, Bishop Museum Press
  1971   *People Movements in Southern Polynesia,*
                Chicago, Moody Press
Toynbee, Arnold J.
  1954   *A Study of History,* (10 vols.) London,
                Oxford University Press. Volume III used.
Villiers, Alan
  1967   *Captain James Cook,* New York, Charles
                Scribner's Sons
Walker, Vernon Lee (Recruiter)
  1878-89   "Private Correspondence from New Hebrides."
                La Trobe Library, Melbourne. Originals
                MS8290, Xerox MS7568, of which the originals
                are at Rhodes House, London
Ward, John M.
  1948   *British Policy in the South Pacific 1786-
                1893* Sydney, Australasian Publishing Co.
Waterhouse, Joseph
  1848-76   "Manuscript Papers"   3 Folders.
                Letters 1848- April 1850
                    "   April 1850 - 1851
                    "   1852 - 1876
                Typescript and Photographs. Turnbull Library.
                MS. Pap. #203. Originals in M.O.M. Archives
                Mitchell Library, Sydney

Wawn, Wm. T.
  1893   *The South Sea Islanders and the Queensland
              Labour Trade: a Report on Voyages and Ex-
              periences in the Western Pacific from 1875-
              1891,*   London, Swan Sonnenschein
Weaver, Raymond M.
  1921   *Herman Melville: Mariner & Mystic,*   New York,
              G.H. Doran Co.
Westermarck, Edward
  1891   *History of Human Marriage,*   London, Macmillan
              & Co.
Williams, Thomas
  1860   *Fiji and the Fijians,*   Vol. I   "The Islands
              and their Inhabitants"   London, Alexander
              Heylin
Williamson, J.A.
  1946   *Cook and the Opening of the Pacific,*   London,
              Hodder & Stoughton

Page from Joeli Bulu's autobiographical life history. (See p.196)

9

MISSIONARY RESOURCES
and
ISLAND LIFE HISTORIES

One of the criticisms often made of the older types
of Pacific missionary is that they wrote up their own exploits more than those of the Pacific islanders who worked
with them - the "Native Agents" as they were called.   The
missionaries are often depicted as rather self-assertive,
dogmatic and biased. For this reason many anthropologists
and some historians have rejected the missionary records as
reliable source material.

This has been unfortunate and has invariably given
an opposite bias to their own writing. Writing the essays
in this book has convinced me of the great value of missionary documents on the Pacific. However, as with any research
tool, one has to learn how to use them. One has to realize
the variety of their types and functions, and evaluate them
according to their basic purposes.

Missionary records need to be evaluated in the following manner -
(1)   Official Reports intended for publication.
(2)   Official Correspondence not for publication.
(3)   Private Correspondence.
(4)   Private Journals.
(5)   Printed Books.
The moment the character and function are apparent the researcher should know how to allow for any bias - recognizing,
of course, that all writing has some bias, including that of
the administrative officer and the anthropologist.

Official reports and correspondence published in
England or America (e.g. in *Wesleyan Magazine* or *Missionary
Herald*) may be regarded as written with this possibility in
mind, but where I have been able to compare the printed

letter with the original, I have not found them edited for publication. The printed books vary in value. Those with imprints of the Mission Society have been prepared for the missionary-minded reader at home. Books from a secular pub-lisher may be assumed to have a wider audience than the mis-sionary constituency. The significance of the audience is important in evaluating a book. The book is more likely to have been edited than the letter or report. It may be pro-motional or educational - i.e. for raising support or for interesting reading. Both are of value to the ethnohistor-ian, but one must first establish what the purpose is.

For the ethnohistorian the missionary journal is the most valuable of all these sources. The missionaries recorded their feelings and impressions and were frank in their descriptions, especially about things regarded as too delicate for putting in a book. They lived in the midst of the raw life of paganism, sometimes only 10 to 20 feet from the cannibal ovens, and they were good observers. Sometimes their book editors removed items and substituted a phrase like "too disgusting to mention". In a later day these have been rejected by secular scholars as "exaggeration" or "mis-sionary bias". Yet in the journals one frequently finds ev-idence of the reality of that "too disgusting" culture trait. Unfortunately this elimination was needed at the time as a corrective to the idea of the 'Noble Savage'.

Not all journals are of equal value. One has to measure one off against another. Fiji is rich in this kind of material - Williams, Hunt, Jaggar, Lyth, all of them avail-able in one repository, and all very much in agreement.   A little later on (in the 1860s) one finds a wider difference in the missionary personality types. From then on over the years some men stand out as recorders of the changing way of life - Fison, Horsley and others. From the same missionary continuum one can identify good observers and men with an-thropological insights: Fison from the 1870s to the first decade of the new century and then Deane later on. Fison was a contemporary of E.B. Tylor, Lewis Henry Morgan, R.H. Cod-rington and Sir J.G. Frazer, and corresponded with them all. Fison and Deane left proper anthropological discussions.

Each repository has its own unique corpus of mis-sionary documents and journals quite apart from the housing of mission archives.[1] In the Turnbull Library, Wellington, one can work on missionary journals and papers of Buller, Woon, Colenso, Kendall, Selwyn, Williams, Yate, Hall and oth-ers, between 1800 and 1900, and also many reels of microfilm

together with several files of mission society papers which
have been alienated from their own archives.

The ABCFM records and correspondence of Hawaii and
Micronesia, and files of individual missionaries may be used
at the H.M.C.S. repository in Honolulu; amplified by the superb island collection of books, theses, documents and micro-
films at the Gregg Sinclair Memorial Library at the University of Hawaii, and the Library of the Bishop Museum. These
places between them offer many missionary journals - Chamberlain, Mrs. Ruggles and others, mission station reports and
many rare pamphlets.

In Sydney, Wellington or Honolulu one can work on
missionary material to his heart's content - more than any
man can use in his lifetime.

Indigenous Sources

The Fiji missionaries did not bypass the "Native
Agents" in their writings. They knew well that the small
staff of British missionaries could not do the job that was
opening up before them, and they recognized their dependence
on the native agency. They did not bemoan this necessity
but rejoiced in it. They recognized the superiority of the
nationals for breaking new ground with the Gospel and used
them at every level of Christian education. The missionaries recognized their ability to endure the climate better
than a white man, better ability to mix with the people
and better communication through superior knowledge of the
language (Calvert, 1860:430). A few select men were given
posts of oversight at an early date. Twenty years later,
Calvert wrote of the 1848 decision to admit 4 islanders as
assistant missionaries with all the rights of the minister-
ial office -
> We were somewhat timorous of taking this step; but it
> answered well, and many have been chosen for the work
> since that time..... There are now 44 of these devoted
> and useful men, already thus ordained, or on trial"
> (Calvert, 1870:562-563).

Calvert updated this in 1884 when the missionaries, eleven in
all, were outnumbered by 51 Fijian ministers, 32 catechists
and 1,729 local preachers (laymen) (1884:xiv).

If these Fijian agents received little publicity in
England, it was because the folk there wanted to know about
"our missionaries", i.e. the men "we send forth and support".

But in the private records of the missionaries their Fijian
colleagues figure prominently and the missionaries themselves frequently inspired the island leaders to write down
their stories. In this way Fison acquired the autobiographical account of James Havea and Joeli Bulu. The latter being of book length, he translated it for publication.   Fison's translation retains the character and rhythm of the
original - I have read them both (1871). R.H. Codrington
did the same with the autobiography of Clement Marau, the
Melanesian deacon. Fison's little book on Sefanaia Bilivucu
is probably also a translated autobiography - it has the
music of Fijian narrative about it.

        The life story of Ligeremaluoga (Osea) has been
translated by Ella Collins and published under the title
The Erstwhile Savage. It is a New Ireland story told in a
delightfully conversational style, even to his impressions
of the preaching of a Fijian missionary (78-80), and his
experience in connection with preaching his own first sermon (80-81).

        During my Solomon Island research in 1964 I came
across a small book *From Heathen Boy to Christian Priest*
about Taloifuila, which although written by a missionary,
A.I. Hopkins, was a biography which seemed to have been
built up on reminiscences. There are of course, many biographies written by missionaries, like R.C. Nicholson's
Son of a Savage, based on the life of Daniel Bula; and biographical articles, for instance, "Harry Raeno," "Solomon
Damusoe" and "Timothy Loe" &c., among the *Metcalfe Papers*,
which have now been microfilmed by Pacific Manscripts Bureau.

        The biographies written by missionaries may offer
an appreciation or evaluation from the angle of a westerner;
but when the rhythm and idiom of the prose strongly suggests
translation, it may be assumed that much autobiographical
material has been included. This usually stands out very
clearly to one who knows the vernacular language. Sometimes
a missionary narrated his own experiences, identifying them
throughout with an island fellow-worker. Paton's *Lomai of
Lenakel* is a good example of this type. Such works do point
up the personal cross-cultural relationships between Chris-
tain workers, at least from the missionary side, and within
such limits are valid evidence.

        Also not to be overlooked are the memoirs published
immediately after the death of some prominent islander,
a life story reconstruction by a writer who knew the deceased

personally, and in a book which was circulated among others who knew him. The most famous of these was Dwight's *Memoir of Obookiah*. It has been recently republished as a paperback after a century and a half.

Another source of indigenous autobiographical material is the large excerpts from their accounts translated by some missionary for inclusion in his own book. A good example of this is the "Narrative of Peter Vi," fairly literally translated in West's book on Tonga (1865:360-368). I found this important data for my study of the people movements in Southern Polynesia (1971: 79-82).

R.H. Codrington and Lorimer Fison were not the only anthropologically orientated missionaries to set out to preserve the biography of outstanding islanders. Another was George Brown, author of *Melanesians and Polynesians* (1910). In 1898 he wrote an article "Life History of a Savage" which reconstructed the story of a New Britain individual from his birth to his death, not the narrative of a particular identified person, although he had assembled it from observing people he actually knew.

The methodology for handling biographical and autobiographical data of this kind has been discussed by Kluckhohn (1945: 79-173). He points out the need for exploring the potential of these documents and how research based on them maybe developed, controlled and tested (79). He also believed that because these documents are so widely scattered their "collective bulk is probably not appreciated, even within the profession" (80). Annotation should be done by a person familiar with the material, the culture (146) and the language used in the documents.

There is no short cut to this kind of research, at least to those who pioneer the field. Even if someone has paved the way by translating a manuscript one still should know the language and be able to feel the rhythms and emotions of the translation. One only has to listen to an evening entertainment of both Polynesian and Melanesian artists to realize that all Polynesians are not rhythmically identical even though they borrow from each other.

Kluckhohn is certainly correct about the scatter of these mission documents. The observation raises another question - what can be done about the restoration of the integrity or wholeness of archival collections: *respect des fonds* as the archivists call it? Supposedly it is desirable

(Muller *et al.*, 1940: 34, 38), but is it ever possible? One
thing which impressed me on my travels around the manuscript
repositories of the Pacific was the presence of *archival
strays*. I came across a collection of letters in one place
which had strayed from the Methodist Overseas Mission Archives in Sydney. They were all letters to the General Secretary. One might presume he had left them behind in New
Zealand *en route* to the islands or on his way home. Four,
at least, of the letters were important to me. One was the
only letter I know in the handwriting of Crawford, a young
missionary who died really before getting into 'harness'. It
is the only historical portrait I know of his personality.
Another was a letter of Calvert's on a political issue of
some significance, on which we badly need confirmation. Another was a letter of Edward Martin, a fugitive seaman converted under the influence of Hazelwood in Fiji, and who
trained as a printer there and stayed for many years of noble service. I know all the handwritings except Crawford's
and so the genuineness is in no doubt. We can only hope
that the new accessibility of documents will expose other
items like this; because some of these archival strays speak
to major anthropological and historical problems that are
still unsettled.

Richards, at Lahaina in 1824, produced a *Memoir
of Keopuolani*, Queen of the Sandwich Islands, within four
years of the commencement of the mission. The first two
chapters thrust back into the pre-mission period, and the
material must have been gathered from Keopuolani herself or
other Hawaiians who knew her well. In any case it is a
good picture of Hawaii at the mission contact period.

I have often thought that every Pacific mission-
field should produce a good volume of essays devoted to its
most fascinating indigenous characters. This would require
much research but it could be done. If Joeli Bulu, Ratu
Cakobau, Sefanaia Bilivucu, Henry Obookiah, Daniel Bula,
Clement Marau, David Vule and Jack Taloifuila can provide
enough material for a whole volume each, the men who planted
the Church in Fiji, say, like Ilaija Varani, Paula Vea,
Ra Esekaia, Solomoni Raduva, Josua Mateinaniu and the missionary, Wilisoni Lagi, could at least provide material for
an essay on each.

Oscar Mauer's useful little booklet, *Three Early
Christian Leaders of Hawaii* (1945) is an interesting example of what I mean - but it is only a small sample. The
three men Maurer selected were Bartimea Lalana Puaaiki, the

blind preacher of Maui; David Malo, Hawaiian preacher of
social righteousness, and James Kelela, first ordained
Hawaiian minister and a missionary to the Marquesas. The
most important of these studies is the third because
Maurer is able to quote Kekela verbatim at some length,
which gives the man's personality a chance to break through
nicely. The extent to which this may be done would surprise many researchers. Twenty years ago in writing a
long monograph, *The Christian (Fiji 1835-67)*, I found that
a great many letters of indigenous Christians and their
reports had been preserved for the use of anyone with the
patience to search them out. At the time the Fijian Church
was moving towards independence, and the process of discovering its own selfhood was not confined to the present
and future. The people were aware that their own forebears had contributed much to the spread and building of
the Church. I made it a rule of my life to have a fund of
anecdotes about the great Fijians of the past to use on
all kinds of occasion, and I never once failed to get a
hearing. Furthermore, I must confess, that I became more
and more impressed with the character and calibre of these
pioneer Fijian Christians. Some day they must claim a
major volume. No history of the islands is adequate which
passes them by.

As for those which were written at the time the
subjects were remembered by the readers, many of these
might well be reprinted now that we seem to have entered
the age of facsimiles - with an introductory essay perhaps.
The republication of the memoir of Obookiah to commemorate
the sesquicentennary of his death was a good idea, and
likewise the introduction by Albertine Loomis and the fifteen historic illustrations. This work is largely comprised of Obookiah's correspondence, and this throws much
light on the character of his conversion and the burden on
his heart. It shows up the historic role he played in in-
spiring the Church in America to undertake the mission to
Hawaii. "Slender and simple as it was," says Miss Loomis,
"this book shaped the future of Hawaii"(1968:xi).

This article makes no attempt at a comprehensive
survey of missionary material. For example, I have not discussed material in private hands to any great extent, letter books, newspaper cuttings books, obituaries, book reviews and vernacular publications for purposes of Christian
growth of converts, translations of Scripture and hymns,
all of which exist in abundance. There are enough editions
of the Fijian Scriptures and hymnbooks to study semantic
change in them over 150 years. I have merely intended to

make two points, namely that (1) the primary sources are
there for any who undertake to prepare themselves to use
them, and (2) there is far more historical and anthropological raw material of very high value in the missionary
sources than has generally been realized.

Notes:

1   These usually require the special permission of the
     mission concerned. The Methodist Overseas Missions
     Pacific documents, for example, are in the Mitchell Li-
     brary, Sydney, and in the Fiji Government Archives in Suva,
     beside Roman Catholic Mission material. The M.O.M.
     collection includes much personal material assembled by
     missionaries - Royce, Jaggar, Hunt, Baker, Billings,
     Heighway, to mention only a few of them. The Mitchell
     Library itself has many others to go with these. I have
     mentioned only one Society.   The early record of Pacific
     Missions involves one in the study of the L.M.S., the
     C.M.S., the Melanesian Mission and several horizontal
     structures like the B.F.B.S., and the Protestant Missions
     Medical Aid Society. The Northern Pacific was the domain
     of the A.B.C.F.M., and some Presbyterian activity was lo-
     cated in the southwest. Catholic activity was widespread
     and involved four or five Societies - Marists, Picpus,
     Capuchins, Sacred Heart and old Spanish Missions and
     Jesuits if we cover the entire Pacific. A researcher
     will do well to cover the records on any one of these in
     his lifetime.   Many of them have now microfilmed their
     materials and therefore are available in more than one
     repository, and some have xeroxed duplicate sets: thus,
     for example, the A.B.C.F.M. records are both in America
     and in Honolulu.

References Cited:

Brown, George
   1898   "Life History of a Savage," *Proc. Australian
                 Association for the Advancement of Science*
                 7:778-790
   1910   *Melanesians and Polynesians: Their Life His-
                 tories Described and Compared,* London,
                 Macmillan & Co.
Bulu, Joeli
   n/d   *Ai Tukutuku ni Noqu Bula,* Manuscript
   1871   *Joel Bulu: The Autobiography of a Native*

Minister in the South Seas, London, Wesleyan
Mission House   (Translated by Lorimer Fison).

Calvert, James
  1860   *Fiji and the Fijians,* Vol. II   *Mission History,* London, Alexander Heylin
  1870   *Fiji and the Fijians,* Vol. II *Mission History.* Supplement to the 3rd Edition   559-567
         (Copy used 4th edition. Chas H. Kelly, London)
  1884   *Fiji and the Fijians,* (One volume edition). Preface to 4th Edition   viii-xxii, London, Charles H. Kelly

Dwight, E.W.
  1830   *Memoir of Obookiah, a Native of Owhyhee.....* Philadelphia, American Sunday School Union (Died 1818. 1st Edition issued immediately)

Dwight, Edwin (Ed. Albertine Loomis)
  1968   *Memoirs of Henry Obookiah, a Native of Owhyhee, &c.....* Honolulu, Woman's Board of Missions for the Pacific Islands, Hawaii Conference, United Chruch of Christ (Edition commemorating 150th Anniversary of his death)

Fison, Lorimer
  n/d   *Old Sefanaia, the Fijian Herald,* by a friend of his. London, Charles H. Kelly (Data collected in 1870, probably published c. 1895)

Havea, Jemesa
  n/d   *Ai Tukutuku ni Noqu Bula,* Manuscript

Hopkins, A.I.
  1949   *From Heathen Boy to Christian Priest,* London S.P.C.K.

Kluckhohn, Clyde
  1945   "The Personal Document in Anthropological Science" in *The Use of Personal Documents in History, Anthropology and Sociology,* by Gottschalk, Kluckhohn & Angell, New York, Social Science Research Council   Bull. 53   79-173

Loomis, Albertine
  1968   "Introduction" to Dwight, 1968

Mauer, Oscar E.
  1945   *Three Early Christian Leaders of Hawaii,* Honolulu, Board of the Hawaiian Evangelical Association

Metcalfe, John F.
  n/d   Unpublished Manuscripts
         "The Three Brothers"
         "Harry Raeno"
         "Solomon Damusoe"
         "The Gumi Family"

"Timothy Loe"
(Microfilmed by P.M.B.)

Ligeremaluogo, Osea
1932   *An Account of the Life of Ligeremaluogo*, (published under the title *The Erstwile Savage*, Melbourne, F.W. Cheshire (Translated by Ella Collins)

Marau, Clement
1894   *The Story of a Melanesian Deacon*, London, S.P.C.K. (Translated by R.H. Codrington)

Muller, S., J.H. Feith and R. Fruin
1940   *Manual for the Arrangement and Description of Archives*, New York, The H.W. Wilson Co. (Translated by A.H. Leavitt)

Nicholson, R.C.
1924   *Son of a Savage: The Story of Daniel Bula*, London, The Epworth Press

Paton, H.L.
1903   *Lomai of Lenakel: A Hero of the New Hebrides* New York, Fleming H. Revell Co.

Richards, W.
1825   *Memoir of Keopuolani, Late Queen of the Sandwich Islands*, Boston, Crocker & Brewster

Rycroft, Harold R.
1926   *From Savagery to Christ: The Story of David Vule*, London, Epworth Press

Tippett, A.R.
1954   *The Christian (Fiji 1835-67)*, Auckland, The Institute Publishing Co., for the Methodist Church in Fiji
1971   *People Movements in Southern Polynesia*, Chicago, Moody Press

Vi, Peter
n/d   *"Peter Vi's Narrative"* in *Ten Years in the South-central Pacific Islands (Friendly Islands)*....   London, J. Nisbet & Co. 1865, 360-368

Waterhouse, Joseph
1866   *The King and People of Fiji.... Life of Thakombau....*   London, Wesleyan Conference Office

INDEX